£10 95

E

Autism

DISCARD

DEVELOPMENTAL CLINICAL PSYCHOLOGY AND PSYCHIATRY SERIES

Series Editor: **Alan E. Kazdin,** *Western Psychiatric Institute*

In the Series:

Autism

Laura Schreibman

Volume 15.
Developmental Clinical Psychology and Psychiatry

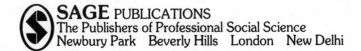
SAGE PUBLICATIONS
The Publishers of Professional Social Science
Newbury Park   Beverly Hills   London   New Delhi

For information address:

SAGE Publications, Inc.
2111 West Hillcrest Drive
Newbury Park, California 91320

SAGE Publications Inc.   SAGE Publications Ltd.
275 South Beverly Drive   28 Banner Street
Beverly Hills   London EC1Y 8QE
California 90212   England

SAGE PUBLICATIONS India Pvt. Ltd.
M-32 Market
Greater Kailash I
New Delhi 110 048 India

Printed in the United States of America

Library of Congress Cataloging-in-Publication Data

Schreibman, Laura Ellen.
    Autism.

    (Developmental clinical psychology and
psychiatry ; v. 15)
    Bibliography: p.
    Includes indexes.
    1. Autism.   I. Title.   II. Series. [DNLM:
1. Autism.   2. Autism, Infantile. W1 DE997NC v.15 /
WM203.5 S378a]
RJ506.A9S4   1988   616.92'8982   88-1926
ISBN 0-8039-2809-2
ISBN 0-8039-2810-6 (pbk.)

FIRST PRINTING 1988

CONTENTS

SERIES EDITOR'S INTRODUCTION

Interest in child development and adjustment is by no means new. Yet, only recently has the study of children benefited from advances in both clinical and scientific research. Advances in the social and biological sciences, the emergence of disciplines and subdisciplines that focus exclusively on childhood and adolescence, and greater appreciation of the impact of such influences as the family, peers, and school have helped accelerate research on developmental psychopathology. Apart from interest in the study of child development and adjustment for its own sake, the need to address clinical problems of adulthood naturally draws one to investigate precursors in childhood and adolescence.

Within a relatively brief period, the study of psychopathology among children and adolescents has proliferated considerably. Several different professional journals, annual book series, and handbooks devoted entirely to the study of children and adolescents and their adjustment document the proliferation of work in the field. Nevertheless, there is a paucity of resource material that presents information in an authoritative, systematic, and disseminable fashion. There is a need within the field to convey the latest developments and to represent different disciplines, approaches and conceptual views to the topics of childhood and adolescent adjustment and maladjustment.

The Sage Series on *Developmental Clinical Psychology and Psychiatry* is designed to serve uniquely several needs of the field. The Series encompasses individual monographs prepared by experts in the fields of clinical child psychology, child psychiatry, child development, and related disciplines. The primary focus is on developmental psychopathology which refers broadly here to the diagnosis, assessment, treatment, and prevention of problems that arise in the period from infancy through adolescence. A working assumption of the Series is that understanding, identifying, and treating problems of youth must draw on multiple disciplines and diverse views within a given discipline.

The task for individual contributors is to present the latest theory and research on various topics including specific types of dysfunction, diagnostic and treatment approaches, and special problem areas that affect adjustment. Core topics within clinical work are addressed by the Series. Authors are asked to bridge potential theory, research, and clinical practice, and to outline the current status and future directions. The goals of the Series and the tasks presented to individual contributors are demanding. We have been extremely fortunate in recruiting leaders in the fields who have been able to translate their recognized scholarship and expertise into highly readable works on contemporary topics.

The present monograph considers *Autism*, a severe and pervasive disorder that emerges early in the course of development. In this book, Dr. Laura Schreibman details multiple facets of the disorder. The impact of autism on child, parent, family, and community functioning are presented in a way that integrates clinical material and contemporary research. The full range of symptoms of the disorder is elaborated. In addition, current research related to diagnosis, etiology and treatment, as well as alternative methods of assessment, are detailed. Diverse conceptual views, together with their evidence and limitations, are conveyed in an even-handed and scholarly fashion. Dr. Schreibman, who has contributed substantially to the research in this area, cohesively weaves diverse strands of evidence in a superb book.

— *Alan E. Kazdin, Ph.D.*
Series Editor

PREFACE

Autism. Few behavior disorders in adults or children have stimulated such genuine fascination as has this severe form of psychopathology in childhood. The unique set of behaviors characterizing the syndrome, its resistence to treatment, and its elusive etiology—all seem to have given autism more attention than might be expected of a disorder that is numerically a rather infrequent occurrence. Indeed, the tremendous impact autism has on the child, the family, the schools, and the community has served to challenge a broad range of professionals and lay personnel.

The intense interest in autism has generated an abundant, and often controversial, literature relating to all aspects of the disorder. This book attempts to acquaint the reader with the current state of knowledge concerning autism. Chapter One presents a discussion of the history of the diagnosis since infantile autism enjoys a rather rich and unusual history in terms of its conceptualization as a distinct diagnostic entity and its hypothesized etiology. Also, such a historical context allows the reader to see ties between research and clinical conceptualizations and prevailing theoretical positions at various points in time. Next comes a discussion of the specific behavioral characteristics associated with the syndrome which should give the reader a good idea of what autism is in terms of its behavioral manifestations. This is followed by a discussion of diagnostic issues which, like almost everything pertaining to the disorder, have not been without controversy and disagreement. The subsequent section on the etiology of autism describes both nonempirical hypothesized relations between the child and his/her social environment as well as data-based hypotheses focusing on organic factors. The investigation of the cause or causes of autism has been particularly lively of late and while no answer has yet been found, it is hoped that the reader will gain an appreciation of the range of work in this area. The discussion then turns to issues of treatment. The main treatment models that are, and have been, applied to autism are presented first, followed by more extensive details describing the specifics of one such model—the behavioral model. The emphasis on behavioral research and treatment in this volume is a reflection of both the author's theoretical orientation and, more importantly, the tremendous volume of literature supporting the contributions of this work to our understanding of autism and its treatment. Thus behavioral interventions are discussed in relation to specific behaviors exhibited by these children. Related to the general treatment procedures is the description of

9

extended treatments for autism, which include parent training and classroom programs. These extended treatments reflect the acknowledgment that to a great extent generalized treatment gains depend upon application of the treatment to wide areas of the children's functioning and multiple environments. The book concludes with a brief discussion of what the future holds for autistic children at this time. Prognostic issues are addressed throughout the volume but are summarized here to give the reader an understanding of those factors that are now known to be significant prognostic indicators.

The author had multiple incentives for undertaking the task of writing this book. First, the desire to provide a concise yet comprehensive and up-to-date discussion of autism for the reader who may have little or no knowledge of the disorder, yet who is somewhat sophisticated in terms of child psychology and research issues. Second, she hopes to give the reader a sense of her own utter fascination with this syndrome. Her first exposure to autism occurred during an undergraduate psychology course at UCLA. Since then the author has been intrigued by, challenged by, and educated by the study of these children and their treatment.

The author would like to acknowledge the many contributions of others to this effort. Alan E. Kazdin, Ph.D., the Series Editor, provided the opportunity to write this volume as well as the encouragement, patience, and editorial acumen that made all the difference. Invaluable comments and suggestions on an earlier draft of this manuscript were provided by Marjorie H. Charlop, Ph.D., Glen Dunlap, Ph.D., and Robert L. Koegel, Ph.D. An extra special thanks is owed Robert Koegel who for over 20 years has been a wonderful colleague, collaborator, and friend. In addition, the author acknowledges the National Institute of Mental Health Research for Grants MH 28231, 39434 and 28210, which supported some of the research reported in this book and facilitated the preparation of this manuscript.

The author is also indebted to Amy B. Good for her many valuable contributions to the preparation of this manuscript and to N. Jennifer Oke and Bertram O. Ploog for additional comments. Last, but never least, the author is indebted to her husband, Dennis W. LaDucer, who read every word of the manuscript and offered editorial suggestions, pointed questions, and encouragement. While the editorial suggestions and pointed questions may not have been always graciously accepted, the encouragement certainly was.

— *Laura Schreibman*
La Jolla, California

1

AUTISM: A HISTORICAL PERSPECTIVE

The history of the diagnosis of autism is an important component to the overall picture of this disorder since, as we shall see, it relates to many aspects of it. Unlike some other forms of psychopathology, which have had a rather long and uncomplicated history, the diagnosis of autism is characterized by a relatively short history rich in detail, controversy, and theoretical confrontations. Thus, perspectives on etiology and treatment have been constantly entwined in the historical skeins of prevailing philosophies. Fortunately, the more recent emphasis on the scientific investigation of autism has had a steadying effect on the field and we can note a more directed approach to the study of autism, its etiology and treatment. While these factors will be addressed in the subsequent sections of this volume, it might be helpful to have a brief introduction to the historical perspectives.

"Early infantile autism" was first identified as a distinct diagnostic entity in 1943 when Leo Kanner of Johns Hopkins University described the behavioral characteristics of 11 children whom he felt were not adequately described by existing diagnostic criteria. In his initial report (1943) he gave a very comprehensive and detailed description of each of the children. What he described was a group of children who were indeed remarkably alike in several behavioral characteristics and yet as a group were quite different from other recognized child clinical populations. The distinct behavioral characteristics identified by Kanner included an inability to develop normal relations with people and situations in life (extreme autistic aloneness), a delay in speech acquisition, the noncommunicative nature of speech if it developed (e.g., echolalia), pronominal reversal (e.g., substituting "you" for "I"), repetitive and stereotyped play activities, a compulsive demand for the maintenance of sameness in the environment, a lack of imagination but a good rote memory, a normal physical appearance, and the appearance of abnormalities in infancy (e.g., lack of responsiveness when held). It is interesting that while the specific behavioral criteria for a diagnosis of autism have undergone some debate over the years, Kanner's original criteria have emerged almost unchanged. This is quite a testament to Kanner's perceptive and detailed description of the children he observed and to his ability to identify the seminal features of the disorder.

While Kanner's (1943) was the first description of a new clinical diagnosis, the syndrome had certainly existed long before its official recognition. For example, Itard's (1801) report of Victor, the "Wild Boy of Aveyron," presents us with a description of a child considered retarded but who also exhibited characteristics of autism. He was found in 1799 in the woods of Aveyron, France, when he was 11 or 12 years old. Itard described him as filthy, affected with spasmodic movements, body rocking, and resistive to contact with others. He showed no affection and did not seem to attend to his environment. He failed to focus on objects or people. He would sometimes appear to be deaf yet respond quite readily to certain sounds such as those associated with food (e.g., the cracking of a walnut). He did not play with toys. When he desired something, he would lead someone by the hand to the location of the desired object. He showed a compulsive demand for sameness in his environment and resisted any change in the location of objects in his room. These are but some of the behavioral similarities to Kanner's syndrome that lead one to suspect that Victor was autistic (Itard, 1801; Wing, 1976). In addition, Kanner's paper (1943) led to the recognition of several other prior cases of the disorder (e.g., Darr & Worden, 1951; Haslam, 1809; Vaillant, 1962).

Kanner's use of the term "autism" has proven to be somewhat unfortunate because of its association with the term as used by Bleuler (1919, 1950) to describe the withdrawal into an active fantasy life adopted by adult schizophrenics. Actually, as Wing (1976) points out, the concept of "autism" as used by Kanner describes the opposite of Bleuler's "autism" in that it is the very absence of any creative fantasy life which characterizes the withdrawal of such children. Hence, clinicians and diagnosticians have worked to differentiate autism from other identified disorders. For example, Bender (1947) thought that autistic children represented the earliest expression of adult schizophrenia and thus the diagnostic label "childhood schizophrenia" was coined. Berta Rank (1955) used the term "atypical ego development," emphasizing the psychoanalytic perspective. Similarly, Mahler (1952) described the children as suffering from "symbiotic psychosis" and thus a pathological mother-child relationship. More recently, investigators have attempted to delineate potential subfacets of the disorder. For example, Goldfarb (1961) described a continuum from organic childhood schizophrenia to non-organic childhood schizophrenia (assuming an environmental causation) and Anthony (1958) made the distinction between "primary" and "secondary" autism based on the age of onset.

Since there were no known organic pathologies that could be identified as having a causal influence on the disorder, Kanner adopted the prevailing theoretical orientation of the time and looked to the family and the child's early experiences as possible main etiological factors responsible for the development of autism. He provided descriptions (Kanner, 1943, 1949) of the parents of autistic children as highly intelligent, cold, emotionally reserved, highly organized, and mechanistic in their relationship to their child. *Time* magazine, focusing on the "refrigerator type" parent described by Kanner, once wrote that autistic children "were the offspring of highly organized, professional parents, cold and rational," who "just happened to defrost long enough to produce a child" ("Child is Father," 1960). Some early hypotheses, derived from these observations of the characteristics of parents of autistic children, focused on a causal relationship between these parental characteristics and the appearance of autism. Some professionals (e.g., Bettelheim, 1967) speculated that the child's "withdrawal" into its own world of autism was a reaction to parental behavior. Bettelheim speculated that there was some very early event in the parents' behavior that convinced the child that he/she was in mortal danger and the world was a hostile, dangerous place. The child's only defense was to withdraw from the threatening world into an inner world, safe from external influences. The issue of parent-causation has provided a colorful, sometimes animated, debate in the field of autism and will be covered in more detail in our discussion of etiology.

Intimately related to prevailing perspectives on the etiology of autism are the various treatment approaches developed over the years. As Ritvo (1976) points out, the 1940s and 1950s can be characterized as giving rise to several treatment philosophies, each based on the theoretical perspective advocated by the practitioner. Thus, diagnosis, etiological hypotheses, and specific treatments varied. The treatments ranged from psychoanalysis of the parents, institutionalization of the patient, psychotropic drugs, megavitamin regimens, electroshock, and treatments based on learning theory principles (Ritvo, 1976).

Recent years have witnessed a rather dramatic shifting in orientation both in relation to treatment and etiology. Currently, the emphasis on behavioral treatments, first stimulated by the work of Ferster and DeMyer (1961, 1962), reflects the results of a large body of systematic research supporting the effectiveness of these interventions based on learning principles. Further, focus on etiology has shifted toward the identification of biological etiologies reflecting the prevailing attitude that autism is organically, rather than psychogenically based.

As will become apparent to the reader, most of the early forms of treatment, and to a large extent the philosophies upon which they were based, have fallen by the wayside in the face of failure. Autism has proven to be a most difficult puzzle indeed. Specifics of etiology and effective treatments have awaited systematic experimental analyses and documentation. Despite treatment advances, a cure remains elusive. It is fortunate that autism continues to hold fascination for so many. This will surely lead to its continued investigation and, one hopes, firm answers regarding possible prevention and remediation.

2

BEHAVIORAL CHARACTERISTICS

Schopler (1978) points out that the specific behavioral characteristics of interest in the diagnosis of autism may vary with the purpose of the diagnosis. Thus behavioral psychiatrists, speech pathologists, researchers, educators and others are likely to focus on different aspects of the disorder that are of most importance to them. Indeed, as we shall see, one can certainly make a convincing argument for describing autism in terms of specific behaviors and for directing research and clinical efforts toward understanding these specific behaviors (Schreibman & Koegel, 1981).

Also, since Kanner's (1943) early description of the disorder there has been a good deal of discussion in the professional literature concerning which "symptoms" are required for a true diagnosis of autism. (See Rutter, 1978a, b for a more detailed description of this literature.) Yet despite some varying emphases, individuals involved in the study of autism have reached agreement on the behaviors most commonly associated with autism today (Schreibman & Mills, 1983). This chapter presents a detailed overview of these behavioral characteristics.

DEFICITS IN SOCIAL BEHAVIOR

Kanner (1943) originally pointed to the autistic child's inability from the beginning of life to relate in a normal manner to people and situations. It is unanimously agreed that the profound and pervasive deficits in social attachment and behavior displayed by these children are the hallmarks of autism and many have indicated that abnormal social and emotional behaviors are primary to the diagnosis (e.g., Denkla, 1986; Fein, Pennington, Markowitz, Braverman, & Waterhouse, 1986). The nature of this social responsiveness has been investigated (e.g., Bartak, Rutter, & Cox, 1975; Churchill & Bryson, 1972; Hutt & Vaizey, 1966; Sorosky, Ornitz, Brown, & Ritvo, 1968; Wing, 1969; and Wolff & Chess, 1964) and distinct patterns have emerged. There is a definite lack of attachment to others and a failure to bond with parents. Typically, the parents say they feel the child does not "need" them in the true emotional sense. One mother put it concisely when she said: "I am only important to him as one who fulfills his needs. If it were not me, then it could just as well be a total stranger."

It has often been observed that autistic infants do not cry for attention as do normal infants. They are perfectly content to lie alone in their crib and seldom cry unless truly uncomfortable (e.g., hungry or wet). They are frequently described as "good babies" because they are content to be left alone and rarely demand attention. They may not display the normal postural anticipation of being picked up when the parent is near and may even cry when approached. Indeed, the children not only do not actively seek cuddling, hugging and kissing, but may, in fact, actively resist the affectionate overtures of others. Some parents have reported that on being held the child was rigid, like a wooden doll, or flaccid, like a rag doll. Thus, the children typically fail to show the cup-and-mold response associated with normal infants, who mold their bodies to that of the person holding them. Another very early sign, and one that persists throughout their lives, is the failure to establish social eye contact with others. Not only do they not show the normal social response of eye contact when interacting, they very often actively avoid it (Rimland, 1964). This has been termed "gaze aversion" by some investigators and is a most striking behavior. No wonder autistic children do not delight in the "peek-a-boo" games so popular with nonautistic infants and toddlers. Interestingly, while gaze aversion is considered characteristic of many autistic youngsters, recent studies suggest that the behavior is not universal among this population and varies in different situations and across time (Tiegerman & Primavera, 1984; Mirenda, Donnellan, & Yoder, 1983).

An example of the social unresponsiveness of an autistic infant provides a nice illustration of the behavioral characteristics of these infants. One mother reported anecdotally to the author that she had had a difficult time trying to get her infant to eat. She was bottle feeding the infant and every attempt on her part to feed the baby led to fussing, crying, struggling, and the ultimate regurgitation of most of the formula. When the mother contracted a severe cold, the pediatrician suggested she not expose the child to infection. To avoid close contact during feeding, the mother rigged up a pillow arrangement that propped both the baby and the bottle in such a way that the child could feed. During this time the mother noted the child no longer cried, fussed, or struggled but instead seemed very happy while eating. Upon the mother's recovery and subsequent return to normal bottle feeding, the child reverted to the previous problematic behaviors. It was apparent that the child was most content when not in contact with the mother. This intolerance, or passive acceptance, of physical contact has commonly been associated with autism and the literature abounds with accounts like the one described above, although some investigators (e.g., Howlin, 1986) suggest that the emphasis in clinical literature on avoidance of physical contact may have been overplayed. Nonetheless its occurrence serves to dramatize the social deficits in these children.

This preference for being alone continues to be evident as the child grows older. Such children are often described as "loners". Such a child might wander away from other family members to be by him/herself. Typically, the child is not upset when the parents go out for an evening and leave him/her with a sitter, or drop him/her at school. Similarly, parents have reported that the child may be indifferent to their return, perhaps not even noticing that they have, indeed, returned. The child displays no spontaneous affection and may actively resist such contact or passively accept it with no apparent pleasure.

Another striking characteristic of autistic children is their failure to derive comfort from their parents. Unlike normal children who run to their parents when upset, autistic children typically do not seek them out when hurt or frightened. In short, these children show minimal involvement with their parents, which is in striking contrast to the intense, dependent, and affectionate emotional attachment demonstrated by nonautistic children.

This failure to develop social attachment and behavior is also evident in their lack of peer contact and interactive play (e.g., Rutter, 1978a, b). They usually avoid play situations with peers and, if in the same area, will engage in solitary activity. If they do express interest, it is often only to watch the activity without social initiation or reciprocation. Predictably, most autistic children do not show the social imitation so necessary to the acquisition of appropriate interaction with peers (e.g., Varni, Lovaas, Koegel, & Everett, 1979).

While true social attachment and responsiveness is grossly deficient in autistic children, this does not mean they do not engage in social behavior. It is frequently reported that autistic children relate to people as "objects" rather than as people and hence treat them as such (e.g., Rimland, 1964). An autistic child may stand on her mother's lap to reach a cookie jar but will do so without establishing eye contact or in any way acknowledging the mother as anything but a piece of furniture. A child might also lead people by the hand (without looking at them) to gain access to a desired object or activity (e.g., Schreibman & Mills, 1983).

Perhaps one of the most impressive features of this lack of social behavior is that the children may form strong attachments to inanimate objects, such as rocks, small toys, pencils, and be very upset if these are taken away. Kanner (1943) provides a vivid description of the social detachment and object attachment of one of his original cases of autism.

> The most striking feature in his behavior was the difference in his reactions to objects and to people. Objects absorbed him easily and he showed good attention and perseverance in playing with them. He seemed to regard people as unwelcome intruders to whom he paid as little attention as they would permit. When forced to respond, he did so briefly and returned to his absorption in things. When a hand was held out before him so that he could not possibly ignore, he played with it briefly as if it were a detached object. He blew out a match with an expression of satisfaction with the achievement, but did not look up to the person who had lit the match. When a fourth person entered the room, he retreated for a minute or two behind the bookcase, saying, "I don't want you," and waving him away, then resumed his play, paying no further attention to him or anyone else. (Kanner, 1943, p. 10–11).

The profound social deficits so characteristic of the disorder can be identified in autistic adults and "high-level" autistic individuals (those with minimal or no retardation and mild appearance of the psychopathology). The social behavior of these individuals is characterized by a lack of interest in establishing friendships, lack of responsiveness to the subtle social cues so important in normal social behavior, and continued interest in being alone. Such individuals remain for the most part social isolates, may say or do socially inappropriate things (e.g., Rutter, 1978a, b) and be labeled "eccentric" (if fortunate) or "weird" (if not so fortunate).

SPEECH AND LANGUAGE

Another identifying characteristic of autistic children is a specific pattern of speech and language. Often it is the child's failure to acquire language that first alerts the parents that something is wrong. Kanner (1943) considered the delay or failure in the acquisition of language to be of primary importance in autism. Approximately 50% of autistic individuals never develop functional speech (Rutter, 1978a, b) and those who do speak characteristically display speech that is qualitatively different than the speech of normal children and children with other language disorders (e.g., Bartak *et al.*, 1977; Ricks & Wing, 1975; Rutter, 1965, 1966a, 1978a, b; Wing, 1976). In addition, it is often reported that such children begin to speak, learning to say "Mama," "Dada," and other labels but suddenly lose the acquired speech and fail to progress linguistically. This language loss tends to occur between 18 and 30 months of age.

Speaking autistic children commonly display *echolalia*, the repetition of words or phrases spoken by others (Fay, 1969). Typically, this form of speech is noncommunicative in nature. There are several distinctions within the speech anomaly of echolalia, the most common being immediate and delayed echolalia (Carr, Schreibman, & Lovaas, 1975). Immediate echolalia occurs when the child repeats a verbal stimulus just heard. For example, an adult approaches a child and says "How are you, Kenny?" to which the child echoes "How are you Kenny?". In delayed echolalia the child repeats a verbal stimulus heard sometime in the past. Thus it could be something heard a few minutes ago, a week ago, a year ago, or even several years ago. Because the situation where the child echoes is usually different from that of the original verbal stimulus, the speech is contextually inappropriate (Carr *et al.*, 1975). The child might be working with her teacher and suddenly repeat the words of a television commercial heard days before. Sometimes the delayed echolalic response is so far removed from the original stimulus situation that the speech sounds quite bizarre. One child known to the author was working with his therapist on some rather difficult material. The frustrated child suddenly blurted out "So what if I drink beer!" Obviously, any relationship between the original verbal stimulus and the present situation was, indeed, remote.

Echolalia, *per se*, is not peculiar to autistic children nor is echoic responding necessarily pathological. Children who are essentially retarded and/or display delayed language development often exhibit echolalic speech. Normal language development includes a phase of echoic responding, peaking at about the age of 30 months (Van Riper, 1963; Zipf, 1949).

However, when this echoing persists past the age of three or four years, it is considered to be pathological (Darley, 1964; Fay, 1967; Ricks & Wing, 1975). While the variables affecting delayed echolalia are as yet poorly understood, there are data suggesting that immediate echolalia is related to the comprehensibility of the verbal stimulus (Carr *et al.*, 1975; Schreibman & Carr, 1978). That is, if an echolalic child is presented with a stimulus for which he has an answer (e.g., "What's your name?"), he is likely to respond correctly (e.g., "Bobby"). If, however, the child is presented with a stimulus for which he has no response, (e.g., "Who is the President?"), he will probably echo all or part of the stimulus (i.e., "Who is the President?" or "President?"). Echolalic speech is often the first manner in which language is used by autistic children and its existence, especially if it occurs before the age of five years, is associated with a more positive response to language intervention (Howlin, 1981; Rutter & Lockyer, 1967).

Pronominal reversal is another distinctive characteristic of the speech of speaking autistic individuals (e.g., Bartak & Rutter, 1974; Ricks & Wing, 1975; Rimland, 1964; Rutter, 1978a, b). Typically, the child will refer to him/herself as "you" or by name. For example, a child named Alan who has sufficient speech for communicative purposes might ask for a glass of juice by saying "Do you want a glass of juice?" or "Want some juice, Alan?" This pronominal reversal is undoubtedly related to echolalia, and the reversal of pronouns is not surprising in that other people typically refer to the child as "you" or by name. In the example above it is quite likely that the child has heard his mother say "Do you want a glass of juice?" in a situation associated with obtaining juice.

The speech and language of autistic individuals is abnormal in other respects as well. Their comprehension may be severely impaired (e.g., Ricks & Wing, 1975) and when they speak, it is often not for communicative purposes. Speech may serve a self-stimulatory purpose (e.g., Lovaas, Varni, Koegel, & Lorsch, 1977) where it seems only to function to provide sensory feedback. In such cases, autistic children may repeat certain sounds, words or phrases over and over with no apparent intent to communicate. Their use of speech in communication is typically quite limited and they seem to have great difficulty talking about anything outside the immediate situation or events (e.g., Rutter, 1978a, b). They do not easily relate past or future events and remain concretely in the here-and-now. Even the speech of high-functioning autistic individuals with relatively sophisticated language seems devoid of expressions of emotion, imagination, or abstraction. One 22-year-old autistic man was asked how he felt during various events in his life (e.g., when he was teased at school, when his mother died). His responses consisted entirely of unemotional statements, such as "It was OK," "I don't know". When he did answer with an "emotional" statement, such as "I felt bad" when his mother died, one had the impression that he was merely mouthing an expected answer.

Another oft-reported speech characteristic is the almost total literalness with which speech is comprehended and produced (e.g., Wing, 1976). Analogies and metaphors are particularly problematic and often misunderstood. If you say that it is raining cats and dogs outside, the autistic child is likely to look for animals falling from the sky. One five-year-old boy provides another illustration of the literalness of speech. This child was having difficulty learning the name of one of his therapists. For some unknown reason he kept calling the therapist "Poster". Finally, after several frustrating attempts to have the child use his correct name, the therapist said: "Kenny, my name is not Poster!" A few minutes later, when asked the therapist's name, the child answered "Not Poster". In fact, the child referred to him as "Not Poster" ever after.

The speech of most speaking autistic children is characterized by *dysprosody* (e.g., Baltaxe, 1981; Baltaxe & Simmons, 1975; Schreibman, Kohlenberg, & Britten, 1986; Simon, 1976). The speech is characterized by inaccurate pitch, rhythm, inflection, intonation, pace, and/or articulation. This is particularly true of children who are nonverbal but have acquired speech through training, although echolalic children also display errors in the prosodic (non-content carrying) characteristics of speech. The result is that even children who have relatively sophisticated language skills often sound abnormal when they speak.

ABNORMALITIES IN RESPONSE TO THE PHYSICAL ENVIRONMENT

Another behavioral characteristic often observed in autistic children is an unusual responsiveness to the sensory environment (e.g., Ritvo & Freeman, 1978; Schreibman & Mills, 1983; Wing, 1976). This is evident by under- or overreaction to various sensory events, or even to the same events on different occasions. In Kanner's (1943) original paper he describes Paul G. as a child who, "when spoken to, . . . went on with whatever he was doing as if nothing had been said. Yet one never had the feeling that he was willingly disobedient or contrary. He was obviously so remote that the remarks did not reach him" (p. 212). One might predicate from such behavior that many autistic children have histories of suspected, but unconfirmed, deafness or blindness. The child might fail to respond to a loud noise or startle stimuli or to his/her name. This, and the absence of language, are the primary reasons parents often give for suspecting their child suffers from some hearing impairment. Similarly, a child may seem totally oblivious to salient visual events in the environment, such as the comings and goings of people, approaching cars, and so on (e.g., Schreibman & Mills, 1983). Of great significance is that this unresponsiveness to the environment can be highly variable in nature (e.g., Lovaas, Schreibman, Koegel, & Rehm, 1971; Ornitz & Ritvo, 1968). The child who fails to respond to his name or to loud noises may cover his ears and scream at the sound of a turning newspaper page or come running at the sound of a soda pop can being opened. The child who does not seem to notice events in the visual environment might be obsessed with following patterns in floor tiles, watching lint fall in the light, or be able to spot a piece of candy several feet away. This variability of responsiveness has led some researchers to refer to this pattern of responding as "apparent sensory deficit" to convey the idea that the deficit is evident in behavior but not tied to known deficits at the receptor level (Lovaas, Schreibman, Koegel, & Rehm, 1971).

Unusual sensory responsiveness is noted in other modalities as well. In the tactile modality, autistic children might be over- or underresponsive to touch, pain or temperature (Ritvo & Freeman, 1978). Attenuated response to pain is apparent when the child falls or otherwise injures him/herself and, seemingly oblivious to pain, continues in the ongoing activity. In the area of vestibular functioning, autistic children may show an over- or underresponsiveness to gravity stimuli (e.g., being lifted in the air) and be fascinated with spinning objects. They may gaze intently into fans, clothes dryers, and flushing toilets or repetitively spin objects such as saucepan lids and ashtrays. In addition, their response to gustatory stimulation may be unusual; they may lick, mouth, or sniff objects, have very limited and idiosyncractic food preferences, and be very sensitive to different food textures (e.g., Ritvo & Freeman, 1978).

To understand this unusual responsiveness to the environment and how it might relate to the problems these children show in learning new behaviors, much research has been addressed to the parameters of this responsivity. Several studies (e.g., Koegel & Wilhelm, 1973; Lovaas, Schreibman, Koegel, & Rehm, 1971; Lovaas & Schreibman, 1971; Reynolds, Newsom, & Lovaas, 1974; Schreibman, Kohlenberg, & Britten, 1986; Schreibman & Lovaas, 1973) have demonstrated that autistic children typically respond to only a very limited amount of the available, relevant, sensory information in learning situations. This phenomenon has been called "stimulus overselectivity," indicating that when presented with simultaneous multiple cues, autistic children often attend to only a limited portion of the cues. Because learning usually requires responding to simultaneous cues, it is certainly not surprising that a deficit in this area would have profound implications for the acquisition of new behavioral repertoires. If someone points to a woman and says "That's mother" it is crucial that both the verbal stimulus "mother" and the referent, that particular woman, be understood. In overselective attention one or the other stimulus would go unheeded. Overselective attention is thought to play an important role in many abnormal behaviors so characteristic of autism. For example, Wing (1976) speculates that overselectivity might account for the tendency of autistic children to select a single, trivial aspect of a stimulus for attention. She cites, as an illustration, the case of one child who was fascinated with church steeples and refused to look at pictures of anything else.

Stimulus overselectivity has thus been advanced as a potential explanation of the variability in the responsiveness of autistic children and as a basis for their difficulty in learning new behaviors. Specifically, it has been implicated in the difficulties of acquiring new discriminations (Koegel & Covert, 1972), in generalizing new behaviors (Rincover & Koegel, 1975), in social behavior (Schreibman & Lovaas, 1973), in learning from traditional prompting procedures (Rincover, 1978; Schreibman, 1975), and in learning through modeling (Varni et al., 1979). As we shall see in later sections of this book, research in the area of overselective attention in autism has had considerable impact in the design and implementation of behavioral treatments (Lovaas, Koegel, & Schreibman, 1979).

DEMAND FOR SAMENESS IN THE ENVIRONMENT

One of Kanner's primary characteristics of autistic children was their compulsive preoccupation with the "preservation of sameness" in their environment (Eisenberg & Kanner, 1956; Kanner, 1943). These children are very sensitive to specific arrangements and to order and may become very upset when the environment is altered. As young children they display limited and rigid play patterns that lack the variety and imagination one might expect in normal children (Rutter, 1978a, b; Schreibman & Mills, 1983; Wing, 1976). They may play with blocks or toy cars only to the extent of lining them up in neat rows, perhaps by color and size, and become distressed if their orderly arrangement is disturbed. They might collect certain objects such as tiny toys, rocks, or pencils and hold them constantly, as a normal child may hold onto a favorite blanket or teddy bear. Any attempt to take away these favored objects will likely be met with a severe tantrum. The demand for sameness is frequently evident in the children's resistance to changes in furniture arrangements. Often even the smallest change will be noticed and lead to a tantrum and/or attempts to return the situation to its former state. Autistic children are apt to notice that a picture has been shifted just a few inches, or a particular object is missing. Anyone who has worked with autistic children can easily provide many, many examples of this demand for sameness. The author remembers one child who became extremely upset at any of the following: an open Cheerios box, an open drawer in the house, her father's open briefcase, the reclining chair left in the reclining position. Any of these events would cause her to scream hysterically until her frantic family found the offending situation and corrected it.

Many autistic children display a demand for sameness in routes of travel and/or routine. Parents often comment that if they try to take another route to a familiar place, the child becomes quite upset. Similarly, autistic children are usually not very flexible about changes in their daily routine and many parents work very hard to ensure a consistency in routine so the child will not be upset.

Sometimes autistic children develop certain ritualistic preoccupations, such as memorizing calendars, timetables, or patterns (Rutter, 1978a, b). Often they become obsessed with letters or numbers and may spend a good deal of time memorizing, reciting, or writing these symbols. One child, for example, was so attached to numbers that she insisted on taking plastic magnetic numbers to bed with her every night. While some autistic children may be extremely precocious in the use of these symbols, which is related to their "special abilities" (to be considered below), typically these skills are limited to compulsive rituals as opposed to creative endeavors. These rituals are also evidenced by such behaviors as insistence on eating particular foods, using particular eating utensils, wearing only certain clothing, touching particular objects, or repeatedly asking the same questions, which must be answered in a particular fashion (Rimland, 1964; Rutter, 1978a, b). The intensity of these compulsions can be very strong. One child insisted on wearing a particular T-shirt, long after he had outgrown it. His mother said he tore off any other shirt she put on him. Another child would only eat

McDonald hamburgers at McDonald restaurants. He would eat no other foods at a McDonald's nor would he eat McDonald hamburgers at home. This pattern persisted for a period of three years during which time the parents took the child to McDonald's for every meal.

Little wonder that this demand for sameness in autistic children remains one of the most fascinating aspects of the disorder. Kanner (1943) considered it one of the most essential features of the disorder and it still remains one that is consistently associated with the diagnosis (e.g., Rutter, 1978a, b). But while this behavioral characteristic continues to fascinate, it remains poorly understood.

SELF-STIMULATORY BEHAVIOR

Another behavior very frequently seen in autistic individuals is repetitive, persistent, stereotyped behavior that seems to serve no other function than to provide sensory or kinesthetic feedback (e.g., Lovaas, Litrownik, & Mann, 1971; Rincover, 1978; Stanley, 1985). This behavior is often viewed as a defining characteristic of autism (Rimland, 1964) and was noted by Kanner (1943) in his original description of the disorder. The behavior has been variously labeled self-stimulation (the term that will be used in this volume), stereotypic behavior, or disturbances in motility. At the gross motor level, typical behaviors include rhythmic body rocking (standing and rocking from foot to foot, sitting and rocking the upper torso, or rocking back and forth while on hands and knees), jumping, darting or pacing, head bobbing, arm or hand flapping, or posturing. At a more subtle level, the behavior may include gazing at lights, gazing or "regarding" the cupped hand, staring out of the corner of the eye, moving or rolling eyes, tensing muscles, finger wiggling, waving fingers in front of the face, hair twirling, or grimacing. Autistic children often incorporate objects in their self-stimulatory behavior; for example, spinning objects such as saucepan lids or coins or repeatedly flipping the pages of a book. They may tenaciously hold particular objects or rotate a block in a repetitive manner. While much of this behavior provides kinesthetic feedback (e.g., rocking, jumping, flapping), a good deal involves visual and auditory feedback. Common visual self-stimulatory behaviors include gazing at lights or gazing at flickering lights (by waving an outstretched hand in front of the eyes). They may twirl pieces of string, wave pencils in front of their face, pick lint from sweaters or stuffed animals, or spin the wheels on a toy car. Frequently observed auditory self-stimulatory behaviors include repetitive vocal patterns (nonsense sound patterns or particular words or phrases), tapping objects, and listening to particular songs.

There are other defining characteristics of self-stimulation. First, these children may spend a high proportion of their waking hours engaged in this activity. The behavior seems to be extremely important to them to the extent that some autistic individuals engage in little else. Indeed, they resist attempts to discourage the behavior and will sometimes even risk pain or loss of food while engaging in self-stimulation (e.g., Lovaas, Litrownik, & Mann, 1971). Second, this behavior differs significantly from the normal "play" behaviors associated with normal childhood. It typically looks unusual or bizarre, as when the child jumps up and down while waving his arms repeatedly. The behavior may involve grotesque body movements and facial grimacing that are particularly bizarre when the individual is older. Another difference between the normal play behaviors of children and the self-stimulation of the autistic child is that there are data indicating that the occurrence of the self-stimulation interferes with the child's responsiveness and the acquisition of more normal behaviors (Koegel & Covert, 1972; Koegel, Firestone, Kramme, & Dunlap, 1974; Lovaas, Litrownik, & Mann, 1971).

The fact that this behavior interferes with the children's responsiveness to environmental input has the support of both empirical investigations (e.g., Koegel & Covert, 1972; Lovaas, Litrownik, & Mann, 1971; Rincover, 1978) and anecdotal observations (Kanner, 1943). It is quite striking to see an autistic child sitting alone in a corner rocking or twirling a string while the room around him is filled with active children playing with toys. The child is truly oblivious to the surrounding activity. It is not surprising that children so absorbed in isolated activity are often described as "in their own world" or "in a shell".

Unresponsiveness has drawn the attention of researchers and clinicians because of the important implications this problem has for treatment. Self-stimulation serves as a major obstacle to treatment and, as we shall see in our discussion of treatment below, understanding and remedying this aspect of autism has proved most difficult.

SELF-INJURIOUS BEHAVIOR

While the above description of behavioral characteristics certainly includes an assortment of severe behaviors, none of the behaviors manifested by autistic (or other) individuals is more dramatic than self-injurious behavior (SIB). SIB involves any behavior in which the individual inflicts physical damage to his/her own body (Tate & Baroff, 1966). The most common forms of SIB in the autistic population include head banging and self-biting of hands or wrists (Rutter & Lockyer, 1967). Other common SIB behaviors are elbow or leg banging, hair pulling or rubbing, face scratching, and self-slapping of face or sides. Sometimes the children tear out their fingernails with their teeth, gouge at their eyes, and progressively bite off their fingertips.

Self-injury can vary in intensity and therefore the amount of damage incurred can range from slight to extremely severe. Some individuals who slap their faces, bang their heads, bite their wrists, and so forth, leave bruises, redness and/or calluses. Other children engage in this type of behavior so intensely, or engage in a form of the behavior that is so severe (e.g., running into walls, head first) that they suffer fractured skulls, detached retinas, broken jaws or noses, and loss of large quantities of flesh from their bodies (e.g., Carr, 1977; Lovaas & Simmons, 1969). It is quite possible for an individual to kill him/herself as a result of SIB. It is important to note that such a death can hardly be termed "suicidal" since death was not the intended result. Rather, death is sometimes the tragic result of engaging in this kind of behavior. For example, one child known to the author was a severe head-banger, seeking out metal bed frames on which to beat his head. Eventually he suffered extensive brain damage and died as a result.

While the direct effects of SIB may be obvious, others are not as apparent but just as serious. First, infections are a serious hazard, often resulting from the open wounds caused by SIB. Second, with some children the behavior is so intense and life-threatening (e.g., severe head banging) that they must be physically restrained to prevent this type of behavior. In such cases, the children may be tied down to their bed, be placed in a camisole ("straitjacket"), have splints placed on their arms, have their hands tied to their waist, and so forth. When such restraints are prolonged (e.g., periods of months or years), structural changes such as demineralization of bone, shortening of tendons, and arrested motor development result from nonuse of limbs (Lovaas & Simmons, 1969). A third kind of damage resulting from SIB is that the latter restricts the child's psychological and educational development. Besides the restraint that prevents the child from engaging in social and educational activities, parents and staff members dealing with SIB children are often reluctant to place demands on them for fear of precipitating an SIB episode (Carr, 1977). Under such circumstances, the children miss important opportunities for productive interaction with their social and physical environment.

Treatments for SIB have included drugs, restraints, and reassuring affection. None of these has proven effective in alleviating SIB and, indeed, some (e.g., reassuring affection) have exacerbated it (e.g., Carr, 1977; Lovaas & Simmons, 1969). More successful treatments have involved operant techniques such as extinction and punishment. For comprehensive reviews of the treatment of SIB, the reader is referred to Carr (1977), Bachman (1972), Smolev (1971), Frankel and Simmons (1976), Iwata, Dorsey, Slifer, Bauman, & Richman (1982), and Murphy & Wilson (1985).

SIB is certainly not peculiar to autism. It has been reported in four to five percent of the psychiatric populations (Frankel & Simmons, 1976). Nevertheless, it remains a significant problem for autism researchers and one which clinicians have also spent considerable energy addressing. However, it is one behavior that can be called a success story in that research has led to a fairly good understanding of it and, more importantly, to the design of effective treatments. These will be discussed in our coverage of treatment.

SPECIAL SKILLS

One oft-reported characteristic of autistic children is the appearance of isolated skill areas. Many of these children display isolated areas of exceptional performance that are incongruous with their otherwise depressed level of functioning. Sometimes these behaviors reflect normal levels of functioning which only appear exceptional in contrast to the lower levels of functioning in other areas. Sometimes, however, they may be truly exceptional. These abilities most commonly lie in the general areas of musical, mechanical, or mathematical skills (e.g., Applebaum *et al.*, 1979; Rimland, 1978). One child may be able to remember and reproduce complex melodies and song lyrics. Another child may demonstrate an ability to assemble difficult jigsaw puzzles (perhaps picture-side down), or to assemble or dismantle complicated pieces of machinery (Wing, 1976). One nine-year-old child known to the author was an expert at assembling and disassembling vacuum cleaners. Some children seem obsessed with memorizing bus schedules, mathematical tables, issues of TV Guide, or random number or letter sequences. "Calendar calculation," the ability to determine on what day of the week a particular calendar date will fall, is exhibited by some autistic children.

Interestingly, Kanner (1943) noted the autistic child's excellent rote memory and hypothesized that it suggested the capacity for normal intelligence. He also suggested that the "serious expression" of the children indicated intelligence. He viewed the children's intellectual retardation as a consequence of their failure to establish social relationships (Rutter, 1978a, b). This is one of the few areas in which more recent data have not upheld Kanner's early observations. It is now apparent that the excellent rote memory often seen in these children falls into the category of isolated skill (Rutter, 1978a, b; Schreibman & Mills, 1983). Rimland (1978) refers to the autistic "savant" (à la "idiot savant") and draws a parallel between the isolated savant skills observed in many autistic individuals and those noted in the retarded population. Thus, what we have here is a behavior or behaviors that in all likelihood bear no relation to the level of skill apparent in other areas of functioning. Indeed, many of these children display exceptional skill in one area that would have little obvious utility in their environment (e.g., memorizing schedules for busses they never see, calendar calculation) and relatively few skills in more adaptive areas of functioning. For example, one seven-year-old autistic child was a true musical genius. He could play many instruments and on hearing a melody could instantly reproduce it on any of his instruments. He could also immediately transpose the tune into any key desired and compose appropriate harmonies. While few would doubt that this child had musical talent, the usefulness of his skills was questionable; he was neither toilet trained, nor able to say his name, nor to respond to a simple command such as "close the door."

INTELLECTUAL FUNCTIONING

Many researchers have long believed that autistic children are not retarded, that it is only their deficits in other areas of functioning which make them seem intellectually handicapped, i.e., perform poorly on standardized intellectual assessments and demonstrate difficulty in learning new behaviors. This belief dates back to Kanner's (1943) original thesis that these children possessed normal intelligence. Their good rote memory, serious facial expressions, and the absence of physical abnormalities supported this hypothesis (Rutter, 1978a, b). Unfortunately, however, the data acquired to date indicate that the majority of autistic children are mentally retarded. According to Ritvo and Freeman (1978), current research estimates indicate that approximately 60% of autistic children have measured IQs below 50, 20% between 50 and 70, while 20% measure 70 or above.

Intellectual assessment of autistic children is difficult because of the extreme variability of performance on portions of the assessment instruments.

These children tend to perform best on tests and subtests measuring manipulative or visual-spatial skills and rote memory, and do least well on tasks requiring abstract thought and symbol or sequential logic (Ritvo & Freeman, 1978). One of the main differences between autistic children who score in the retarded range and children whose primary diagnosis is retardation, is the difference in the pattern of performance on different tests and subtests. Retarded children score poorly on most or all assessments. The performance of autistic children is typically characterized by significant variability, scoring very poorly on tasks measuring symbolic thought (e.g., language) and perhaps at a normal or high level in areas involving rote memory, mathematics and/or music (e.g., Applebaum et al., 1979).

Another fact suggesting that the poor performance of autistic children is due to retardation are data indicating that IQ in autistic children has the same properties as it does for other children (Rutter, 1978a, b). It tends to remain stable throughout childhood and adolescence (DeMyer et al., 1974; Lockyer & Rutter, 1969; Gittelman & Birch, 1967) and tends to be predictive of future educational accomplishments (Bartak & Rutter, 1974; Lockyer & Rutter, 1969; Rutter & Bartak, 1973). Based on this information it appears that although autism and retardation are separate conditions, they often coexist in the same child.

AFFECT

Autistic children often display flattened, excessive, or otherwise inappropriate affect (e.g., Rimland, 1964; American Psychiatric Association, 1987). They may have an almost constant, placid expression and seem totally emotionally detached, coasting through life. These children show little or no differential emotional reactions in varying situations. At the other extreme are children who display erratic emotional behavior, ranging from giggling and hysterical laughter to fury to inconsolable sobbing. These emotional responses often seem to be totally independent of environmental events, and the child can rapidly vacillate from one to the other without apparent reason (Schreibman & Mills, 1983). In fact, many parents complain that their children "fly into" intense and lengthy tantrums without obvious provocation. Some of this unusual emotional behavior seems tied to the lack of appropriate social behavior and the failure to respond to the social cues provided in their social environment. The child might laugh when another person is hurt, or cry when others laugh (Schreibman & Mills, 1983). Bernard Rimland (1964) provided a succinct description of the emotional detachment of autistic children when he observed that childhood schizophrenics are "disoriented" in that their response to the environment is apparent but confused, while autistic children are "unoriented" in that they totally fail to respond directly to their environment.

Autistic children may display irrational fears; sometimes these seem to be related to their demands for sameness. Their extreme reactions to disturbances in environment, routes of travel, or routine sometimes take the form of fear or anger. They may be terrified by objects or events that other people see as harmless and which have not been associated with unpleasant experiences for the child. Take the case of a child who was afraid of an empty paper towel holder in the kitchen, of dining room drapes left half-opened, of certain doorways in the house, and of punched computer cards. Another child was terrified of tortillas, yellow ducks, balloons and sesame seed hamburger buns (regular buns were OK). The relation of fears to demand for sameness in this last child was evident by the fact that he insisted on having his bedspread arranged in a particular manner, because in other positions it appeared white and circular—like a tortilla.

SUMMARY

The syndrome of autism is just that—a combination of specific behavioral characteristics that constitute a specific pattern. The most commonly associated behavioral characteristics of the disorder include severe and pervasive deficits in social behavior, delays and deficits in the acquisition of speech and language, unusual responsiveness to the environment, a demand for the maintenance of sameness in the environment, self-stimulatory behavior, self-injury, isolated special skills, impaired intellectual functioning, and unusual affect. While not every autistic child necessarily exhibits all these behaviors, they are the characteristics most closely associated with a diagnosis of autism.

The behaviors described above comprise the "syndrome" of autism. While it is the combination of these behaviors that distinguishes autism from other disorders, the specific behavioral characteristics described above are not equally important for the diagnosis. Thus self-stimulation, SIB, inappropriate affect, impaired intellectual functioning and certain language characteristics are represented in other populations. However, the profound deficits in social attachment and behavior, the demand for sameness, certain speech characteristics and the highly uneven profile in a range of functioning areas are more unique to autism, and may weigh more heavily in diagnosis. In the next chapter we shall address how these behavioral characteristics are fitted together in formulating the diagnosis.

3

DIAGNOSIS AND EVALUATION

DIAGNOSIS

Despite Kanner's (1943) clear and detailed description of his population of autistic children, the diagnosis of the disorder has progressed through an evolution fueled by the study of more children and the application of some rigorous scientific investigations. In this chapter we shall look at the evolution of the diagnosis of early infantile autism, the features differentiating this disorder from other developmental disorders, and the psychological evaluation procedures commonly applied to autistic children.

Evolution of the Diagnosis

Kanner's (1943) original paper described a group of children who represented a form of childhood psychosis which differed significantly from other types of childhood disorders, but maintained many of the similarities with what was then called childhood schizophrenia. Basically, he described the syndrome as characterized by the following:

1. *Extreme autistic aloneness.* This involves the failure during infancy to develop normal relationships with parents, general unresponsiveness to people, failure to interact with peers, and the failure to acknowledge the presence or absence of parents or others. This characteristic was assumed to be present from birth.
2. *Language abnormalities.* This includes mutism, echolalia, pronominal reversals, and the ability in verbal children to demonstrate an excellent rote memory by repeating names of objects, nursery rhymes, songs, and lists.
3. *Obsessive desire for the maintenance of sameness.* Autistic children are highly sensitive to daily routine, arrangements of furniture or objects, precise wording of requests, and broken or incomplete objects. Changes in these events may be quite upsetting to the children. This category also includes stereotypic, self-stimulatory behaviors, and preoccupation with certain objects.
4. *Good cognitive potential.* Kanner noted the intelligent and serious facial expressions of the children, their excellent rote memory, and good performance on the Seguin Form Board.

5. *Normal physical development*. This included the normal appearance and good fine motor skills of the children.
6. *Highly intelligent, obsessive, and cold parents*. Kanner (1943) reported that most of the parents of his sample were professionals with advanced degrees, who appeared aloof, overly organized (to the point of being mechanistic), withdrawn, emotionally insulated, and unhappily married.

Kanner's (1943) work served well to delineate characteristics of the syndrome and reflects psychiatry during that time (Newsom & Rincover, 1982). Unfortunately, however, such a description is problematic in that no clear, objective criteria were proposed. Thus it is not surprising that after Kanner's original paper the diagnosis of autism has undergone changes. Three major areas of controversy emerged. These included: (a) whether autism was indeed a separate entity that could be differentiated from other forms of childhood psychosis; (b) what the diagnostic criteria were; and (3) the role of parents in its etiology and as a diagnostic factor (Schreibman & Charlop, 1987).

Kanner later reduced the essential symptoms of autism to extreme aloneness and preoccupation with the preservation of sameness (Eisenberg & Kanner, 1956). It is interesting, but somewhat puzzling, that language abnormalities, considered so important in the earlier papers, were no longer listed as essential characteristics (Rutter, 1978a, b).

While Kanner steadfastly asserted that autism was distinct from childhood schizophrenia (Eisenberg & Kanner, 1956), others noted the similarities between autism and childhood schizophrenia and hence the terms were sometimes interchanged. The British Working Party, as summarized by Creak (1961), proposed nine points for the diagnosis of "childhood schizophrenia" (including autism). These criteria included:

1. Gross and sustained impairment of emotional relationships with people;
2. Apparent unawareness of personal identity (for example, pronominal reversals, self-stimulation, and SIB);
3. Pathological preoccupation with particular objects or certain characteristics of them;
4. Resistance to change;
5. Abnormal perceptual experience—unpredictable response to sensory stimuli or insensitivity to pain or temperature;
6. Acute, excessive, and seemingly illogical anxiety (inappropriate or absence of appropriate fear);
7. Speech abnormalities;
8. Distortion in motility patterns (self-stimulatory behavior);
9. A background of serious retardation in which islets of normal, near normal, or exceptional intellectual function or skill may appear.

These British Working Party diagnostic criteria are very important because, as can be seen, they recognized the importance of abnormalities in language. They reinstated what Kanner had dropped. Also, unlike Kanner, they proposed that such children's intellectual functioning was impaired (Schreibman & Charlop, 1987).

It is also noteworthy that the British Working Party criteria say nothing about the parents of autistic children as a factor in the diagnosis or etiology of the disorder. Kanner (1949) continued to stress the possibility of psychogenic factors in autism. He described mothers of autistic children as mechanistic, lacking in warmth toward their child, unemotional, obsessive, and perfectionistic. In a period when psychoanalysis was enjoying great popularity, it is hardly surprising that other individuals of a psychodynamic bent agreed (e.g., Bettelheim, 1967; Goldfarb, 1961; Kaufman, Rosenblum, Heims, & Willer, 1957). Empirical evidence was later provided which contradicted psychogenic factors in association with autism (e.g., Creak & Ini, 1960; Koegel, Schreibman, O'Neil & Burke, 1983; Kolvin, 1971; Rutter, 1968).

Current Diagnostic Criteria

The evolution in diagnostic criteria for autism has served several purposes. In addition to the need to specify more precisely the nature of autism and how it differs from other childhood disorders, the change in diagnostic criteria has also led to an increase in the number of children diagnosed as autistic (Schreibman & Charlop, 1987). If autism had continued to be defined in strict accordance with Kanner's criteria, then too few children would "qualify" for the diagnosis. As Newsom and Rincover (1982) point out, this would make research on the syndrome quite difficult since too few subjects so identified would be available for appropriate investigations. In fact, "Kanner's syndrome" or classic autism represents only a relatively small portion of the children who receive the diagnosis. The broader diagnosis has also served an important social and economic function; parents and educators needed larger numbers of autistic children to justify the need for special education for them and to qualify for government funding (Schreibman & Charlop, 1987).

While some disagreement as to the exact criteria to be used in applying a diagnosis of autism persists, nevertheless three main sets of diagnostic criteria are currently in wide use. [The interested reader is referred to Newsom and Rincover (1982) for a synopsis of the various diagnostic criteria employed in prominent research and treatment centers, and to Schreibman and Charlop (1987) for a detailed comparison of diagnostic criteria used since 1943.]

One set of diagnostic criteria, advanced by Rutter (1978a, b) and based on previous definitions and research, includes:

1. Onset before the age of 30 months;
2. Impaired social development that is not due to the child's impaired intellectual level. Included here is lack of affection and eye contact;
3. Delayed and deviant language development. Included here are lack of comprehension, immediate and delayed echolalia, pronominal reversal, and lack of conversational speech;
4. Insistence on the preservation of sameness which is indicated by stereotypic actions, preoccupations with certain objects or activities, rigid routines, and resistance to environmental change.

Rutter's (1978) list of criteria represents a compilation of research. Another set of criteria, however, was devised to serve administrative and legislative purposes. These criteria were proposed by the National Society for Autistic Children (this organization is now called the Autism Society of America) and presented by Ritvo and Freeman (1978). The five criteria proposed in this definition are based on clinical observation and professional consensus rather than a summation of the literature (Newsom & Rincover, 1982; Schreibman & Charlop, 1987) and include the following:

1. Age of onset before 30 months;
2. Disturbances of developmental rates and sequences in the areas of motor, social-adaptive, and cognitive skills;
3. Disturbances of responses to sensory stimuli. This includes hyper- or hypo-reactivity in audition, vision, tactile stimulation, motor, smell, and taste. Self-stimulatory behavior is included here;
4. Disturbances of speech, language-cognition, and nonverbal communication. Included here are mutism, echolalia, and failure to use abstract terms;
5. Disturbances of the capacity to appropriately relate to people, events, and objects. Included here are lack of social behavior, affection, and appropriate play. Interruption of the idiosyncratic or perseverative use of objects will result in upsetting the child. There may be an awareness of the sequence of events with interruption of the sequence resulting in discomfort or panic.

While it is apparent that there is some overlap in these definitions, there are some significant differences. Rutter (1978a, b) emphasizes insistence on sameness as a requisite characteristic, while NSAC emphasizes developmental delays and sensory abnormalities. As Schopler (1978) points out, because of the different purposes and audiences for the definitions, both sets of criteria are appropriate.

The third definition of autism was proposed by the American Psychiatric Association and is presently in the *Diagnostic and Statistical Manual of Mental Disorders—Revised* (DSM III—R, 1987). This set of criteria, based on consensus of clinical impressions, is the most widely used and probably constitutes the "official" classification system. Unlike prior versions of the DSM, the new revision includes autism as a subtype of the more general diagnostic classification of Pervasive Developmental Disorder (PDD) and describes the syndrome in éxplicit behavioral terms. This emphasis on specific behaviors will undoubtedly clarify the diagnosis for researchers and clinicians alike. One noteworthy change in the criteria cited by the revised DSM III is the specification that the onset of the disorder must occur prior to three years of age, rather than 30 months as earlier specified. The DSM III—R criteria are presented in Table 3.1.

Other Factors in Diagnosis

As evident from the above discussion, autism is a behaviorally defined syndrome because no definite, specific set of biological factors common to all cases has been identified. Like all syndromes, the diagnostic category of autism is considered to comprise several subtypes, each perhaps having distinct etiologies and pathologies (Freeman & Ritvo, 1984).

Two types of clinical onset have been identified in autism. One type

TABLE 3.1
Diagnostic and Statistical Manual of Mental Disorders III-Revised (1987) Criteria for
Autistic Disorder

At least eight of the following sixteen items are present, these to include at least two
items from A, one from B, and one from C.

NOTE: Consider a criterion to be met *only* if the behavior is abnormal for the person's
developmental level.

A. Qualitative impairment in reciprocal social interaction as manifested by the following:

(The examples within parentheses are arranged so that those first mentioned are
more likely to apply to younger or more handicapped, and the later ones, to older
or less handicapped, persons with this disorder.)

  (1) marked lack of awareness of the existence or feelings of others (e.g., treats a
  person as if he or she were a piece of furniture; does not notice another
  person's distress; apparently has no concept of the need of others for privacy)

  (2) no or abnormal seeking of comfort at times of distress (e.g., does not come for
  comfort even when ill, hurt, or tired; seeks comfort in a stereotyped way, e.g.,
  says "cheese, cheese, cheese" whenever hurt)

  (3) no or impaired imitation (e.g., does not wave bye-bye; does not copy mother's
  domestic activities; mechanical imitation of others' actions out of context)

  (4) no or abnormal social play (e.g., does not actively participate in simple games;
  prefers solitary play activities; involves other children in play only as "mechanical aids")

  (5) gross impairment in ability to make peer friendships (e.g., no interest in
  making peer friendships; despite interest in making friends, demonstrates lack
  of understanding of conventions of social interaction, for example, reads phone
  book to uninterested peer)

B. Qualitative impairment in verbal and nonverbal communication, and in imaginative activity, as manifested by the following:

(The numbered items are arranged so that those first listed are more likely to apply
to younger or more handicapped, and the later ones, to older or less handicapped,
persons with this disorder.)

  (1) no mode of communicaltion, such as communicative babbling, facial expression, gesture, mime, or spoken language

  (2) markedly abnormal nonverbal communication, as in the use of eye-to-eye
  gaze, facial expression, body posture, or gestures to initiate or modulate social
  interaction (e.g., does not anticipate being held, stiffens when held, does not
  look at the person or smile when making a social approach, does not greet
  parents or visitors, has a fixed stare in social situations)

  (3) absence of imaginative activity, such as play-acting of adult roles, fantasy
  characters, or animals; lack of interest in stories about imaginary events

  (4) unreasonable insistence on following routines in precise detail, e.g., insisting
  that exactly the same route always be followed when shopping

  (5) markedly restricted range of interests and a preoccupation with one narrow
  interest, e.g., interested only in lining up objects, in amassing facts about
  meteorology, or in pretending to be a fantasy character

D. Onset during infancy or childhood.

Specify if childhood onset (after 36 months of age).

includes children who display pathological behaviors evident from the first few weeks or months of life. The second type includes children who seem to develop normally, acquiring some speech and other appropriate behaviors, but rather suddenly lose previously acquired behaviors (e.g., language) and begin to display other characteristics of the syndrome that may not have been evident earlier. This rapid deterioration is typically reported to occur at approximately 12 to 24 months of age (e.g., Anthony, 1958; Freeman & Ritvo, 1984; Wing, 1976).

While the specific behaviors responsible for an initial diagnosis of autism may fluctuate in intensity or even disappear, if the behaviors were present prior to the age of 30 months, the diagnosis of autism remains (Freeman & Ritvo, 1984). However, it is also important to note here that it is very rare to find a "recovered" autistic individual. Autism is a very severe disorder that is generally expected to persist throughout the lifespan although effective treatment may significantly lessen the severity of the handicap.

Because autism is not associated with any particular physical disabilities (although the condition may coexist with other disorders), it is not characterized by problems that would lead to a reduced lifespan. Autistic children are typically reported to be healthy, good looking, and well coordinated (e.g., Rimland, 1964).

Differential Diagnosis

A major result of the evolutionary process of diagnosis, of the appearance of different sets of diagnostic criteria, and of differing motivations for diagnosis (e.g., research, education, economic considerations), is that diagnosis is not applied in a consistent manner. This has resulted in a tremendously heterogeneous population of autistic children. Few children who are eventually diagnosed as autistic display all the characteristics described by Kanner (Kanner 1943; Rimland 1964), and autistic youngsters can vary widely as to level of severity of the disorder (Wing, 1976).

The heterogeneity in the autistic population has not only led to some confusion in diagnosing autistic children but also in conducting research on the disorder. Since different investigators are likely to study different subgroups of autistic children, the problem becomes one of trying to specify a subgroup of children that will be as comparable (i.e., homogeneous) as possible with the group being studied. An example of this strategy is provided by Coleman (1976), who has subclassified the population into three main groups: the classically autistic (i.e., Kanner's syndrome), childhood schizophrenics with autistic features, and neurologically impaired autistic children.

An additional reason for the heterogeneity is that there appears to be an overlap between autism and other childhood disorders (Rimland, 1964; Rutter, 1978a, b; Schreibman & Charlop, 1987; Schreibman & Mills, 1983). It is becoming apparent that autism may be a byproduct of a known organic pathology such as congenital rubella or phenylketonuria (Coleman, 1976). In other instances autism coexists with another identified pathology such as Down's syndrome (Wakabayashi, 1979).

Yet another cause for heterogeneity in the population is the fact that autism shares several central features with other childhood disorders. Impaired cognitive ability is a feature autism shares with mental retardation. Deficits in language are evident in autistic, retarded, and aphasic children. It is apparent that the diagnosis of autism overlaps with other diagnoses and one must address the important question of whether or not it is necessary, or useful, for clinicians and researchers to make the differentiation between autism and other developmental disorders. While there are valid arguments to both sides of this issue (as we shall see later in this chapter), many investigators (e.g., Rimland, 1964; Rutter, 1978a, b) provide evidence that it is helpful to make the distinction. The five major developmental disorders with which autism is most frequently associated are: childhood schizophrenia, pervasive developmental disorder, developmental aphasia, mental retardation, and environmental deprivation.

Childhood Schizophrenia

While this term is no longer considered a valid diagnostic category (DSM III—R, 1987), it has been in use for many years and warrants being considered here. Childhood schizophrenia has served somewhat as a catch-all term used as a broad diagnostic category for several different types of children (Menolascino, 1971; Ornitz & Ritvo, 1976; Rutter, 1972; Wing, 1976). While schizophrenic and autistic children share several features, such as sustained impairment in social relations, resistance to change in environment, speech abnormalities, and constricted or inappropriate affect, there are differences that do allow for a differential diagnosis between Infantile Autism and Schizophrenia, Childhood Type (American Psychiatric Association, 1987). One of the main differences is age of onset. It is now apparent that children develop psychoses in two waves. The first wave evidences symptoms before the age of three and the second between the ages of five and 15 (Kolvin, 1971). Those children of the first wave, that is those who show symptoms of the disorder before the age of 30 months, typically have the characteristics of autism. If these children manifest the criterion behavior characteristics before this time, they will probably receive a diagnosis of autism. Children of the second wave, those who have some period of normal development before the onset of the full syndrome between the ages of 30 months and 12 years (American Psychiatric Association, 1987), more closely resemble schizophrenic adults in symptomology. These children would probably be diagnosed as having childhood schizophrenia. In general, autism is characterized by early onset (before three years of age), less common family history of mental illness, normal or above-average motor development, lower IQ, no period of normal development preceding the appearance of the symptoms, good physical health, and failure to develop complex language and social skills. In contrast, childhood schizophrenics are characterized by a later onset of the disorder, a family history of mental illness, poor physical health, poor motor performance, higher IQs than are typically found in autistic children, periods of remissions and relapses (and a period of normal development preceding the appearance of symptoms), higher levels of language skill, and the presence of delusions and hallucinations (as are found in adult schizophrenics) (Mesibov & Dawson, 1986; Rimland, 1964; Wing, 1976). Related to the presence of delusions and hallucinations is the creation of a fantasy life or inner world. Such behavior is associated with childhood schizophrenia, for example, the child reported by Bettelheim (1967) who thought he was a machine. This development of an inner world is not associated with a diagnosis of autism (Clarizio & McCoy, 1983).

Pervasive Developmental Disorder

As mentioned above, this category has been incorporated in the classification system of the DSM III—R for children who neither manifest the behaviors of schizophrenia nor the specific features of autism. Children who fall into this category differ from autistic children in other ways as well (American Psychiatric Association, 1987; Mesibov & Dawson, 1986). Impairment in social relationships is present but does not necessarily take the form of unresponsiveness. The language problems of these children may be less severe or different from those seen in autism. Also, motor abnormalities and other behavioral oddities are usually observed in this population more often than in autistic children.

Developmental Aphasia

In developmental aphasia the children fail to develop, or are delayed in the development of, comprehension and vocal expression of language. Aphasic children share with autistic children echolalia, pronominal reversal, sequencing problems, and difficulties in comprehension (Churchill, 1972). Because of these language deficits, such children may display secondary problems with social relationships (Ornitz & Ritvo, 1976). However, the language deficits of autistic children are more severe and widespread than those typically seen in aphasic children (Churchill, 1972; Rutter, Bartak, & Newman, 1971). In addition, aphasic children generally make eye contact (American Psychiatric Association, 1987), achieve meaningful communication through the use of gestures (American Psychiatric Association, 1987; Wing, 1976), exhibit emotional intent (Griffith & Ritvo, 1967), and engage in imaginative play (Wing, 1976). These characteristics are not typical of autistic children. In addition, language-disordered children are more likely to be of normal intelligence than are autistic youngsters (Shea & Mesibov, 1985).

Mental Retardation

Like childhood schizophrenia, mental retardation is a catch-all diagnosis broadly applied to individuals showing developmental delays. Both autistic children and children who would receive a primary diagnosis of mental retardation share poor intellectual ability that persists throughout their life (e.g., Lockyer & Rutter, 1969; Rutter, 1978a, b). Similarly, many mentally retarded children exhibit behaviors typically seen in autistic children (Wing, 1976). These often include echolalia, self-stimulatory behaviors, SIB, and attentional deficits. There are, however, several characteristics that differentiate the two diagnoses. First, many retarded children exhibit appropriate social behavior. For example, a child with Down's syndrome is likely to be very affectionate and strive for the approval and attention of others. Similarly, retarded children are often communicative; even though their abilities to communicate may be limited, the intent and motivation are apparent. In addition, autistic children typically show a normal physical development, while mentally retarded children do not. One seldom sees the delays in acquisition of motor milestones and other motor behaviors in autistic children, which are so common in retarded children (Schreibman & Mills, 1983). Another difference is apparent in the pattern of intellectual impairments seen in the two types of children. While it is common for retarded children to show impairments over a wide range of functioning, autistic children usually display a more variable pattern. For example, autistic children tend to score poorly on assessments of the use of language meaning and concepts (Rutter, 1978a, b), but score higher on nonverbal assessments, such as those measuring visual-spatial abilities. Also, autistic children may show some isolated areas of outstanding functioning in the areas of music, mechanical ability, rote memory, and mathematics (Applebaum et al., 1979; Rimland, 1964). While the two disorders can be differentiated, it is apparent that most autistic children are retarded. When both syndromes are present, the child typically receives both diagnoses. Therefore, most autistic children have a secondary diagnosis of mental retardation.

Environmental Deprivation

Features of autism have been likened to characteristics often seen in children suffering from various forms of environmental deprivation. Maternal deprivation, anaclitic depression, and hospitalism are all characterized by developmental delays resulting from neglect, abuse, and/or institutionalization. In fact, deprivation in the form of parental emotional abuse or neglect has even been cited as a potential causative factor in autism (e.g., Bettelheim, 1967; Kanner, 1943). Spitz (1945) and others have documented the effects of such psychological trauma. Children subjected to environmental deprivation appear to be withdrawn and disinterested in their surroundings. They may display delays in motor skills and speech development, engage in unusual motor activity, and show little interest in toys (Ornitz & Ritvo, 1976). While these behaviors are similar to those seen in autistic children, deprived children typically show marked improvement once the environment is enriched. One often sees that these children catch up on language and motor skills, and regain an interest in social relationships (Ornitz & Ritvo, 1976; Schaffer, 1965). There is as yet no agreement on whether the deficits seen in neglected children are caused by maternal deprivation specifically or by lack of environmental stimulation per se (Bronfenbrenner, 1979). There is, however, substantial agreement that autism is not caused by neglect and that the behavioral similarities between autistic and neglected children are limited. Neglected children do not display the repetitious, stereotypical play, echolalia, pronominal reversal, and avoidance of social contact characteristic of autistic children (Ornitz & Ritvo, 1976).

Prevalence

There are differing estimates of the prevalence of autism. These are undoubtedly the result of the different ways in which subjects are gathered and classified in epidemiological studies. One type of study involves looking at an entire population of children in a community and determining how many of these children are autistic. One of the most well-known of these studies (Lotter, 1966) surveyed the entire 8- to 10-year-old population of the former county of Middlesex in England. Using a different methodology,

Lotter (1978) later surveyed children, or the administrative records of children, who had been institutionalized in six countries of Africa. Studies of exclusively institutionalized populations have their limitations in the assessment of the prevalence of autism because not all developmentally delayed children are brought to the attention of the authorities (e.g., Schopler, Andrews, & Strupp, 1979), and administrative records may rely on, and fail to delineate, different criteria for the diagnosis of autism. Despite their limitations, studies employing this latter methodology are the most common and can be very useful in determining characteristics within a population of autistic individuals such as male/female ratio and first-born/later-born.

Not surprisingly, another factor contributing to the difficulty in determining the prevalence of autism is that studies do not always classify their subjects according to the same criteria or diagnoses. In some studies the number of cases of childhood psychosis has been reported with no distinction made between childhood schizophrenia and autism (Kolvin, 1971). In contrast, Treffert (1970) excluded from his classification of autism any child who had not been diagnosed as autistic by a clinic and those with known organic pathology. One way around this problem, and one that will doubtless enjoy popularity in the near future, is to subclassify autism and to report statistics relevant to each subclassification. The classical Kanner syndrome could be one subclassification, children with many, but not all, of the classical Kanner syndrome features could be another, and so forth (Lotter, 1966, 1978; Treffert, 1970).

Thus, because of these variations in studies conducted to date there are really no reliable estimates of the prevalence of autism. Given that much of what is known about autism is controversial, it seems inevitable that prevalence, too, will be another bone of contention. Existing studies have put the prevalence of autism between 3.1 and 5.0 per 10,000 live births (Schreibman & Mills, 1983). The most oft-quoted statistic is Lotter's (1966) finding of 4.5 per 10,000 children in Middlesex, England. This population included children with the classical Kanner syndrome and children with many autistic features. Lotter's statistic has been supported by other studies in Denmark (Brask, 1970) and London (Wing and Gould, 1979). While Treffert (1970) reported a lower figure 0.7 per 10,000 classically autistic children and 3.1 per 10,000 autistic or schizophrenic for children in Wisconsin, these figures are probably artificially lowered due to reliance on administrative records from clinics and institutions. In contrast, when one broadens the diagnostic criteria to include children with social impairments characteristic of autism, regardless of other physical or mental disability, the prevalence rises to approximately 21 per 10,000 (Wing & Gould, 1979).

Researchers have also been very interested in other statistical features of autism such as male/female ratio, birth order, and concordance rates. One very consistent finding is that autistic boys outnumber autistic girls by about three or four to one (Ando & Tsuda, 1975; Dunlap, Koegel, & O'Neill, 1985; Janicki, Lubin, & Friedman, 1983; Kanner, 1954; Lotter, 1966, 1978; Rutt & Oxford, 1971; Spence, Simmons, Brown, & Wikler, 1973; Treffert, 1970). Some have speculated that this weighting toward the male is due to biological factors (Tsai, Stewart & August, 1981), but no specific causative factors have been identified to date. Kanner (1954/1973) has reported that almost 60% of 100 cases of autism were first-born or only children. Subsequent studies have not replicated this birth-order effect (Ando & Tsuda, 1975; Lotter, 1966, 1978; Spence *et al.*, 1973; Treffert, 1970). The rate of occurrence of autism in siblings of autistic children has been consistently reported as around two percent (Coleman & Rimland, 1976; Hanson & Gottesman, 1976) or the percentage to be expected from chance alone (Hanson & Gottesman, 1976). Among identical twins both are afflicted in about 82 to 86% of cases, while the rate for fraternal twins is about 25% (Hanson & Gottesman, 1976). We shall consider the role of genetic variables more extensively in our discussion of etiology in Chapter Four.

After reviewing the epidemiological data on autism and related factors, Wing (1976) adopted a strategy of subclassifying autistic children into two major groups. Members of the first group, relatively few in number, function in the normal to mildly retarded range on nonverbal assessments, are most likely to conform to Kanner's original description, most likely to show a high boy:girl ratio, least likely to show overt neurological pathology, and probably have parents of high socio-economic status. The second, larger group, of children typically function in the severely mentally retarded range, conform less to the classical Kanner syndrome, show less boy:girl ratio, are more likely to display neurological problems, and are less likely to have parents of high socio-economic status.

EVALUATION

Psychological evaluation of children has traditionally involved a battery of tests designed to assess functioning in a variety of areas. These tests assess the child's social maturation, intellectual abilities, expressive and receptive language, physical development and developmental milestones, family inter-action and parental behavior, and emotional responding. Specific assessment tools include standardized IQ tests (e.g., Wechsler Intelligence Scale for Children, Stanford-Binet Intelligence Scales, Bayley Scales of Infant Development), standardized language tests (e.g., Peabody Picture Voca-bulary Test), and tests to determine level of emotional adjustment (e.g., Children's Apperceptive Test, Rorschach, Draw-A-Person Test). While incorporating these tests in a comprehensive assessment battery is appro-priate for many children, and even for children who suffer from a variety of disorders, such tests may be inappropriate for (or impossible to administer to) children suffering from severe psychopathology. Severe withdrawal from environmental stimulation, noncompliance, language deficits, hyperactivity, lack of motivation, and attentional deficits are all important features of severe psychopathology that can seriously interfere with obtaining accurate test scores or meaningful interpretation of these scores. It is apparent that evaluation based on such a battery of traditional assessments may be of limited value in assessing children suffering from severe psychopathology (Schreibman & Charlop, 1987). Typically, therefore, in considering the severely handicapped child only selected tests of such a battery (e.g., Peabody Picture Vocabulary Test) are used in conjunction with other evalu-ation techniques.

For severe forms of psychopathology, such as autism and other childhood psychoses, assessment and diagnosis generally depend upon determining the presence of behavioral characteristics associated with the disorder. Therefore, the use of diagnostic criteria (presence or absence of relevant behavior characteristics) and later the use of behavioral checklists, has become the major mode of psychological assessment of severe forms of child psychopathology (Newsom & Rincover, 1982).

As we shall see, the specific type of evaluation employed to assess autistic children is based on three factors. First, based on the behavioral limitations of the child, which assessments could be expected to provide meaningful information for diagnosis? Here the presence or absence of diagnostically relevant symptoms is helpful and can be determined from a variety of sources including parental report, direct observation, and behavior checklists. Second, which more traditional and/or standardized assessments could be used with the child that would provide supplementary information about the child's level of functioning in specific areas? One might administer a nonverbal language test (e.g., the Leiter International Performance Scale) to derive an intelligence quotient for a nonverbal child. Third, and possibly most important, how can evaluation be aimed at measuring later improvement in functioning? While many of the above-described assessments could be used for this purpose, another form of evaluation, typically behavioral in nature, involves the presence or absence of specific behaviors (not necessarily diagnostically relevant) in a given child. For example, one might measure the amount of self-stimulation, appropriate play, tantrums, and social interaction a child manifests after, as compared to before, treatment. This would allow for an evaluation of treatment effectiveness as determined by positive changes in the child's behavior.

Evaluation Strategies

Clinical Interview and Observation

The initial stages of psychological evaluation usually include gathering information from parents, teachers, and informal observations of the child. Information commonly obtained from parental interviews includes the following which assists the clinician or investigator in determining whether autism is an appropriate diagnosis for the child (Schreibman & Charlop, 1987):

1. Prior developmental history. To get an indication of age of onset and/or unevenness in development, the clinician or investigator often obtains a developmental history of the child, including a description of any prenatal or perinatal difficulties, presence of apparent sensory deficit (suspicion of deafness or blindness), acquisition of developmental milestones (e.g., when did the child sit unassisted, when did the child walk), affect during infancy (e.g., molding to parent's body when held).

2. Social behavior. As an infant, was the child responsive to people? Did the child seem "different" (e.g., overly rigid or flaccid) when held or resist or seem indifferent to such contact? Was there eye contact with others? Was the child content to be alone or did he/she cry or demand attention? Do the parents feel their child is truly "attached" to them and would be unhappy if they were not around? Is the child affectionate with the parents and does he/she seek them for

comfort if hurt or frightened? Would the parents describe the child as wanting to be with others or as a "loner"? Does the child interact with peers? If so, what is the nature of this interaction?

3. Speech development. Does the child have speech? Has he/she ever spoken in the past? Does the child display echolalia, pronominal reversals, extreme literalness in comprehension and expression? In the parents' estimation, what is the extent of the child's language abilities?

4. Self-stimulation or self-injury. Does the child engage in or has he/she ever engaged in any of these behaviors?

5. Affect. Does the child have any irrational fears? Does the child have any appropriate fears (e.g., fear of moving vehicles on busy street)? Does the child seem to laugh or cry at unusual times or for no apparent reason? Does the child show rapid, typically inexplicable, mood swings?

6. Insistence on maintenance of sameness. Does the child become upset if furniture is rearranged or if other aspects of the environment are altered? Does the child become upset at changes in routes of travel or routine? Does the child have any compulsive rituals, unusual food demands (e.g., will only eat one or two foods, demand to eat out of only one particular bowl, refuse to eat crackers or cookies if they are broken)? Is the child unusually attached to an object or objects (e.g., demands to carry certain objects at all times, refuses to relinquish an outgrown garment)?

7. Isolated skills. Does the child show particular skill at a certain task? Is he/she a whiz at assembling puzzles? Does the child demonstrate unusual ability in music? Is there evidence the child has a very good memory?

8. What is the child's behavior like at home and at school?

9. Behavior problems. Does the child have severe tantrums? Is he/she toilet trained, able to eat without assistance, and/or able to dress him/herself? Is the child aggressive, noncompliant, manipulative?

While the input from the parents is crucial, particularly regarding the child's behavioral history and behavior in the home, it is also necessary for the clinician or investigator to observe the child during an observation/ interview session to (a) establish the reliability of some of the parental information and (b) to assess the child's behavior in a different setting and with an unfamiliar person. During such an interview and observational session the interviewer will obtain the following types of information:

1. Will the child engage in eye contact either spontaneously or with a request to do so?

2. Does the child interact with toys? If so, is it appropriate play or self-stimulation? Does the child interact with the parents? Does the child have any speech and if so, what is the nature of the speech? Is the child compliant with commands from the parents or interviewer?

3. Does the child engage in inappropriate behaviors such as self-stimulation, echolalia, SIB, tantrums, noncompliance?

4. What is the nature of the child's interaction with parents? Does he/she notice the parents? Does he/she initiate any affectionate contact with the parent (e.g., sit on the parent's lap and hug or kiss the parent)? If the parent has to ask the child for a hug does the child respond appropriately, or does he/she fuss or turn away and "back into" the parents' arms? Will the child hug the interviewer?

5. What is the nature and extent of the child's receptive and expressive speech? For example, the interviewer will gather preliminary information about language abilities by asking the child to name common objects (e.g., toys, body parts) or to respond receptively to them.

Behavior Checklists and Observational Schemes

The information derived from the parental interview and observation sessions is useful in determining the appropriateness of an autism diagnosis and for identifying specific characteristics of the child. In addition to these methods, several evaluation checklists and observational schemes have been developed by various research groups. These have the advantages of ensuring some uniformity in the information collected and also provide the opportunity to gather information on many children without the family being present (i.e., for demographic purposes, etc.). While some of these checklists and observational schemes have been widely used (e.g., Rimland's E-2 Checklist), they are most appropriately used as a screening measure in conjunction with additional assessment procedures.

Rimland's Diagnostic Checklist for Behavior-Disturbed Children is a questionnaire pertaining to the child's behavior and development. The original form, Form E-1, was later revised to include questions applying to a child five years and older (Form E-2) (Rimland, 1964). Rimland's Checklist contains 80 questions about the child's birth history, social responsiveness, speech and so forth. Scoring consists of a plus for each response consonant with a diagnosis of autism (e.g., child avoids social contact) and a minus for each response indicating behavior not characteristic of autism. Rimland (1971) reported scores from 2,218 forms, ranging from −42 to +45, with a score of +20 as indicative of autism.

Interrater reliability has not been assessed for the Rimland Checklist. However, reliability between parents' and teachers' reports suggests that teachers score children as more abnormal than do parents (Prior & Bence, 1975). Internal consistency, test-retest reliability, content validity, and concurrent validity have not been addressed (Parks, 1983) and discriminant validity is still open to question (Davids, 1975; DeMeyer, Churchill, Pontius, & Gilkey, 1971).

Ruttenberg's Behavior Rating Instrument for Autistic and Atypical Children (BRIAAC) is an evaluation instrument based on observations in a psychoanalytically oriented daycare unit (Ruttenberg, Dratman, Fraknoi, & Wenar, 1966; Ruttenberg, Kalish, Wenar, & Wolf, 1977). The checklist is divided into eight scales measuring the relationship to an adult, communication, drive for mastery, vocalization and expressive speech, sound and speech reception, social responsiveness, body movement, and psychosexual development. Wenar and Ruttenberg (1976) report interrater reliabilities have ranged from .85 to .93 for the eight scales of the BRIAAC. Internal consistency and content validity of the instrument have been established, while concurrent validity, discriminant validity, and construct validity remain questionable (Parks, 1983).

The Autism Behavior Checklist, part of the Autism Screening Instrument for Educational Planning (ASIEP), is a composite scale comprised of behaviors selected from a variety of checklists and instruments for identifying autism, including Rimland's E-2 checklist, the nine points of the British Working Party, the BRIAAC, and Kanner's original criteria (Krug, Arick, & Almond, 1979). A resulting total of 57 behaviors, weighted in terms of prediction ability, are grouped into five symptom areas. These include sensory, relating, body and object use, language, and social and self-help. Also included are components to obtain samples of vocalizations, an interaction assessment, an educational assessment, and a prognosis of learning rate.

The reliability and validity of this instrument are as yet unproven. Initial interrater reliability reports are high but based on a small sample of 14 children. Internal consistency, test-retest reliability, content validity, concurrent validity, discriminant validity, and construct validity have not been demonstrated (Parks, 1983).

The Behavior Observation Scale for Autism (Freeman, Ritvo, Guthrie, Schroth, and Ball, 1978) utilizes both a checklist and direct observations of the child's behavior. The child is observed while in a room with toys and the observer records the occurrence of 67 operationally defined behaviors in nine 3-minute intervals. The investigators responsible for this scale base their measure on the premise that autistic children, like all children, are continually changing and developing. Thus the assessment should be conducted often and the children repeatedly compared to normal and mentally retarded populations.

Interrater reliability is acceptable for 55 of the 67 behaviors. Additional issues of reliability and validity remain to be addressed (Parks, 1983).

The Childhood Autism Rating Scale (Schopler, Reichler, DeVellis, & Daly, 1980) represents another evaluation procedure that includes both checklist assessment and observations. The child is observed in a structured session and his/her behaviors scored on a scale ranging from "normal" or "severely abnormal" for each of 15 subscales. Total scores range from 15 to 60 with scores above 30 considered to be indicative of autism. The scale is based on the diagnostic criteria of Kanner, the British Working Party, Rutter, and NSAC.

Interrater reliability has been reported at .71 (Schopler *et al.*, 1980). Internal consistency has been demonstrated to be high, but test-retest reliability, content validity, discriminant validity, and construct validity need to be addressed. Reported correlations for concurrent validity are high (Parks, 1983).

The Psychoeducational Profile (PEP) is an instrument developed by Schopler and Reichler (1979) to identify and assess uneven and idiosyncratic learning patterns in autistic and other developmentally disabled children. The test is designed to serve both as a diagnostic tool and as an assessment of developmental functioning. Diagnostically the test measures the degree of pathology in several areas including affect; relating, cooperating, interest in others; interest in materials and play; sensory modes; and language. For assessment of functioning the test provides information in the areas of imitative skills, perception, fine and gross motor skills, eye-hand integration, cognitive performance, and cognitive verbal skills. This assessment of developmental functioning allows for the specific identification of the child's strengths and weaknesses, relative to developmental age norms, and thus is useful in the preparation of his/her individualized educational program.

The PEP uses toys and play activities administered by an examiner who also observes, evaluates, and scores the child's responses on the test items. The child's scores are then distributed among the seven developmental scales and the pathology scale. While no formal reliability or validity data have been collected, the PEP has been shown to correlate highly with some intelligence tests (e.g., Merrill Palmer, Vineland Social Maturity Scale, Bayley Scales of Infant Development, and Peabody Picture Vocabulary Test).

Behavioral Assessment

The use of checklists alone, or in conjunction with observations, can lead to very important information about the appropriateness of an autism diagnosis based upon specific diagnostic criteria. The presence of sufficient behavioral characteristics indicative of autism usually leads to the child receiving that diagnosis. While this is very useful for classification purposes, there are some important limitations to depending on these measures for identifying treatments for a specific child (Schreibman & Charlop, 1987). First, because of the heterogeneity of the population of autistic children, just knowing that a child has a diagnosis of autism does not provide sufficient information about the behavioral characteristics and needs of that particular child. For example, one child may have fairly sophisticated language skills, minimal self-stimulation, and some appropriate play. Another child may be completely nonverbal, have pervasive self-stimulation, and no play skills. Despite quite different behavioral repertoires, both these children are labeled autistic. Second, the diagnoisis of autism does not suggest a treatment. There is no treatment for "autism" per se. While professionals may agree on a specific treatment approach (i.e., behavior modification), treatment techniques are typically aimed at particular symptoms or characteristics of autism (e.g., tantrums, language), not for the syndrome as a whole. Third, a diagnosis of autism does not suggest a prognosis for a specific child. Some children may show significant improvement with treatment while others do not (Lovaas, Koegel, Simmons, & Long, 1973; Schreibman & Koegel, 1981).

The behavioral model of assessment represents an attempt to remediate the above problems by providing a functional definition of the syndrome as it relates to a specific child. Schreibman and Koegel (1981) have suggested three steps in the behavioral assessment of autism. First, the individual behaviors of a particular child are operationally defined which permits reliable measurement. The focus is not only on the autistic characteristics of the child, but also on specific behaviors comprising the characteristic. For a particular child, demand for sameness means that she becomes upset when her carefully placed rows of blocks are disturbed or if her bedtime routine is altered.

The second step in the behavioral assessment consists of identifying the variables controlling the specific behaviors identified in the first step of the assessment. For example, a child may show SIB only at school when the teacher makes demands upon him. The child may echo the speech of others only when they ask a question for which he has no appropriate response.

The third step involves grouping specific behaviors in terms of common controlling variables. For example, head banging, self-biting, and arm-banging may make up the child's SIB. Arm-flapping, body-rocking, and finger-wiggling may make up the child's self-stimulatory behavior.

As one might expect behavioral assessment neatly fits into the behavioral treatment of autism. It specifies, in precise terms, exactly what the child does and does not do, specifies the variables controlling the behaviors, and suggests what alterations in the environment might effectively lead to changes in the child's behavior. The information necessary for this assessment comes from a variety of sources, including parental and/or teacher reports, diagnostic observations, behavior checklists, and most importantly, from direct observations of the child. Since the goal of the assessment is to specify the behaviors the child lacks (deficits) and the inappropriate behaviors the child should not have (excesses), the use of a structured observation system such as that described below is extremely helpful.

Structured Observations

This structured observation was developed by Lovaas et al. (1973) and is presented as an example of this assessment technique. The procedure involves placing the child in a room with chairs and toys. The observation period is 30 minutes, during which the child is observed in three main situations. During the first 10 minutes the child is observed alone in the room. During the second 10 minutes an adult is present in the room but does not initiate interactions with the child (the adult, however, responds if the child initiates an interaction). During the third 10-minute segment the adult attempts to have the child respond to commands (e.g., Give me the ball.), or to have the child speak (What's your name?). Also during this period the adult attempts to get the child to play with toys.

During this session, observers are continuously recording the presence of behaviors that are grouped into eight categories considered important in the assessment and treatment of autism (Lovaas et al., 1973) and that have been socially validated (Schreibman, Koegel, Mills & Burke, 1981). These include appropriate verbal behavior, inappropriate vocalizations (e.g., echolalia), social/nonverbal behavior (e.g., affection, compliance), self-stimulation, appropriate play, exploratory play (a lower level of interaction with play materials such as holding or carrying), noncompliance, and tantrums. Importantly, these behaviors are operationally defined for each individual child. Two raters observe the session so interrater reliability can be obtained. Response definitions describe the scored behaviors in sufficient detail to ensure that independent raters can agree on the presence or absence of specific behaviors. Table 3.2 presents examples of scoring definitions. The observation sessions can be conducted with different adults (mother, therapist, stranger) to determine the stimulus control of specific individuals over the child's behavior.

At the end of the assessment the observers have a record of the percentage of time the child was engaged in each of the identified behaviors. The clinician has a profile of the child's behavioral excesses and deficits which can be used to plan a treatment strategy. The clinician can now select appropriate

TABLE 3.2

Operational Definitions for Scoring Scheme of Structured Observation
of Autistic Children in Free Play Setting

Appropriate Verbal

This is simply intelligible, nonrepetitious, in-context speech. Occasionally an answer
can be an echo, like confirming a question (e.g., "Where is the frog?" answered by
pointing to the frog and saying "Frog"). In this case Appropriate Verbal is scored. This
is rare, though, and must be very convincing, so for our purpose the echoic response
must be paired with physical evidence (like the pointed finger). Also, the adult can ask
for an echo (e.g., "Say Mississippi"). A reasonable response (like "Mississippi" but not
like "Bull's eye") is scored as Appropriate Verbal. A question that is answered
incorrectly is scored only if it is definitely a good attempt (e.g., if the question is "What
color is your shirt?", the incorrect but appropriate response could be the wrong
color—"Blue" to a black shirt). Unintelligible speech, yelling, and playful noises are
not scored.
EXAMPLES: reading aloud, conversing, answering or asking questions, or just
making an in-context comment.

Psychotic Speech

Unmeaningful or out of context speech—word salad or delayed and immediate
echoing—are scored as Psychotic Verbal, but here again, unintelligible speech is never
scored.
EXAMPLES: words that do not belong together, such as "clouds more piglet purple,"
the answer "Name" to the question "What is your name?" and delayed echoing as in
"Bull's eye, bull's eye".

Social Nonverbal

Here the child responds to the presence of the adult. For our purpose, there are four
forms of Social Nonverbal behavior, all of which focus on the adult in the room and not
some other dimension of the situation: (1) *Compliance* (if the child follows instructions), (2) *Cooperation* (if the child alters his/her behavior in order to conform to the
activity of the adult), (3) *Initiation* (if the child approaches or questions the adult), and
(4) *Affection* (if the child spontaneously engages in physical contact with the adult). This
is, then, essentially interpersonal interaction which has no ulterior motive on the part of
the child.
For example, a good rule of thumb is to watch for a reaction by the child that occurs
before the adult asks again or gives up. If the child fails to react within a reasonable
amount of time (usually just several seconds), score Noncooperation (see below under
Noncooperation). And be sure to score the behavior in the interval where it occurs
rather than where the instructions occur.
EXAMPLES: grabbing the adult's hand, physically initiating a game, moving to sit in
the adult's lap.

Noncooperation

If the adult asks or commands the child to do something, and the child has the
opportunity but does not comply, score Noncooperation. Sometimes the child actually

---

(*continued*)

TABLE 3.2 continued

has no chance to do as the adult invites (e.g., the adult may list several tasks or quickly change the suggestion about which toy to use); if this happens, score nothing. Watch for the child ignoring the adult and continuing with whatever he/she was doing prior to the adult's suggestion. Also look for indirect orders by the adult, like questions. They too are often ignored and scored Noncooperation. The score should be placed in the interval where the adult gives up or repeats the suggestion.

Do not score Noncooperation when the child is simply incorrect in responding unless it is a drastic error (e.g., the adult asks for the telephone and the child takes another toy from the table and begins to play with it). And if the child answers the adult with a "no," score Noncooperation and Appropriate Verbal.

EXAMPLES: ignoring the adult, saying "No," or attempting to appease the adult by approximating the correct response.

---

treatment targets for the child, and through analyses of present environmental contingencies, determine appropriate treatment procedures (Schreibman & Charlop, 1987; Schreibman & Koegel, 1981). Identified behavioral deficits such as lack of language, attentional deficits, and lack of play skills need to be remediated by increasing language, breadth of attention, and appropriate play. Similarly, behavioral excesses such as self-stimulation, SIB, and tantrums need to be reduced or eliminated. Since the behavioral clinician has at his/her disposal an arsenal of procedures that can be used to treat these behaviors, the treatment strategy consists of choosing those procedures appropriate for these behaviors under existing conditions. Further, by repeating the behavioral assessment at regular intervals the clinician can evaluate treatment effectiveness and the child's long-term progress.

The amount of information gathered by such an observational scheme is limited only by the range of behaviors identified and included in the assessment. Such an assessment also has the advantage of allowing continued assessment of both specific as well as more global changes. This information is useful for the continued evaluation and evolution of the child's treatment.

SUMMARY

The criteria for a diagnosis of autism have undergone several adjustments since Kanner's original description. Whereas Kanner originally included in his diagnostic criteria the good cognitive potential and normal physical development of the children and the presence of intelligent, obsessive and emotionally cold parents, he later reduced the criteria to extreme autistic aloneness, language abnormalities and obsessive desire for the maintenance of sameness. Others have given specific characteristics more or less emphasis, leading to variations in the list of criteria applied. Also, similarities with other disorders such as childhood schizophrenia have led to the use of these different diagnostic terms interchangeably. Current diagnostic systems again specify the distinct nature of autism and are relatively similar in the specific behaviors included.

Since there is so much heterogeneity within the autistic population itself and since autism shares behavioral characteristics with other disorders, the issue of differential diagnosis becomes very important. Autism can be differentiated from other disorders that share some features with it. These include childhood schizophrenia, pervasive development disorder, developmental aphasia, mental retardation and the effects of environmental deprivation.

The heterogeneity of the population and lack of agreement about diagnostic criteria over the years have made estimates of the prevalence of the disorder difficult. Nonetheless, it is generally accepted that at present the figure is approximately 4.5 per 10,000 children.

The limited utility of traditional assessment methodology with this population has led to the development of assessments specifically designed for the autistic population. These include clinical interview and observation data, behavior checklists, observation schemes, and an emphasis on behavioral assessment.

Because of the tremendous heterogeneity of the autistic population, unevenness of application of diagnostic criteria, and the potential existence of subgroups, the fact remains that at present a diagnosis of autism may tell us very little about a particular child. Future research may enable us to better identify subgroups and thus be more precise in our diagnostics, which would certainly lead to diagnostic labels that communicate more precisely about individual children.

4

ETIOLOGY

The precise basic pathology underlying infantile autism has not yet been determined. This lack of a definite etiology has led to the proliferation of theories accounting for the severe and characteristic pattern of behaviors that make up the diagnosis. As Wing (1976) points out, these theories range from the realistic (e.g., organic factors) to the blatantly bizarre (e.g., autistic children are beings from outer space). As one might predict, the absence of a known etiology has allowed the theories of etiology to reflect the popular conceptualizations of the times. We therefore see progression from psychogenic hypotheses, reflecting the popularity of psychodynamic thought, to the more modern emphases on genetic and biological factors. This progression reflects the same factors that have influenced the field of psychology as a whole. As the limitations of psychodynamic conceptualizations have been realized, and as our appreciation and understanding of how learning and organic factors influence behavior increases, the move toward a more empirical, experimentally based approach is the most logical one.

Over the years, researchers and theorists have focused their attention on three fundamental mechanisms in attempting to identify the etiology of autism. First, the relation between autistic children and their surrounding social environment has stimulated much lively debate. Second, the potential etiological factors in cognitive deficits and abnormalities have received attention. Third, attempts to relate basic biological factors to the disorder have recently led to important discoveries.

SOCIAL ENVIRONMENT

Psychodynamic Theory

Perhaps the most emotionally charged theory in the study of the cause of autism is the idea that the disorder is caused by the parents and the social environment they provide. The reasons for this, the earliest of the theories, can be traced to two basic events. First, psychodynamic thought was the prevailing trend in psychiatry at the time autism was first identified. As predicted from this theoretical orientation, disorders that could not be tied to definite organic causes were often considered a function of the child's early social environment. Second, Kanner provided a very intriguing picture of the parents of his first sample of children. He described them as cold, detached, aloof, obsessional, and lacking in emotional warmth (see Kanner, 1943). Given the psychodynamic climate of the time it is certainly not surprising that theorists related the emotional characteristics of these parents to the severe withdrawal of their children.

As mentioned, the first evidence cited to support parental involvement in the etiology of autism was provided by Kanner in his observations of the parents of autistic children (Kanner, 1943; Eisenberg & Kanner, 1956). Kanner found that these parents differed as a group from parents of other disordered children. He described his population of families as coming mainly from Jewish or Anglo-Saxon stock, being highly intelligent, well educated, unusually professionally qualified (i.e., many fathers were doctors, professors, lawyers, etc. and many mothers had advanced degrees), and generally sophisticated. However, he also described their personalities as cold, bookish, formal, introverted, disdainful of frivolity, humorless, detached, highly rational, and objective. They were considered compulsive to the point of being almost mechanistic in child rearing, lacking warmth and affectionate behavior. The term "refrigerator parents" was coined to succinctly describe the emotionally insulated, cold personalities of these parents. Despite representations to the contrary (e.g., Ward, 1970), Kanner never speculated that "refrigerator parents" were the sole cause of autism. Rather, he felt that autism was either a biosocial phenomenon in which a predisposing organic condition interacts with unfavorable social conditions (Eisenberg & Kanner, 1956), or that autistic children suffer from a more exaggerated version of a familial tendency toward social isolation (Kanner, 1954). Thus, he felt that autism was present from birth and its development was the result of organic factors or the interaction of organic predispositions with specific environmental events.

A proliferation of theories hypothesizing relationships between family environment and autism followed Kanner's observations. Some of the specific factors proposed in these theories as playing causative roles in autism are parental rejection, child responses to deviant parental personality characteristics, family breakup, family stress, insufficient stimulation, and faulty communication patterns (Cantwell, Baker, & Rutter, 1978; Cox, Rutter, Newman, & Bartak, 1975; Ward, 1970). Much of the literature in this area has been of a psychoanalytic persuasion, although the same concept has also been expressed in more behavioral-ethological terms (e.g., Zaslow & Breger, 1969). The environmental viewpoint is favored by psychoanalysts because they see autism, characterized by the absence of relations with the physical and social environment and a preoccupation with inner stimuli, as characteristic of the first stage of normal development. The shift from "primary narcissism" to object relations is seen as being accomplished through nurturing maternal acts (Spitz, 1965). It follows that a failure to progress through the appropriate developmental stages can be attributed to inadequate mothering.

While several individuals have related the personality characteristics of the parents to the development of autism, the most notable proponent of this position is Bruno Bettelheim. A description of his theory will serve as an excellent example of the parent-causation hypothesis in the etiology of autism. Basically, Bettelheim (e.g., 1967) proposes that parents of autistic children and parents of nonautistic children differ in that the parents of the autistic children have a psychological pathology causing them to react to their children's natural behaviors in an abnormal manner. The young infant is actively engaged in exploring and reaching out to people and objects in his environment. During several critical developmental periods, which roughly correspond with nursing, recognition of parents, and toilet training, the child may react to any number of real or imagined threats and frustrations from the environment. That these threats could be imagined is also suggested by Mahler (1952), Rank (1955), and Weiland and Rudnick (1961). At these times, the infant becomes more withdrawn and less responsive. Bettelheim (1967) suggests that mothers with no psychological pathology react to this withdrawal with "mothering acts" such as rocking, cuddling, feeding, stroking. This is the normal response and is necessary for the continued emotional bonding of the child and mother. In contrast, however, parents with psychological pathologies (i.e., parents of autistic children) respond to the infant's withdrawal with extreme negative feelings, rejection, and perhaps counterwithdrawal. This behavior is interpreted by the child as hostility and the child responds with inner rage, a feeling of powerlessness in a threatening environment, and by an intensification of the withdrawal. This cycle continues until the child completely withdraws into what Bettelheim refers to as "chronic autistic disease". It is important to note that the child's initial withdrawal is caused by normal environmental events that lead to withdrawal in normal infants, and is not caused by the mother. Rather, it is her extreme negative reaction to the child which compounds the withdrawal. Other theorists hold a modified view of this theory in that it is not the mother's psychopathology but rather the child's misinterpretation of the mother's reaction that leads to the withdrawal (Mahler, 1952; Rank, 1955; Weiland & Rudnick, 1961).

The basic assumption here is that the withdrawal is the child's way of defending against a threatening and hostile reality represented by the mother (Bettelheim, 1967; O'Gorman, 1970; Rank & MacNaughton, 1950; Ruttenberg, 1971). As the child's withdrawal intensifies, all libidinal energy is used for protection. This results in an arrest of ego development (Weiland & Rudnick, 1961). Since experiencing certain environmental events would be too painful, the child keeps these events out of awareness by avoiding any direct interaction with the environment. Thus certain overt symptoms of autism such as self-stimulation, echolalia, and insistence on the maintenance of sameness are really attempts by the child to maintain a homeostatic psychic environment (Ruttenberg, 1971). Others (e.g., Bettelheim, 1967; Kugelmass, 1970) further emphasize that the very behaviors symptomatic of autism are themselves suggestive of the etiology. In other words, inadequate mothering is considered to be the crux of the disease, autistic social withdrawal and associated behaviors express hostility and indifference to the parents.

Key assumptions in this hypothesized developmental process are: (1) children actively interpret their experiences at very early ages; (2) children who become autistic are unusually sensitive to their experiences; (3) children who become autistic have parents who are either unwilling or unable to provide satisfactory responses to their child; and (4) withdrawal is a willful act on the part of the children. Important in this parent-causation hypothesis is the fact that Bettelheim does not agree with Kanner's position that autism is due to "innate" inabilities and is present from birth. Bettelheim believes many autistic characteristics noted in the first weeks of life are a reaction to parenting that has already taken place (Schreibman & Mills, 1983).

The parental-causation hypothesis was popular from 1943 until late into the 1960s and even has its proponents today. However, the perspective of time and the accumulation of more systematically obtained data have contributed to the decline of this hypothesis as viable in the etiology of autism. One of the main reasons for re-evaluating this hypothesis is that it rests heavily on the assumption that the parents of autistic children have abnormal personalities. Kanner was quite clear in his early papers about the characteristics he observed in the parents of the children he explained. Subsequent authors have also given descriptions of abnormal personalities of parents of autistic children, but as Wing (1976) points out, these accounts tend to be anecdotal rather than empirically based (Bettelheim, 1967; Despert, 1951; Goldfarb, 1961; Rank, 1955; Zaslow, 1967). Another major criticism of the hypothesis is that the deviant interactions considered so essential in the development of autism have never been systematically observed. Some authors have adopted *ad hoc* theories of causality in the absence of any empirical support (e.g., Bettelheim, 1967; Zaslow & Breger, 1969). Others have inferred parental rejections or parental deviance from self-report or projective techniques. The reliability and validity of these methods are questionable since the demand characteristics of a psychiatric interview session might well prompt parents to shade their accounts of family or emotional life in the direction of the interviewer's expectancies (Orne, 1962; Yarrow, 1963). Another very important factor often overlooked is the effect of a deviant child on the parents. Thus the direction of causality (if causality is in fact present) may be in the opposite direction. It has been widely demonstrated that a child's behavior has effects on the behavior of the caretakers (e.g., Bell, 1968, 1971; Yarrow, Waxler, & Scott, 1971). It is certainly reasonable to assume that any lack of social responsiveness evidenced by the parents might be a reaction to the lack of social behavior, excessive tantrums, and bizarre behavior of their autistic children (e.g., Rimland, 1964; Rutter, 1968; Schopler & Reichler, 1971).

Perhaps the most important and damaging evidence against the parental-causation hypothesis has come from more recent and methodologically sound studies (Cantwell *et al.*, 1978; Cox *et al.*, 1975). Studies using adequate experimental controls have demonstrated that parents of autistic children do not differ from parents of normal children or parents of children from other clinical populations (such as developmental aphasia and retardation) on measures of personality and social interaction (Cantwell *et al.*, 1978; Cox *et al.*, 1975; Creak & Ini, 1960; DeMyer, Pontius *et al.*, 1972; Freeman & Ritvo, 1984; Koegel *et al.*, 1983; L'Abate, 1972; McAdoo & DeMyer, 1978; Pitfield & Oppenheim, 1964; Rutter *et al.*, 1971; Schopler & Loftin, 1969;

Schopler & Reichler, 1971). For example, Rutter *et al.* (1971) compared the parents of normal IQ autistic children with parents of normal IQ receptive aphasic children on a variety of measures using interviews and questionnaire data. These investigators found no differences between the parents on measures which included psychiatric illness, obsessional behavior, emotional warmth towards their children, and empathy. While neurotic or depressive disorders occurred in one-half of the mothers in both groups, this was seen as probably reflective of the stress of raising a handicapped child rather than a causative factor in the child's disorder.

There has been another actively debated characteristic of the parents. This refers to Kanner's repeated observations that the parents of classically autistic children tended to be of higher intelligence, socio-economic status (SES) and occupational level than would be expected of the general population (Kanner, 1943, 1949; Eisenberg & Kanner, 1956). Eisenberg and Kanner (1956) found that 12 years and 120 families later, their original finding with respect to parent socio-economic status was maintained. A majority of parents were well-educated professionals of distinction, compared to parents of other child patient populations. This finding has been corroborated by other investigators (e.g., Cox *et al.*, 1975; Kolvin, 1971; Levine & Olson, 1968; Lotter, 1966; Rimland, 1964; Schopler *et al.*, 1979; Treffert, 1970). However, several studies have not replicated the finding of higher SES in the parents of autistic children (Schopler *et al.*, 1979). Schopler *et al.* (1979) proposed several possible explanations for the finding of higher SES among parents of autistic children. First, high SES individuals have more detailed information about child development, are more likely to detect their child's disability at an earlier age, maintain more detailed records of their child's developmental history, and will travel further for help. Their own study (Schopler *et al.*, 1979) confirmed these factors. Thus, Schopler and his colleagues suspect that researchers are more likely to come into contact with high SES parents because of a systematic sampling bias. On the other hand, several of the studies appear to be well controlled for these sources of bias (e.g., Cox *et al.*, 1975; Kolvin, 1971; Lotter, 1966; Treffert, 1970). Indeed, the DSM III stated that autism is found more often in certain socio-economic groups (American Psychiatric Association, 1980). However, more recent research (Gillberg & Schaumann, 1982; Tsai, Stewart, Faust, & Shook, 1982), which was more adequately controlled for biasing factors, has found no relationship between autism and social class. The revised DSM III (American Psychiatric Association, 1987), in acknowledgment of this research, states that autism is not more prevalent in upper socio-economic level families. Freeman and Ritvo (1984) have concluded that autism is ubiquitous, occurring in all parts of the world, in all races and colors, and in all types of families.

Abnormal child-rearing practices, independent of any basic psychopathology in the parents, have also been mentioned as a possible etiological factor in autism. While he acquired no data to support his anecdotal observations, Kanner (1954) nevertheless suggested that parents of autistic children dealt with their children in a rigid manner. He noted the tendency for parents to "go by the book" in child rearing. Since one can readily imagine cold, aloof, overly compulsive parents behaving in this manner, this view seemed to fit in nicely with the notion that parental behavior is influential in the development of the disorder. More systematically derived data have failed to support the notion that parents of autistic children rear their children in any particular, or unusual, manner. In a classic study, Pitfield and Oppenheim (1964) compared the child-rearing attitudes of parents of 100 Down syndrome, 100 autistic, and 100 normal children. The investigators used attitude questionnaires and measured attitudes such as overprotectiveness, rejection, strictness, and objectivity. These investigators found very few differences between the three groups of parents and further suggested that the minor differences noted were due to differences in the characteristics of the children, not to differences in the parents' attitudes. These results were corroborated by DeMyer, Pontius, *et al.* (1972), who conducted a retrospective study of the child-rearing practices of parents of autistic, normal and brain-damaged children.

The importance of the child-rearing argument for the etiology of autism is that it is based on the contention that the overly structured, mechanical manner in which parents are said to interact with their children would somehow allow autism to develop. Yet as Wing (1976) points out, this aspect alone is hardly likely to produce a disorder such as autism. Children raised in institutional environments where child-rearing practices are typically highly routinized and structured, and where there is little opportunity for the child to develop a close and stable relationship with a caretaker, are no more likely to develop autism then children from normal homes. In fact, children who suffer from "hospitalism" (Spitz, 1945) do not display the behavioral characteristics of autism and often recover when placed in an adequate social environment.

On a more general level, the psychogenic hypotheses are not of the quality one might expect of experimentally based theories because they are based on implicit assumptions (e.g., infant interpretations and motivations) not amenable to empirical verification (Schwartz & Johnson, 1985). This makes any scientific test of these hypotheses essentially impossible, and without such verification they are of little or no use.

Learning Theory

Another theory relating problems in the social environment to the etiology of autism was formulated in learning theory terms by Charles Ferster (1961). This formulation represents an attempt to account for the behavioral deficits and excesses seen in autistic children in terms of the learning environment of the child during the first years of life. Basically, Ferster's discussion relates known, laboratory-validated principles of behavior (e.g., positive and negative reinforcement) to the low frequencies of appropriate behavior seen in these children (e.g., social and language behaviors), the relative high frequencies of atavistic behaviors (e.g., tantrums, self-injury) and meaningless behaviors (e.g., self-stimulation). In this interpretation the child's parents do not provide frequent positive reinforcement for emerging behaviors such as language and social behaviors. This is because the parents exhibit a predisposition to be generally depressed, or are occupied with other activities, or there are other factors which lead to according a low priority to reinforcing their child's behavior. Conversely, the child's negative, atavistic behaviors, such as tantrums, are attended to by the parents because of their aversive properties. The parents act to terminate the child's aversive, disruptive behavior. Ferster then describes how more severe disruptive behavior may be shaped and differentially reinforced. In addition, behaviors not having an impact on the parents, such as self-stimulation, are likely to be ignored and uninterrupted by the parent. Unlike social, language, and play activities, self-stimulation leads to an immediate environmental effect. Thus, these behaviors are strengthened while insufficient reinforcement or extinction schedules attending appropriate behaviors lead to the weakening of these behaviors or the failure of their ever being acquired. This formulation also attempts to account for the "sameness" demands of autistic children by explaining that the child's behavioral repertoire may be conditioned to very specific environmental stimuli, and change in the environment may lead to severe disruption of behavior and concomitant emotional behavior. Finally, Ferster explains that people acquire conditional reinforcing properties because of their association with many reinforcers for many behaviors. Since the parents of autistic children do not provide sufficient consistent reinforcement, they (and social behaviors such as a smile, "good girl," etc.) fail to acquire the properties of generalized conditioned reinforcers.

In Ferster's (1961) hypothesis, the severe behavioral deficits so characteristic of autism are attributed to a faulty conditioning history and, since parents are the early deliverers of reinforcers, it stands to reason that this theory be interpreted as implicating the parents in the cause of autism. Yet, like the psychodynamic explanation of the etiology of autism, Ferster's learning theory approach is also not supported by empirical data. While Ferster presents a theoretical position based on possible learning environments that could lead to some of the specific behaviors evidenced in autism, it is important to emphasize that the specific parental interactional patterns presented by this theory have never been objectively observed in the behaviors of parents of autistic children. It has also been noted that this theory does not lend itself to explaining some of the other severe problems in autism, such as particular and widespread cognitive deficits. As shall be seen in our discussion of treatment, Ferster's ideas have had a greater impact on the evolution of treatment for autistic children than they have had on the theory of etiology of this disorder. Although Ferster's ideas began the behavioristic approach to dealing with autistic children, and while the application of learning principles has been invaluable in the design of treatments, it is important to remember that the success of behavioral treatments for autism does not imply that learning *per se* was the causative factor in the development of the disorder.

Interactional Position

In an attempt to deal with the observation that parents of autistic children often have children who are normal, some theorists have attributed the development of autism to an interaction between a biologically or psychologically susceptible child and parental psychopathology. Kanner (1949) specifically mentioned he believed the development of autism might be due to some organic predisposition exacerbated by parental personality. Tinbergen and Tinbergen (1972), on the basis of their ethological studies, have suggested that perhaps an extremely oversensitive and socially fearful child is paired with a parent who is insensitive to the child's fears and thus fails to protect him/her from stressful social situations. Because of the intensity of the child's fears and the failure of the parents to ease them, these fears are generalized to other social stimuli such as faces and smiles. The Tinbergens suggest that autism could be caused by the child's overarousal due to chronic fear.

The main problems with the foregoing "interactional" theories are the lack of empirical evidence to support specific interactions and lack of explanations for the specific cluster of behaviors seen in autism (Wing, 1976). Thus one can argue effectively for the lack of any systematic evidence that autism is caused by the parents' personalities or behavior. This is not to say that parental behavior is unimportant in the form certain behaviors take, but the development of "autism" as a diagnostic entity lies elsewhere. Rimland (1964) summarized the main arguments against the psychogenic causation view of autism, most of which are still defensible today:

1. The oft-cited absence of physical or neurological abnormalities in these children does not indicate that the disorder is psychogenic in origin, but rather that the presence of such abnormalities has still to be ascertained or, perhaps, that another factor is the culprit.
2. Both the parents' and the child's behaviors could be genetically or biologically determined.
3. An analogy between "hospitalism" and autism cannot be drawn.
4. The argument that the child's behavior is meant to "punish" or "retaliate against" the parents is not valid since these behaviors are *symptoms*, not etiological factors. These behaviors could be organically determined.
5. The argument that autism can be tied to some "traumatic event" (e.g., birth of a sibling) is weak because many normal children experience such events and do not become autistic. Also, such events, do not occur in the history of many autistic children.
6. The form of treatment prescribed by a psychogenic theory of autism (e.g., psychotherapy) has proven to be ineffective. Even if it proved effective in individual cases, this would not serve as *pro forma* evidence that the cause of the disorder is psychogenic. It could very well be organic.

COGNITIVE DEFICITS AND ABNORMALITIES

A growing body of literature considers that many of the characteristic autistic behaviors are the result of a fundamental cognitive deficit and/or abnormality. Although a specific basic cognitive defect has not been identified, several theories have been advanced and investigated. This work is wide ranging, including an impressive amount of research on perceptual and attentional processes, intellectual functioning, and language processes. Central to all of this work is the effort to identify and describe some syndrome-specific cognitive problem with comprehensive implications for autistic functioning. We shall look at each of these areas briefly.

Perceptual and Attentional Functioning

Basic to many areas of academic, language, and social functioning is the ability to accurately perceive stimuli in the environment and to have one's attention directed in such a way that normal development in these areas can occur. Evidence exists that autistic children have deficits in these areas and many authors consider such deficits basic to the development of autism (e.g., Ornitz, 1969). Obviously, the identification of a deficit in these areas, and one specific to autism, would go far in accounting for many of the cognitive deficits reported in other areas of functioning.

It is generally agreed most autistic children have no identified problems in sensory functioning at the receptor level. Their sensory equipment seems to be intact (e.g., Prior, 1984; Schreibman & Mills, 1983). It is the manner in which the child responds to sensory input that is abnormal. As described earlier in our discussion of behavioral characteristics of autism, one of the most frequently cited characteristics of the disorder is an unusual responsiveness to the physical environment. Even at a very early age autistic children exhibit disturbed perception in virtually any modality including auditory, visual, tactile, olfactory, gustatory, and vestibular stimuli (e.g., Rimland, 1964). That these children have an attenuated response to pain has also been frequently observed and reported (e.g., Prior, 1984).

Prior (1984) accurately points to a very important feature of the unusual responsiveness of autistic children. She notes some children appear "not to register a large proportion of surrounding stimuli but may be acutely aware of specific stimuli in an idiosyncratic and inconsistent way" (Prior, 1984, p. 6). She therefore identifies two main topics of research and speculation in the areas of perception and attention—inconsistent responding to sensory stimulation and attention to an overly restricted portion of the available environmental stimulation.

One line of research has focused on "stimulus overselectivity". As discussed earlier, stimulus overselectivity refers to an attentional pattern in which autistic children utilize only a very limited amount of available information in a learning situation (see Lovaas et al., 1979). The problem seems not to be one of perceiving or responding to any particular type of stimulus; rather, it arises when the child must respond to the stimulus in the context of other stimuli (Lovaas et al., 1971). Thus, when confronted with a situation involving simultaneous multiple cues, the autistic child often will respond to only one of the cues. It is readily apparent that such a deficit has profound implications for learning, when one considers that learning almost invariably involves the ability to respond to simultaneous multiple cues (e.g., unconditioned and conditioned stimuli in a classical conditioning paradigm, transfer of stimulus control in an operant paradigm). Indeed, stimulus overselectivity has been found when simultaneous cues occur in different modalities (e.g., Lovaas & Schreibman, 1971; Lovaas et al., 1971), within the visual modality (e.g., Koegel & Wilhelm, 1973; Schreibman, 1975), or within the auditory modality (e.g., Reynolds et al., 1974; Schreibman, 1975; Schreibman, Kohlenberg, & Britten, 1986). In fact, the overselective manner of responding of many autistic children has been implicated in difficulties these children have in learning new discriminations, generalization of acquired behavior, social recognition, transfer from prompt stimuli, and observational learning (see Lovaas *et al.*, 1979).

It is important to note that while stimulus overselectivity has been demonstrated in many studies involving a range of stimuli and behaviors, and across multiple laboratories, it remains a fact that this phenomenon cannot be considered a behavioral pattern specific to autism. Some autistic children do not appear to be overselective while some nonautistic children are (e.g., Lovaas *et al.*, 1979). It appears that overselectivity is more a function of developmental level than of any particular diagnosis. Wilhelm and Lovaas (1976) compared the performance of three groups of children differing in IQ level in responding to three simultaneous components of a complex cue in a discrimination task. The low IQ group responded, on the average, to 1.6 of the cues; the middle IQ group responded, on the average, to 2.1 cues; and the normal IQ group responded to all three cues. These findings are consistent with the data on normal and retarded children which indicate that the number of simultaneous stimulus components which control responding is a developmental phenomenon (Eimas, 1969; Fischer & Zeaman, 1973; Hale & Morgan, 1973; Olson, 1971). It is likely that stimulus overselectivity is so often noted in autistic children because so many of this population function at a low developmental level.

Another interesting area of study is that of stimulus preference. For example, some investigators have hypothesized a "hierarchy" of stimulus preference based on observations that autistic children seem to be more attuned to tactile, olfactory, and gustatory stimulation than to auditory and visual stimulation. This preference hierarchy seems to parallel the ontogenic and phylogenic pattern of moving from dependence on near receptors (e.g., olfactory, tactile) to dependence on distance receptors (e.g., vision, audition). Autistic youngsters are viewed as being developmentally delayed and functioning at an earlier ontogenic stage than would be the case if they functioned at their chronological age. Therefore, this preference for near-receptor stimulation is a reflection of an earlier stage of sensory development (e.g., Goldfarb, 1956; Schopler, 1965).

An additional area of research relates to determining responsiveness to particular sensory modalities. Hermelin and O'Connor (1970), for example, reported that their studies on stimulus preferences in autism seemed to indicate particular distortions in perception of auditory stimulation. These investigators found evidence that autistic children differed from normals and mentally retarded controls in their lack of response to auditory stimulation and their preference for tactile stimulation. As noted earlier, suspected deafness is a very common feature of the early history of many autistic children. Hermelin and O'Connor (1970) emphasize that disturbances in auditory perception could have implications for the failure of so many of these children to acquire language.

While we may conclude that research on perceptual and attentional deviations in the autistic population has provided some very important leads to understanding how these children respond to their environment, it is not certain that a specific pattern peculiar to autism has been identified. While the deficits reported above may, in fact, have implications for some of the cognitive areas discussed, the exact nature of any deficit underlying the cognitive deficits is not known. What is known is that perceptual and attentional peculiarities are in evidence from a very early age (e.g., Prior & Gajzago, 1974) and it would not be surprising if they were either consequences of, or played a functional role in, the etiology of autistic behavior. While these results and implications are provocative, we must also remember that they are based on correlational data. We cannot be certain whether these perceptual and attentional deviations are the cause, or the result, of autism.

Intellectual Functioning

As noted previously, the majority of autistic children score within the mentally retarded range on standardized intellectual assessments. Only about 20% score an IQ above 70 on instruments such as the Stanford-Binet and Wechsler Intelligence Scale for Children. One logical question is whether or not we can place much confidence in the results of these tests with this population given the serious behavior problems they may present during testing. These children can be uncooperative, unmotivated, and fail to have the prerequisite skills to understand instructions or give some required response, for example, pointing. Also, some (e.g., Kanner, 1943) have viewed autistic children's poor intellectual performance as a secondary result of disturbances in social relationships, rather than the direct outcome of a true intellectual deficit. A body of data now exists suggesting that poor performance on intellectual assessments is reflective of a true deficit and not reflective of other factors. Rutter (1983) presents a cogent set of arguments along these lines.

First, he points out that if poor intellectual performance were a secondary result of social impairments, then one would expect all autistic children to score in the mentally retarded range on IQ tests. As mentioned earlier, approximately 20% of autistic children have IQs in the normal range.

Second, one would expect if the lower IQs of autistic children are valid, then these scores would function in the same manner as IQ scores obtained by other children. Indeed, it has been documented that like scores for other children, scores for autistic children are moderately stable after pre-school years and correlate well with IQ scores attained at maturity. Also, IQ scores for autistic children are moderately predictive of future scholarly achievement and show a positive correlation with the occupational level and level of social competence in adulthood (DeMyer et al., 1973; Lotter, 1978; Rutter, 1970, 1983). Third, if one holds the position that poor intellectual performance is secondary to the "autism" with which a child is afflicted, then one could predict that an improvement in the psychiatric state of the child (reduction of "autism") would correlate with improvement in the IQ. Again, the evidence suggests this is not the case and that the IQ remains relatively stable despite changes in the child's condition (Hemsley et al., 1978; Rutter, 1983; Rutter & Bartak, 1973; Rutter, Yule, Berger, & Hersov, 1977).

Fourth, it could be argued that the autistic child's performance may be artificially lowered because of poor motivation or perhaps negativism (i.e., the children know the answers but refuse to give them). Research designed to investigate this possibility has found no support for this position. Clark and Rutter (1977) found the performance of the children went up and down in relationship to the level of task difficulty and found no evidence that negativism was a typical feature of their performance. The fact that the children may lack some prerequisite skill, such as understanding of instructions, has been addressed by the use of tests not requiring the child's direct participation (e.g., Vineland Social Maturity Scale). Such tests, too, typically show the same pattern of results, indicating that most of the children are functioning in the retarded range. Another observation difficult to explain in terms of motivational or social withdrawal factors is that a substantial number of autistic children develop seizures during adolescence and the likelihood of later seizures is related to the level of retardation in the child. Bartak and Rutter (1976) reported one-third of the mentally retarded autistic children in their sample developed epileptic seizures versus one in twenty of those of normal intelligence.

The data above suggest many autistic children may have a general cognitive deficit underlying intellectual performance that is not secondary to their severe problems in social relationships (Rutter, 1983). The question remains whether this cognitive deficit can be considered to underlie other features of the autistic syndrome. That such a deficit does function as basic to autistic symptomology is argued by the finding that the risk of autism increases with decreases in IQ (Rutter, 1983; Wing & Gould, 1979). In addition, IQ level seems to be the most predictive of prognosis of any of the features of the syndrome (Lotter, 1978; Rutter, 1970). However, other findings argue that a basic and general cognitive deficit cannot be responsible for the development of autism (e.g., Rutter, 1983). First, as noted above, not all autistic children score in the intellectually impaired range in nonverbal assessments. If the deficit were general to the population, all autistic children would score in the retarded range. Second, the risk of autism seems to be related not only to IQ but to medical condition as well. Other disorders characterized by low IQ, such as Down's syndrome, are rarely accompanied by autism (Wing & Gould, 1979). Thus the general cognitive deficit is one that differs according to the medical condition and is therefore not specific to autism. Third, the cognitive defect seems to follow a distinctive pattern in autistic children. The most common finding is that unlike retarded children who tend to score at a depressed level across all skill areas, autistic children show a variable pattern of performance depending on the skills measured. They tend to score more highly on tests measuring visual-spatial, rote memory, and mechanical skills and less well on tests measuring conceptual and abstraction skills and verbal sequencing (e.g., DeMyer, Barton, & Norton, 1972; DeMyer, 1975; Lockyer & Rutter, 1970).

Specific Language Deficits

As noted previously, language disturbance is commonly considered one of the main defining characteristics of the syndrome of autism. Some investigators (e.g., Churchill, 1972; Rutter, 1965) have identified autism as primarily a communication disorder and see deficits in language functioning as basic to the development of many cases of the disorder. For example, Hermelin and

O'Connor (1970) suggest that the social unresponsiveness so frequently observed in autistic children may be accounted for by poor communication skills due to underlying perceptual and cognitive deficiencies. Thus deficits in language are considered as pivotal to the development and characteristics of autism. Because of this emphasis in the literature, analyses of cognitive factors underlying language have taken a central position in the search for a cognitive deficit or deficits that may hold the key to understanding autism.

There are several features of autistic language upon which most investigators agree. First, a large percentage of autistic children remain mute. Estimates of the prevalence of mutism in autism range from 28% (Wolff & Chess, 1964) to 61% (Fish, Shapiro & Campbell, 1966). Second, when speech does develop, its onset is late, its development is typically very slow, and it is deviant in form (e.g., Mesibov & Dawson, 1986; Prior, 1984). Third, the specific deviant forms of language tend to be relatively common among autistic children and to some extent peculiar to these youngsters (e.g., Bartak et al., 1975; Ricks & Wing, 1975; Rutter, 1965, 1966a, 1978a, b; Wing, 1976). Thus, while children with other language disorders (e.g., aphasia) may show some of the same specific language characteristics as autistic children, there are certain characteristics seen more frequently in this group than in children with other developmental disorders (Mesibov & Dawson, 1986; Prior, 1984). A brief description of these language characteristics will enable us to address the issue of specific underlying cognitive deficits.

Prelinguistic Abilities

There is ample evidence that even at the prelinguistic level autistic children are discriminable from normal and other developmentally disabled youngsters. Motor imitation and the communicative use of gestures are deficient (DeMyer, Alpern et al., 1972). Also, unlike normal infants and mentally retarded children, autistic children do not display expressive noises to convey meaning and show personal, often idiosyncratic ways of expressing emotion (e.g., Ricks & Wing, 1975). Another important prelinguistic behavior found to be deficient in autistic children is the spontaneous initiation of social games such as "peek-a-boo". It is hypothesized that autistic children lack these early social experiences in which the basic rules of interactive communication are acquired. This lack of experience leads to difficulty in learning to use speech in a meaningful and communicative manner (Mesibov & Dawson, 1986).

Echolalia

Echolalia is a speech anomaly characterized by the repetition of words or phrases spoken by others (e.g., Fay, 1969). Even autistic individuals who are relatively skilled in the pragmatic and semantic features of speech may tend to use rigid, repetitive, and noncreative speech forms indicative of dependence on limited, acoustic features of speech rather than on generalized comprehension of language. Some (e.g., Baltaxe & Simmons, 1975; Fay, 1969; Schreibman, Kohlenberg, & Britten, 1986) have suggested that echolalia possibly represents an attempt to communicate based on speech at a phonetic level rather than a true understanding of certain semantic components of speech. As Mesibov and Dawson (1986) and Prior (1984) point out, it is as if instead of using the heard utterances in terms of their basic semantic relationships, the children learn an entire utterance as a label for an associated situation or event. This is illustrated by the case of one boy who said "No, thank you" whenever he wished to express a negative reply. Thus, he answered "No, thank you" to questions such as "Is it raining today?"

Pronominal Reversal

One feature of autistic speech that is often emphasized is the individual's reversal of pronouns. The person may say "you want to go outside" instead of "I want to go outside". From a psychodynamic point of view this speech pattern is seen as a psychological manifestation of avoidance of self-recognition or the denial of the existence of the self (e.g., Bettelheim, 1967). While this interpretation is certainly consonant with the psychodynamic position regarding the etiology of autism, it is not supported by empirical studies. For example, Bartak and Rutter (1974) found no tendency to avoid repetition of the pronoun "I" in their sample of autistic subjects. Silberg (1978) reported that autistic children evidenced a normal progression in their use of pronouns. One likely interpretation of pronominal reversal is that it is a secondary result of echolalia. Since the child hears people refer to her as "you" or "she" or "Lilly" rather than "I," understandably the echolalic child would repeat the name or pronoun heard. However, some researchers (e.g., Fay, 1979) observe that the reversal of pronouns is a complex phenomenon not adequately accounted for by attributing it to echolalia. Fay (1979) speculates that the difficulty relates to difficulties with deixis (language requiring shifts in orientation or perspective).

Semantics

The difficulty autistic individuals have with semantics in language is well documented and the literature is full of examples of semantically inappropriate speech produced by autistic speakers. Simmons and Baltaxe (1975) described several of these problems in a group of adolescent subjects and provided examples, such as "The loopholes can be *livid*," which illustrates inappropriate word usage. Here the word belongs to the proper semantic category but has none of the semantic features of the right word (another adjective). Another example illustrates the idiosyncratic usage of semantics: ". . . or standing up, just like a—just like *lightening to a fireplace standing up to a fire*". The reason for the semantic errors so characteristic of autistic children's speech remains a mystery but several investigators have speculated that the basis for the deficit lies in the children's inability to use symbols which renders the information in high-level abstractions and complex linguistic relationships inaccessible (Ricks & Wing, 1975). The inability of autistic children to utilize semantically related information was investigated by O'Connor and Hermelin (1967a, b) who found that, compared to matched mentally retarded and normal children who were much better at recalling sentences than random words, autistic children showed only a slight tendency to cluster semantically related words in recall. Thus one may speculate that the autistic children did not benefit from the semantic information available in the sentences.

Language and Memory

Much has been made of the importance of language in memory. The ability to encode and organize linguistic material is considered crucial to the ability to retain information. O'Connor and Hermelin's (1967a, b) studies indicated autistic children were just as capable of recalling strings of random words as they were semantically correct sentences. In contrast, MA matched normal and mentally retarded children performed much better with the sentences. Hermelin and O'Connor (1970) and others have speculated that the pattern of performance of autistic children is due to an inability to make use of the semantic features of the stimuli. Thus they are not able to extract the syntactic and semantic information required to benefit from the sentence format. They are also unable to use meaning to facilitate recall (Prior, 1984). However, in an interesting replication, Fyffe and Prior (1978) found high-functioning autistic children could indeed use meaning to facilitate recall but performed at their MA level. It is apparent in this area, as in so many other areas, that one must be very careful about distinguishing autism *per se* from developmental level.

Pragmatics

As Baltaxe and Simmons (1975) point out, even though some autistic individuals become quite sophisticated in their use of many aspects of language (e.g., vocabulary, syntax, semantics) their ability to use language in a socially appropriate and communicative manner remains severely impaired. There is a general failure to adapt speech to the situation or to the listener's cues (Baltaxe, 1977; Ricks & Wing, 1975). One often finds the autistic speaker is not responsive to the subtle social cues governing the speech of most individuals and, consequently, his speech may appear irrelevant, rude, and socially inappropriate. For example, an autistic individual may draw attention to himself by speaking too loudly in a particular situation, may be unresponsive to the cues of the listener that he is boring, or may say something that embarrasses or hurts someone else (quite unintentionally). Evidence also exists that difficulty in pragmatics appears at a very early age. Very early normal development includes the ability to gain, sustain, and direct the attention of others to oneself or to another person or an object. This ability normally develops between birth and two years of age. These behaviors, however, are rarely observed in the spontaneous behavior of autistic infants (Ball, 1978) and some (e.g., Seibert and Oller, 1981) speculate that these problems in early communication may be central to the problems of pragmatics with autistic individuals.

Other Features of Language

The findings on other aspects of the speech and language of autistic people are less definitive than for those aspects mentioned above. It has been reported that compared to the development of other features of language, phonetic development seems to be the least deficient. Some researchers have stated that the phonetic development of autistic children parallels that of retarded and young normal children (Bartak, Bartolucci, & Pierce, 1977; Bartolucci, Pierce, Streiner, & Eppel, 1976).

Addressing the issue of prosody (pattern of intonation), Baltaxe and her colleagues (Baltaxe, 1981, 1984; Baltaxe & Simmons, 1975) and others (e.g., Ricks and Wing, 1975) have reported and described the dysprosody in the speech of autistic children. Basically, the speech tends to be inaccurate in terms of intonation, stress and rhythm. Even when the content of the speech is accurate, the non-content-carrying aspects of the speech may be incorrect and hence the speech still sounds abnormal. Such is the case when previously nonverbal autistic children, who acquire speech through training, display little intonation—with intonation referring to the melody of speech over time. At another extreme, many echolalic autistic individuals speak with varying, even exaggerated, degrees of intonation, while the content of the speech may be contextually and semantically inaccurate (e.g., Schreibman, Kohlenberg, & Britten, 1986).

In addition, Ricks and Wing (1975) report other deficits in verbal and nonverbal communication, such as the absence or idiosyncratic nature of facial expressions, lack of communication with gestures, unusual pitch and voice control, and impaired comprehension of nonverbal communication from others in the environment. Interestingly, these characteristics persist even when there is substantial development of other cognitive and language behavior.

Mesibov and Dawson (1986) point out that the findings in regard to syntactic development in autism are probably unclear because the apparent deficiencies in syntax could reflect difficulties in using language in a complex and changing social context. In other words, it is not entirely clear whether autistic speech in these areas merely reflects a developmental delay rather than a specific pattern of deficit associated with autism.

Cognitive Defect and Language

Since language disorder and deficiency is a hallmark feature of autism, it is important to determine whether language problems are a secondary feature founded in a basic cognitive defect or are due to some other noncognitive factors. In arguing for an underlying cognitive defect, Rutter (1983) carefully rules out the role of social withdrawal and motivational variables as possible culprits behind the specific language deficiencies in autism. In his arguments, Rutter (1983) cites several findings on which he bases his conclusion that autistic language problems are not based on motivational and social withdrawal factors. First, it is important to note the problem is not one of too little speech, it is a problem of *deviant* speech. As discussed above, speech is acquired late and deviant in form when acquired. It is difficult to imagine how a general motivational problem could account for the specific and distinct patterns of speech seen in these children. Second, autistic children's pattern of IQ scores indicates the presence of cognitive deficits above and beyond the failure to use speech. Thus, when one looks at the patterns of performance on nonverbal intellectual tests, one finds it is not just that the children do better on nonverbal tests than on verbal. Rather, the children do better on some nonverbal tests than on others. Third, Rutter (1983) points to the research by Hermelin and O'Connor (1970) cited above wherein autistic children made little use of meaning in their memory and thought processes. Based on these findings, Rutter concludes autistic children have a serious cognitive deficit encompassing language, sequencing, and abstraction; "it is not just a reluctance to speak, it is not a secondary consequence of social withdrawal and it involves far more than an abnormality of speech alone" (Rutter, 1983, p. 521).

The next question to be asked is whether a hypothesized basic cognitive defect is restricted only to language functions, without affecting other behaviors in the syndrome. Rutter (1983) and Prior (1984) emphasize that the only way to accurately address this question is to look at the language of nonretarded autistic children. This is the only manner to avoid confounding the problems of language with the problems associated with cognitive defects relating to general mental retardation. One method of accomplishing this is to compare nonretarded autistic children with other nonretarded children who share many of the same language deficits as those found in autism. In a classic study, Bartak, Rutter, and Cox (1975) compared a group of autistic children to a group of children with receptive language disorder (dysphasia) to study which aspects of cognitive dysfunction were specific to autism. The two groups were matched for IQ and language abilities. The comparisons yielded several interesting results. Of most importance, the groups did not differ significantly in terms of nonverbal reasoning skills or syntactic language skills. The investigators concluded autism is not characterized by a general defect in visual-spatial or perceptual cognition, articulation or the grammatical aspects of language. This means that the presence of a receptive language disorder alone did not suffice to account for the presence of autism (Rutter, 1983). Importantly, the autistic subjects did differ in several respects from the dysphasics. Autistic children were more deficient in measures of understanding language; measures of "verbal-like" skills in thought processes (so-called "inner-language" skills); imaginative play and use and understanding of gesture; and the use of speech in a socially communicative manner. Also significant was the finding that, unlike the dysphasic children, the autistic children showed particular abnormalities in their speech such as echolalia. In contrast, the dysphasics were less behaviorally disturbed and more socially mature and responsive than autistic children. Bartak, Rutter, and Cox (1975) concluded that a severe developmental language disorder was not a sufficient cause of autism, and that autism represents a disorder characterized by both language abnormalities and a cognitive deficit more severe, widespread, and of a different nature than that found in developmental dysphasia.

From a similar perspective, Prior and Isaacs (1979) compared the language acquisition patterns in autistic and developmentally aphasic children. Their findings indicated both groups "shadowed" the normal language acquisition process over time but autistic language acquisition was very deviant in form. It seemed to be a verbatim recital of what had been heard (i.e., reproduction of speech without extraction of the meaning or general linguistic rules). This echolalic, ritualized, stereotypic characteristic of the language is, of course, a familiar pattern and a frequently cited characteristic of the speech of autistic individuals.

Rutter (1983) offers several arguments for considering cognitive deficits in autism as basic to the disorder. First is the finding that some aspect of the deficit is present in virtually every case of autism. Second, there is a close association between the cognitive abnormalities and social and behavioral abnormalities found in autistic individuals. The Bartak et al. (1975) study found autistic children could be differentiated from dysphasic children on the basis of cognitive test performance as well as by behavioral and linguistic criteria. Third, it has been found that language is a strong prognostic predictor; that is, functional language by the age of five years is indicative of a more hopeful outcome. Fourth, since research has shown IQ and language are the least influenced by treatment (e.g., Prior, 1984), it is possible that a basic cognitive deficit underlies the disorder, perhaps at a biological level. Fifth, investigation of concordance for autism in twins found that concordance is higher for monozygotic (identical) compared to dizygotic (fraternal) pairs. This, of course, points to the possible role of hereditary factors. It has also been found that other cognitive problems were more likely to occur in the nonautistic siblings of monozygotic pairs than in nonautistic siblings of dizygotic pairs (Folstein & Rutter, 1977). These results are consonant with the findings of other researchers (August, Stewart & Tsai, 1981; Ritvo, Spence et al., 1985).

Researchers emphasizing a basic cognitive defect in autism point to the foregoing evidence as suggesting that the specific pattern of deficits in autism is peculiar to the disorder and is not a function of developmental level or associated with other disorders. Prior (1984) sums up the situation by saying autistic children are not only delayed in cognitive areas but seem to have a problem with symbolic material that is specific to the syndrome. The problem is common across all intellectual levels, from the most severely retarded to the normally intelligent. Even with normal intellectual abilities, the autistic individual is likely to be concrete and literal in his use of language and is not able to incorporate subtle symbolic information into behavior. Even with a good grasp of the surface aspects of language, a high-level autistic individual will have difficulties with the more complex and abstract aspects of language that give it its uniquely human richness (Prior, 1984). He is likely to remain an outsider to the rest of society even if he has some insight into his own deficiencies.

While investigators continue to speculate on the precise nature of a basic and general cognitive defect underlying autism, none has yet been specifically identified. The difficulties with using symbolic material, the problems in perception and attention, the characteristic language patterns—all these point to potential culprits. However, the identification and specification of any basic cognitive defect underlying the autistic syndrome will need to address several questions. If an autism-specific defect is identified, what form does it take at its most basic level, as opposed to a manifestation or secondary feature of another defect? What is the "cause" of such a defect? Is it organic in nature or is it due to environmental factors? When does this defect have an impact on the autistic child? Is it present from birth, or does it set in later? Since the variability in functioning of different autistic children suggests that some may be more affected than others, what is the nature of the defect, and what are its effects at different levels? Once it is present, can we do anything to attentuate or eliminate the negative impact on the child's development?

BIOLOGICAL FACTORS

The current emphasis on investigating possible biological factors in the etiology of autism can be traced to several causes. First, the accumulating evidence that autism is not psychogenically based has greatly reduced the emphasis on family environment factors. Second, the accumulating evidence that autistic children have various neurological, biochemical, and even genetic abnormalities has given a strong impetus to further investigation of a biological basis or bases for the disorder. Third, our increased technological capabilities now make it possible to investigate biochemical, neuroanatomical, and genetic factors that remained inaccessible until recently.

It is important to point out again that researchers looking into the biological bases of autism acknowledge that one all-encompassing cause is quite unlikely to be found. Autism, as we know it, is probably made up of a subset of disorders, each having its own cause or causes. Thus, it will no doubt serve us best to try to identify these specific subgroups and to then identify contributing etiologic factors. It is further important to note that even for an individual subtype of autistic child, there may not be a single "cause" but, rather, a particular combination of factors leading to the syndrome. It is not difficult to appreciate how very complex the issues are in determining the etiology of autism.

The areas of study into the biological contributing factors in autism can be discussed along four general lines. These include the potential role of various problems during pregnancy and/or birth, genetic involvement, neurological correlates, and biochemical processes. Research into each of these areas will be discussed below.

Pregnancy and Birth

In attempting to isolate specific etiological factors involved in the development of autism, many investigators have conducted studies on the birth histories of autistic children. Many such studies have reported an increased incidence of complications during pregnancy and/or birth than were found in control groups (Gillberg & Gillberg, 1983; Knoblock & Pasamanick, 1962; Ornitz & Ritvo, 1976). Factors found to have an increased incidence include difficult labors, Rh incompatibility, toxemia, vaginal bleeding and maternal illness (Mesibov & Dawson, 1986). Other factors reported in population studies are increased hypothyroidism in mothers or fathers (Coleman & Rimland, 1976), higher incidence of spontaneous abortions and infertility in maternal histories (Funderburk, Carter, Tanguay, Freeman, & Westlake, 1983), and viral infections (Chess, 1977).

Links, Stockwell, Abichandani and Simeon (1980) concluded that existing evidence suggests that prenatal factors, as opposed to perinatal or postnatal ones, are the most significant. An example of this research is provided by Gillberg and Gillberg (1983) who developed an "optimality scale" comprised of 30 pre-, peri-, and neonatal factors. They found that 25 mothers of autistic children showed reduced optimality, particularly regarding prenatal factors, compared to the mothers of 25 normal controls. The most frequently cited adverse factors were maternal age, generalized maternal edema, pre- or post-infant maturity, medication, and uterine bleeding during pregnancy. These findings support Gillberg's (1980) conclusion that like Down's syndrome, there is an increased risk for autism with increasing maternal and paternal age. Another interesting finding of the Gillberg and Gillberg (1983) research is that the same reduced optimality was found in both high IQ and low IQ autistic children. This is noteworthy since these two subgroups of autistic children are often considered to be qualitatively different, and it has been hypothesized that the etiology of the two subgroups differs.

While the findings of research in this area are indeed provocative and have led to investigation in other areas (see below), nevertheless no definite tie between any of these factors and the etiology of autism has been substantiated. These results are correlational and, as Freeman and Ritvo (1984) point out, it is possible that some of these findings, including the "reduced optimality" of Gillberg and Gillberg (1983) might be the result, not the cause, of factors which produce the autism (e.g., primary genetic defect).

Genetic Factors

The possibility of a significant genetic contribution to the development of autism has been suggested since it was first defined. Kanner (1943), in describing his initial clinical sample, suggested that genetic factors might contribute to the etiology of autism in terms of providing a predisposition to develop the disorder. The possibility of genetic involvement has remained an important issue through the years and currently there is a significant body of research suggesting that there may indeed be a subpopulation of autistic children whose disorder might be due to pathogenic genes (Ritvo, Spence, *et al.*, 1985).

While no specific gene marker for autism has yet been identified, several studies of familial factors have suggested a genetic involvement. Bartak, Rutter, and Cox (1975) studied a group of families of autistic children and found a familial history of speech delay in approximately 25% of the sample. Surveys of large populations of autistic individuals indicate between 2 and 6% of autistic subjects have autistic siblings (Ritvo, Freeman, Mason-Brothers, Mo, & Ritvo, 1985) and siblings of autistic children have a 50 times greater chance of being autistic than the general population (American Psychiatric Association, 1987; Rutter & Garmezy, 1983).

Studies of twins have provided perhaps the strongest support for a genetic involvement in a subpopulation of autism. Folstein and Rutter (1977) studied 21 sets of same-sex twins of whom at least one twin in each pair was diagnosed as autistic. Thirty-six percent of the monozygotic (MZ) twins were concordant for autism but none of the dizygotic (DZ) twins were. These investigators also found six of the nonautistic cotwins (5 MZ and 1 DZ) showed a cognitive abnormality in the form of severe speech delay, learning disability, or mental retardation. In 12 of the 17 twin pairs who were discordant for autism, there was evidence that the autistic twin had suffered some form of brain injury whereas in none of the discordant pairs did this occur only for the nonautistic twin. Because of the high concordance rates, Folstein and Rutter (1977) concluded that genetic factors may have played a significant role in the etiology of autism; however, environmental factors (e.g., brain injury) also had to be implicated to account for the nonconcordant cases. This is consonant with the conclusions of Ritvo, Freeman, Mason-Brothers, Mo, and Ritvo (1985), who reviewed the world literature on autistic twins and studied a series of 40 pairs of afflicted twins. These investigators found 22 of 23 sets of MZ twins (95.7%) were concordant for autism compared to 4 of 17 (23.5%) pair of DZ twins. Since autosomal recessive inheritance would predict 100% concordance in MZ twins and 25% concordance for DZ twin pairs, it is apparent other environmental factors must be operating.

Apparently, there is strong evidence suggesting a genetic involvement in at least a subgroup of autistic individuals. It is also apparent that this genetic endowment may not necessarily take the form of autism since investigators have found a significantly high proportion of twins and other relatives with serious problems, such as learning disabilities, language delays, and retardation (Folstein & Rutter, 1977; Ritvo, 1981). August et al. (1981) have concluded, as have other investigators, that there could be a genetically determined spectrum of cognitive disorders, with autism representing the most severe form. Determining that something is inherited is only the first piece of the puzzle. We next need to determine exactly what may be inherited and how this may contribute to the behavioral features that describe autism. Genetic factors could act directly via a recessive gene that transmits a specific enzymatic defect as in PKU or hemophilia. In autism, such a defect could directly produce structural brain abnormalities, neurotransmitter or neuroreceptor pathology, or other types of neuropathology. Indirect genetic influences may also be responsible for other subtypes of autism. Thus, genetically determined decreased resistance to particular viruses may be important.

Recently, investigators have looked at deviations in specific gene structure and the presence of the "fragile-X" chromosome in a few cases of autism has provoked interest (e.g., August & Lockhart, 1984). This abnormality is identified by using a microscope to examine the X sex chromosome and is usually characterized by a weakness or "break" in the structure of the chromosome. While some work seems to suggest the correlation of fragile-X with some cases of autism (Gillberg, 1983), other studies have failed to find such a relationship (Goldfine et al. 1985). Because of our increased ability to detect abnormalities in genetic structure, one might expect that identification of such abnormalities and our understanding of how they affect behavior might lead to some of the most fruitful areas of investigation in the future.

Obviously, we have just begun to appreciate and understand the potential role of genetic variables in the development of autism. It will be most exciting to see which of these leads, if indeed any, enables us to arrive at an identification of the etiology of autism.

Neurochemical Factors

Investigations into biochemical and metabolic factors as possible contributors to the development of autism have continued to be pursued with enthusiasm. Positron Emission Tomography (PET), which measures the rate of metabolism in different parts of the brain, is one of the newest techniques being used. It is being applied only to autistic adults since it cannot be used with children (because of the amount of radiation involved and other technological factors). Initial results indicate that there may be a significant difference in brain metabolism patterns between autistic and normal individuals (Freeman & Ritvo, 1984). However, these results are only preliminary and further investigations are necessary to replicate them and to assess possible parameters of the differences.

By far the most research into biochemical processes in the etiology of autism has focused on the cerebral neurotransmitter serotonin (5 hydroxy-tryptophane—5HT). This cerebral neurotransmitter is also found in the blood where it is easily measured. The level of blood serotonin appears to be an age-related phenomenon; higher levels are found in normal infants, decrease throughout childhood, and stabilize at a lower level in adulthood (Mesibov & Dawson, 1986). A subgroup of autistic individuals, perhaps 30 to 40%, fail to show this expected age-related decrease and show an elevated level remaining hyperserotonemic throughout life (Freeman & Ritvo, 1984). This failure to show a maturational decrease in blood serotonin levels has been interpreted as indicative of immaturity in the autistic neurologic system. Other studies (Campbell et al. 1976) have indicated higher serotonin levels are most clearly related to low intellectual functioning.

One interesting approach to studying the possible effect of elevated levels of serotonin is to reduce the levels of this neurotransmitter and determine covariant behavior changes. Initial attempts along these lines involved the administration of L-dopa, which lowers blood serotonin. Studies investigating the effect of L-dopa found no resulting behavioral changes in autistic children (Campbell et al. 1976; Ritvo et al. 1971).

More promising results have come from studies investigating fenfluramine (an anorectic agent) as a means of reducing blood serotonin levels. Ritvo, Freeman, and their colleagues have conducted several studies in this area. To determine whether hyperserotonemia is linked with symptom expression in autism, these investigators monitored several clinical features after pharmacologic treatments with fenfluramine designed to lower blood and brain concentrations of serotonin. Ritvo et al. (1984) administered fenfluramine to 14 autistic individuals in a double-blind crossover design (1-month placebo, 4-month drug, 2-month placebo). While fenfluramine was administered, blood serotonin values decreased by an average of 51%. In addition, several objective clinical scales (e.g., intellectual assessments, observational recordings) as well as parental reports, showed significant improvements. These improvements included increased social awareness, eye contact, and attention to school work, decreased hyperactivity and decreased repetitive behaviors, such as hand-flapping and spinning, and improved sleep patterns. Unfortunately, not all of these improvements were maintained when the fenfluramine was withdrawn. While it is tempting to interpret these findings as indicative of a serotonin involvement in the behavioral symptomology of autism, Ritvo and his colleagues conclude that the manner by which fenfluramine acts to modify symptoms in autistic individuals is unknown. It may be via the known effects the drug has as a serotonin depleter or inhibitor of the dopamine system or by some as yet undiscovered means. Again, the correlational nature of these findings cannot rule out the contribution of other factors that may be associated with elevated serotonin confounding any relation to autism *per se*. We will return to the findings of fenfluramine during our discussion of treatment.

Some recent preliminary investigations have provided a very intriguing hypothesis about another neurochemical that may influence autism. Sahley and Panksepp (1987) have postulated that the social withdrawal seen in autism may be a function of abnormally high activity within the opioid system in the brain. It has been suggested that opioid peptides, brain chemicals that produce pleasurable effects similar to the effects of morphine, are released when a mother is physically affectionate with her child. Perhaps autistic children have an overabundance of these chemicals, which discourages the youngsters from seeking affection, comfort, and so forth. If this is the case, then administration of an agent that blocks the effects of these natural opioids might be accompanied by decreases in autistic behaviors. To investigate this possibility, Herman and her colleagues (reported by Turkington, 1987) administered an opioid-blocking agent, naltrexone, to autistic children and to children who engaged in severe SIB. Data for five autistic and three SIB cases suggest that naltrexone significantly decreased some abnormal behaviors in the autistic children (i.e., self-stimulation, echolalia, the tendency to cover eyes and ears to block out social stimulation) and increased the children's apparent enjoyment of social behaviors, such as hugging. There were also dramatic reductions in self-injury in the SIB cases studied. As mentioned, these results are preliminary and replication of these effects with more subjects is necessary before firm conclusions may be drawn.

In an intriguing study of the potential influence of other neurochemicals, Kern, Koegel, Dyer, Blew and Fenton (1982) investigated the effects of physical exercise on self-stimulation and appropriate responding to learning tasks in seven autistic children. The children were assessed on these behaviors before and after jogging. Results indicated that the physical exercise was followed by decreases in self-stimulation and increases in appropriate responding. The investigators point out that these results are consistent with other research suggesting that strenuous physical exercise causes physiological changes, such as the release of beta-endorphins and changes in acetylcholine levels. Such changes seem to positively influence motivation, improve attention, facilitate perceptual integration, and counteract the effects of mental fatigue.

While these findings are important and provocative, the specific role of various neurochemical agents remains to be determined. It is apparent, however, that this is an area that will receive increased attention in the future.

Neurological and Neuroanatomical Factors

The role of neurological factors in the etiology of autism has long been suspected. Several indicators have pointed to such involvement (Mesibov & Dawson, 1986). Autism is frequently found in association with other diseases and syndromes affecting the central nervous system including mental retardation (e.g., over 75% of autistic children have severe enough neurological damage that they test in the mentally retarded range throughout their lives), retrolental fibroplasia (Keeler, 1958), tuberous sclerosis (Lotter, 1974), congenital syphilis (Rutter & Lockyer, 1967), phenylketonuria (Knoblock & Pasamanick, 1975), and widespread neurolipidosis (Creak, 1963). In addition, epilepsy, congenital rubella, Down syndrome, fragile-X, hydrocephaly, and microencephaly have all been reported to coexist in patients with autism. While the potential contribution of neurological factors in autism has not been doubted, the precise nature of the neuropathology has remained elusive and has stimulated research in a wide variety of areas.

Neurological pathology is often inferred from the appearance of "*soft signs*" such as hypotonia, poor coordination, and toe-walking. These are characteristic behaviors often associated or correlated with known neurologic pathology. Studies have demonstrated that from 40 to 100% of autistic children show some evidence of neurological problems as indicated by the presence of these soft signs (e.g., DeMyer *et al.*, 1973; Goldfarb, 1961; Knoblock & Pasamanick, 1975). While the significance of these soft signs has been debated, some professionals believe their presence is indicative of neurological damage, immaturity and/or poor organization of the brain (Mesibov & Dawson, 1986). While perhaps suggestive and intriguing, no specific or definitive relation has yet been demonstrated between these neurological soft signs and the syndrome of autism.

Studies focusing on neurologic functioning in autistic children have employed a variety of procedures. Studies assessing the electroencephalograms (EEGs) of the children typically report a higher incidence of *abnormal EEGs* in autistic children compared to nonhandicapped children. The incidence of abnormal EEGs reported in the literature ranges from 20 to 30% (e.g., Kolvin, Ounsted, & Roth, 1971) to 60 to 80% (e.g., Creak & Pampiglione, 1969). DeMyer (1975) compared EEGs of autistic and mentally retarded children and found that whereas only 39% of the retarded children had abnormal EEGs, 65% of the autistic subjects showed abnormal patterns. The specific abnormal patterns most commonly noted in autistic children are focal slowing, spiking, or paroxysmal spike-wave discharges (e.g., Mesibov & Dawson, 1986).

The significance of the higher incidence of abnormal EEGs in autistic children has yet to be adequately determined. The wide fluctuation in reported rates of incidence of abnormal EEGs is probably due to differing diagnoses of autism, inclusion of children with other disorders coexisting with autism, and different criteria for normal *vs.* abnormal EEG. One must also keep in mind that the EEG is still a very gross measure of brain activity and by itself is not a particularly definitive measurement.

One finding that corroborates these reports of abnormal brain wave activity is the often reported incidence of seizure activity in these children. There is little argument that autistic children are more likely to have a seizure disorder than nonautistic children. It is also apparent that these seizures and abnormal EEGs are more likely with increased age. Deykin and MacMahon (1979) found both "partially" and "totally" autistic children had an increased likelihood of seizure onset up to the age of 10, but only the "totally" autistic children had an increased risk of seizure onset during the period of adolescence. Similarly, Bartak and Rutter (1976) reported an increased incidence of adolescent onset of seizures in autistic, as opposed to nonautistic, individuals. They found that one-fourth to one-third of their sample of autistic subjects who had not had seizures during childhood developed them during adolescence. It is noteworthy that Bartak and Rutter found that this pattern of an increased likelihood of seizures with age rarely occurred in children with IQs greater than 70. Freeman and Ritvo (1984) reported that EEG studies confirm their clinical experience in that autistic children are increasingly likely to develop abnormal EEG patterns and seizures with increased age. They found these abnormalities were rarely encountered in children under the age of six years but about 10% of those followed into adulthood subsequently developed such abnormalities and about 5% developed seizures. Thus it is apparent that for many autistic children, particularly those with lower IQs, the risk of developing seizures increases with age. This would suggest a neurological defect although, as with other measures we have discussed, the precise nature of such a defect has not been specified.

One area of the brain frequently postulated to be involved in the development of autism is the reticular activating system (RAS) which regulates arousal. Bernard Rimland (1964) speculated that *underarousal* of the RAS may be the reason for the autistic child's limited, literal encoding of messages and resulant literal and limited response repertoire. Rimland's theory is an interesting one and has attracted attention throughout the years; however, it is purely speculative since there are no supporting empirical data (e.g., Wing, 1976).

Hutt, Hutt and their colleagues (Hutt, Hutt, Lee & Ounsted, 1964; Hutt & Hutt, 1970) have proposed from their EEG studies that problems with the functioning of the RAS lead to nonspecific *overarousal* in autistic children and the behavior of the children may be seen as a reaction to this overarousal. These investigators studied the resting EEGs of autistic children and claimed their findings showed high levels of low voltage irregularity. Their interpretation of these findings included the speculation that some of the more bizarre behaviors of the children (e.g., self-stimulatory behavior) were the child's way of defending him/herself from this chronic overarousal by providing some environmental continuity. However, subsequent investigations carefully comparing autistic children with control groups of normal children have failed to confirm the finding of chronic overarousal as measured by the EEG (e.g., Hermelin & O'Connor, 1970) and the postulated relationship between arousal as measured by the EEG and overt behavior (Hermelin & O'Connor, 1968; Ornitz, Brown, Sorosky, Ritvo, & Diedrich, 1970). Hermelin and O'Connor (1970) also make the important point that the EEG provides only one measure of arousal and we do not know whether in autistic children it correlates with other indices of arousal (e.g., levels of activity in the autonomic system).

Some investigators (Ornitz, 1985; Ornitz & Ritvo, 1968; Ritvo, 1976) have speculated a theory of *perceptual inconstancy* in which autistic children experience variable arousal wherein a particular stimulus is not always experienced in the same manner. This makes it difficult for specific sensory stimuli to be associated with motor output and may be responsible for some of the aberrant behaviors seen in these children. This theory has not received widespread attention and has not been adequately substantiated.

Thus, while the possibility of abnormal arousal regulation in autistic individuals and the potential specific effects of abnormal arousal on autistic behaviors is an interesting one, it remains unsubstantiated. Perhaps Wing (1976) sums it up best in concluding that any chronic aberration in arousal could either be primary (as speculated above) or secondary to some other, correlated, abnormalities. Besides, it is difficult to see how a general state of over- or underarousal could lead to the very specific pattern of impairments and skills found in autism.

In a related direction of research Courchesne (1987) has used event-related potentials (ERPs) to assess response to environmental events. ERPs are direct measures of brain activity evoked by a specified stimulus. Unlike the EEG, which measures ongoing activity, the use of the ERP allows for the exact time of occurrence of a precipitating event. Reviewing the ERP data from the three most carefully performed studies, Courchesne concludes that the development of autism occurs despite normal functioning of pathways that generate brain-stem auditory ERPs. Therefore, we must look elsewhere for the neural systems that must be disordered for autism to develop. This investigator cautiously speculates that the "operation of this apparently otherwise normal neural system is usually abnormally interfered with or hindered by some other system" (Courchesne et al., in press, p. 302). Specifically, he hypothesizes that autism is due to physioanatomical sources of fluctuating aberrant neural activity analogous to, but not necessarily the same as, epilepsy. This interference obstructs the normal functioning of neural systems responsible for attention and awareness. These systems include cholinergic and reticular-thalamic-cortical activating systems. Consequently, normal memory, language, and social functioning are greatly impaired.

Impairment of the *left hemisphere* of the brain has also been implicated as responsible for some of the major cognitive features of autism. Several researchers (Blackstock, 1978; Dawson, 1979; Dawson, Warrenburg, & Fuller, 1982; Prior & Bradshaw, 1979; Tanguay, 1976) have observed that the characteristic language and cognitive deficits in autism are those associated with left-hemisphere functioning. The behavior pattern of the autistic child seems to suggest strength, or minimal handicap, in right-hemisphere-dominated functions, such as visual-spatial abilities; and extreme weakness, or greatest handicap, in left-hemisphere-dominated functions, such as language and formation of abstract concepts (Lockyer & Rutter, 1970; Prior, 1984). In fact, several investigators, employing EEG and dichotic listening assessments have found that many autistic children show an abnormal pattern of hemisphere specialization, i.e., a preference for right-hemisphere dominance for both nonverbal and verbal stimuli (e.g., Prior & Bradshaw, 1979) or dysfunction in the left, or language-dominant hemisphere (Wetherby & Koegel, 1982).

This lateralized pattern of cognitive performance in autistic children could lead to the possible conclusion that there is a specific lesion or maldevelopment in the left hemisphere region. Yet this interpretation is not without its problems. Rutter (1978a, b), for example, argues against this interpretation because the plasticity in the infant brain is such that we would expect the right hemisphere to compensate for any such left-hemisphere deficits. In fact, evidence from children with left-hemisphere maldevelopment from birth or even up to the age of five or six years (Hécean, 1976) suggests that for the majority of these children, the right hemisphere compensates and assumes many of the functions normally conducted by the left hemisphere. If left-hemisphere damage is responsible for many of the cognitive and language deficits characteristic of autism, and if this damage is present from birth or soon thereafter, then why does this right-hemisphere compensation not occur? It would be necessary to postulate bilateral damage to account for this lack of plasticity (Hetzler & Griffin, 1981; Prior, 1984). Also, one must consider that there are other, nonautistic, children who suffer equally severe cognitive deficits but manifest no other features of the autism syndrome. So, while certain cognitive defects may be correlated with lateralization of hemisphere functions, we are far from postulating a specific relation of such functions to autism.

The identification and study of *structural abnormalities* in the brain has been difficult and, until recently, not particularly fruitful. Most of these studies require a postmortem examination of the brain of autistic individuals and few such studies exist. One problem has been that, until relatively recently, the few brain autopsies reported were conducted before the standard diagnostic guidelines for autism were formulated. In addition, the relative rarity of autism in the population and the fact that these individuals tend to lead normal lifespans result in the lack of a significant number of brains for study. Furthermore, since the availability of postmortem brains is mostly limited to adult brains, one must be concerned about the changes in the brain that may have resulted from "having autism" throughout life. Any abnormalities noted might be the result of, rather than the cause of, the disorder. Another problem that has impeded the direct neuroanatomical study of autistic brains is that our rather limited technology has precluded some of the sophisticated assessments such studies require to enable accurate conclusions to be drawn. In recent years, investigators have attempted to overcome these problems. Collaboration among researchers has allowed for the accumulation of several brains, located in different research centers across the country. This allows for the pooling of data and thus more information. Also, our technology for studying the neuroanatomy of the brain has improved substantially.

Bauman and Kemper (1985) present results of an histoanatomic comparison of the brain of a 29-year-old autistic and the brain of an age- and sex-matched control subject. Using whole brain serial sections (a process by which the brain tissue is sliced in very thin sections for anatomical observation under a microscope), these investigators compared gross features of the brain structures as well as cell counts in a number of specific areas of the brain. While there appeared to be no difference between the two brain cortices, there were some significant differences in the cerebellum and structures in the limbic system. The cerebellum is a structure involved with muscle coordination and the regulation of sensory input. The limbic system significantly influences emotion and memory. Specifically, the cerebellum of the autistic man showed a notable loss of Purkinje cells. These cells release certain neurotransmitters that inhibit the action of other neurons. The limbic system, the hippocampus, subiculum, and entorhinal cortex of the autistic brain had more densely packed cells than did the normal brain, and the individual cells were smaller. These investigators note that this cellular pattern of the limbic system is the same as that found in the brains of young normal children, not adults, and perhaps this indicates immaturity of the autistic brain.

The results of studies from multiple research centers on several brains of deceased autistic individuals are now available. The preliminary results of this research show a remarkable correspondence to the data reported by Bauman and Kemper (1985). Ritvo and his colleagues (1986) present data on four autistic brains and those of three control subjects. Importantly, the autistic subjects qualified for the study on the basis of the new diagnostic criteria for autism (i.e., DSM III-R, 1987). The autistic subjects ranged in age from 10 to 22 years at the time of death. The normal control subjects were 3 to 13 years old. The normal control subjects were healthy at the time of death except for one with brain damage due to an overdose of an anti-convulsant drug. Two of the autistic individuals died accidental deaths, one committed suicide, and one died from an undetermined cause. As did Bauman and Kemper (1985), these researchers found abnormalities in the cerebellum of the autistic brains. Again there were significantly fewer Purkinje cells among the autistic subjects. As Ritvo points out, since the cerebellum regulates incoming sensations, its cellular irregularities may account for the sensory deficits so characteristic of autism, such as insensitivity to pain or oversensitivity to sounds and textures.

The fact that relatively consistent findings are being reported by different investigators and centers is encouraging. Also, the direct observation of neuroanatomical anomalies brings us a step closer to relating stucture to autistic behavior and at least reduces some of the speculation necessitated by inferring from indirect observations. Bauman and Kemper state there are several indications that changes in the autistic brains examined by them occurred prior to birth. In a normal brain, neurons begin to push away from each other after birth as their cell bodies develop more and longer dendrites, and glial cells proliferate. It appears this maturational process was impeded or arrested in the autistic brains. In addition, the autistic brains showed a clear zone between two cell layers in the entorhinal cortex (a structure in the limbic system); this anatomical characteristic normally appears during the second trimester of fetal life and disappears by the age of 15 months. Another indication that the autistic brains were affected prior to birth was the finding that a group of cells (the olivary neurons) was intact in the autistic brain whereas postnatal damage to the cerebellum typically results in the destruction of this group of cells.

In a more recent finding, Courchesne, Hesselink, Jernigan and Yeung-Courchesne (in press) used magnetic resonance imaging (MRI) to study the anatomic details of the cerebellum, cerebral cortex, and subcortical struc-tures of a nonretarded, high-functioning, 21-year-old male with autism. This study differs from those discussed above in that a brain-imaging technology applied to a living individual was used, and the fact that the individual studied was autistic (with a diagnosis consistent with the current criteria) without other complicating syndromes, such as mental retardation, epilepsy, history of drug use, postnatal trauma or disease. These investigators argue that many of the prior results with postmortem brains involved individuals with autism and retardation and that the differences noted might be due to the retardation or to some other factors, independent of autism, *per se*. Courchesne and his colleagues report findings which are similar in many ways to those from previous postmortem neuropathology data. They found *in vivo* evidence of both cerebral and cerebellar abnormalities in the brain of this nonretarded autistic individual. Specifically, the right posterior cerebral hemisphere appeared to be abnormal in that its overall size was larger than its corresponding area on the left hemisphere. Also, pathology was found in the cerebellum indicating a decreased or arrested development of several areas within the cerebellum.

While the results of these preliminary investigations are fascinating and strongly tempt one to extrapolate beyond the data to explain the development of autism, it remains a fact that these data are preliminary and need to be considered so. Many more brains must be studied to verify the generality of these findings. Furthermore, the functioning of the many structures of the brain are poorly understood as yet, which certainly inhibits our ability to determine specific relations. Another caveat is that we are still uncertain whether the brain anomalies observed cause autistic symptoms or, in fact, reflect a more widespread brain disorder such as mental retardation (e.g., Courchesne *et al.*, in press).

As can be seen from this discussion of research into a number of areas of the potential biological etiology in autism, few stones have been left unturned. The focus on these areas has allowed us to formulate several interesting hypotheses about the disorder and has helped us to direct our research efforts more effectively. Particularly encouraging is that there seems to be some consensus in findings such as those related to cerebellum and limbic system abnormalities and in evidence that autistic brains may be underdeveloped and immature. Despite such promising findings, however, it is apparent that we have not really come close to understanding the complex issues involved in the development of autism. Rather, the findings of such research have probably served more to give us an appreciation of just how complex and complicated the questions we pose really are.

SUMMARY

While the cause, or causes, of autism have yet to be identified, several hypothetical etiologies have been proposed. The theories postulating abnormal interactions with the social environment can be divided into three positions. The first, and the first historically, is the psychodynamic theory which held that autism was caused by the child's experience with parents who had pathological personalities. The second theory is based on learning principles and was postulated to suggest how autism might be a function of the child's learning history wherein emerging normal behaviors, such as language, are not adequately reinforced while certain abnormal behaviors, such as self-stimulation, are reinforced. Basically, this theory again implicates the parents in that it is assumed that the parents are the ones responsible for providing the inadequate and/or abnormal learning environment. The third basic theory in this area is an interactional position which postulated that autism was a result of the interaction of a biologically or psychologically susceptible child and parental psychopathology. While these theories helped focus attention on the etiology of autism and certainly reflected the dominant theoretical positions of their time, systematic research has failed to support the fact that the social environment, including the parents, plays any role in the development of autism.

A second area that has received attention as a possible etiological basis for autism focuses on basic cognitive deficits and/or abnormalities. Although a specific cognitive deficit has not been identified, several hypotheses have been advanced to account for the development of the syndrome-specific characteristics of autism. These hypotheses have included specific defects in perceptual and attentional behaviors that might suggest a specific central cognitive deficit. Since there is now a body of data suggesting that poor performance on intellectual assessments is reflective of a genuine deficit and not of other factors (e.g., motivation, social difficulties), some researchers speculate that this intellectual impairment is the result of a true cognitive defect. Others emphasize the deficits in language as pivotal to the development and characteristics of autism. The work in the area of cognitive deficits and/or abnormalities is extensive and wide ranging. While investigators continue to speculate on the precise nature of a basic and general cognitive defect that might underly autism, none has been specifically identified to date. There remain several important questions and issues that must be addressed before the argument of a particular cognitive defect as the basis of autism can be supported.

Recent emphasis on the potential organic etiologies of autism has attracted a good deal of attention. This is primarily due to the lack of evidence supporting the psychogenic hypotheses, increasing evidence indicating an organic basis for the disorder, and the increasing technology available to researchers in the biological fields. One area of study has focused on factors relating to pregnancy and birth. While the study of these factors has not led to the identification of specific risk factors in birth histories, several interesting leads have been followed up in other areas. One of these areas relates to genetic factors that might be associated with autism. Data in this area suggest a genetic involvement in at least a subgroup of autistic individuals and further research in this area may lead to the identification of specific variables and their involvement in the development of autism. Another area of study in the biological basis of autism relates to neurochemical factors. Much of this research has focused on the involvement of specific neurochemicals, such as the cerebral neurotransmitter serotonin. Again, while the work in this area is provocative, the case for a neurochemical basis for autism has not been adequately substantiated to date. The role of neurological and neuro-anatomical factors has also received wide attention recently. Abnormal brain wave activity, arousal levels, defects in the ability to respond accurately to sensory input, event-related potentials measured in the brain, impairment of left-hemisphere functioning, and specific structural abnormalities have all been investigated.

Despite some promising leads in some of these areas, the preponderance of evidence does not suport any one of these particular theories and drawing any strong conclusions would certainly be premature at this time. Again we are brought back to the conclusion that the search for a specific etiology of autism may be fruitless. The variation in results, the heterogeneity of the population, and the possible existence of distinct subgroups within the autistic population, suggest that multiple etiologies may be responsible.

5

TREATMENT MODELS

The treatment approaches that have been applied to autistic children can be divided into three categories. First, treatments based on a psychodynamic model follow from the psychogenic hypothesis of the etiology of the disorder. Second, pharmacological treatments typically seek to alter basic biochemical aberrations and thus affect specific and/or general behavioral changes. Third, treatments based on a behavioral model differ from the other treatment models in that the behavioral model does not focus upon a basic "disease" or central cause of the disorder. Rather, this model focuses on the specific behaviors exhibited and on their relation to the child's environment.

PSYCHODYNAMIC MODEL OF TREATMENT

Of all the treatment modalities, the psychodynamic position is the most closely related to a specific hypothesized etiology. As discussed in the chapter on etiology, this position holds that autism is the result of the child's withdrawal from an environment that is perceived as hostile, threatening, and dangerous. Because of psychological pathology in the parent, particularly the mother, the child's normal frustrations and resulting minor withdrawals are met with an extreme negative reaction by the parent. Rather than responding to these normal withdrawals with supportive behaviors such as feeding, cuddling and stroking, these mothers respond with hostility, causing the child to further withdraw into autism. This is the "chronic autistic disease" and involves an arrest in ego development since the child's libidinal energies are spent in defending against the environment (e.g., Bettelheim, 1967).

The most ardent supporter of the psychodynamic model of etiology and treatment is Bruno Bettelheim, and his Sonia Shankman Orthogenic School at the University of Chicago provides perhaps the most representative and comprehensive program based on this theoretical approach (Bettelheim, 1967). Bettelheim pointed out that in most institutions the basic approach is to encourage the child to see the world as it really is, which is precisely what the psychotic child is incapable of doing. Instead, what is needed is to create for the child a world that is completely different from the one he/she abandoned in despair and one which the child can enter exactly as he/she is.

The child is removed from the home, and thus from the parents who are deemed responsible for the child's extreme autistic withdrawal, and placed in a residential setting. Within this setting, the child is tended to by therapists who serve as surrogate mothers who attempt to be what the child's own mother was not. Thus, the child is now in an environment within which he/she is allowed to express feelings and activities with absolutely no fear of the frustration and pressures that characterized the original home environment. The child is encouraged to gradually reach out for experiences and to develop a strong concept of self and of the world. The child's reaching out, even if only in a minimal form initially, is received with acceptance, love, and infinite patience. Importantly, the child's behavior leads not only to acceptance, but also to a reciprocal response from the therapist indicating to the child that his/her behavior does have an effect on others. Thus, the child's sense of his/her own power, lost in the early days with the natural parents, is revived. According to Bettelheim, such a step is essential to the development of autonomy.

To illustrate the importance of the child's developing sense of independence, Bettelheim provides an example in the treatment of one of his children, "Laurie". This child's withdrawal included the refusal of food. On one occasion, Laurie showed independence by reaching for, and eating, a piece of chocolate. Following this, her therapist proceeded to attempt to feed her more chocolate. At this point Laurie bit the therapist. This was viewed as a positive sign in that the child was demonstrating her newly asserted independence. Her behavior was seen by Bettelheim as very encouraging and readily accepted as appropriate.

The psychodynamic approach has deliberately de-emphasized the description or definition of specific procedures. Rather, the children are encouraged through a variety of means to engage in any behavior through which they choose to express their growing autonomy. For example, the child would not be toilet trained since this would involve the imposition of potentially frustrating limits. Instead, the therapist might encourage the child to eliminate at random times, in random locations. Since the psychoanalytic position views the normal child's developing autonomy as closely tied to the anal stage of development, it is believed that the autistic child should go through the same steps toward autonomy. Other examples include encouraging the child to play in his/her own way with materials such as puzzles, crayons, and/or paper, to engage in passive or aggressive behavior depending on the child's desires, and to eat in any manner (e.g., with hands).

As the treatment continues, and the child's expressions of autonomy are met with love, acceptance and understanding, she/he gains a sense of selfness, and other procedures such as tactile and kinesthetic stimulation are used to further encourage growth and the all-important recognition of the presence of nonthreatening others. The child is now able to trust others and the environment. It is through this trust and the re-emergence of the self and a growing sense of autonomy that cognitive areas such as language develop. The child no longer needs to utilize the autistic defenses that were so necessary initially. It is no longer necessary to defend against reality.

Consistent with this position, others (e.g., Hartman, Kris, & Lowenstein, 1946; Rank & MacNaughton, 1950) have emphasized that emotional, perceptual, and cognitive growth in normal individuals depends on the establishment of an object relationship with another person. Approaches based on these and Ruttenberg's (1971) model have sought to provide an environment which allows for complete gratification via contact with consistent and positive mother substitutes. These surrogate mothers, or teachers, develop this relationship by engaging the child in as much tactile, kinesthetic, and vocal stimulation as is possible within the child's tolerance limits. Included here is the imitation of the child's behavior and vocalizations. Once the child begins to accept these surrogate mothers, various self-help and cognitive skill-building programs are introduced. During this process the teacher is very careful to consider the child's overall emotional, functional, and developmental level since expectations above this level could result in frustration and further withdrawal.

While the psychodynamic approach is most clearly illustrated by the work of Bettelheim (1967, 1974), other treatments involve similar techniques. One such treatment approach is that of DesLauriers (1978). He does not view autism as an outgrowth of inadequate mothering but rather as based on a severe sensory impairment. He proposes a form of play therapy emphasizing "body stimulation". This therapy involves sensory-stimulating experiences, which are sufficiently intense to overcome the child's basic sensory deficit. Thus, the therapist engages in highly stimulating activities such as tickling. Such activities are expected to allow the child to learn to experience the world and relate to it more normally.

Evaluation

Many arguments have been presented militating against the use of treatments based on the psychodynamic approach. Foremost among these is the accumulating evidence refuting the assumption upon which the treatment is based.

First, as discussed earlier, there is no empirically validated evidence supporting the hypothesis that the parents are responsible for the development of autism (e.g., Rimland, 1964; Rutter, 1971; Schopler & Reichler, 1971). There is no evidence that the children have been exposed to the extreme negative conditions that analysts feel necessary for the autistic withdrawal that is seen by Bettelheim and others as the essence of autism. Neither is there evidence for greater pathology in parents of autistic children. Again, such pathology is considered basic to the psychogenic hypothesis. Indeed, some have asserted that moving the child away from the home may worsen his/her condition (Lovaas, 1979) and, as we shall see, involving parents and other family members in the child's treatment may be essential.

Second, while Bettelheim claims some impressive success rates with the children seen in his program, the generality of his claims of significant improvement has been challenged in the light of his employment of selection criteria in admitting children to the program and in the absence of empirical verification. In fact, his claims are based on subjective case histories rather than empirical bases (e.g., Greenfeld, 1972; Merritt, 1968; Rimland, 1964; Rutter, 1971; Schopler & Reichler, 1971; Shapiro, 1978).

Third, treatments based on a psychodynamic approach have not stood the test of evaluation. They very nature of psychodynamic with its inferential terminology and lack of precision in describing procedures precludes putting the theory to an empirical test. Indeed, evaluation has been hampered by the failure of Bettelheim and others to describe in any detail exactly what is involved in providing the treatment. This lack of specificity seems to be intentional since the therapist is supposed to be able to progress depending on the responses of the child and this cannot be determined beforehand. In addition, Bettelheim's descriptions of outcome and evaluation criteria are similarly wanting. Despite the difficulties in putting this treatment to the test there have been efforts to do so. Some investigations have been conducted to compare the relative gains made by children in a psychoanalytically oriented treatment program with the gains made by children who received no treatment (Kanner & Eisenberg, 1955; Levitt, 1957, 1963). The results of these investigations showed that the autistic children receiving the psychotherapy did not make greater gains than those receiving no treatment. Similarly, Bartak and Rutter (1973) and Rutter and Bartak (1973) conducted studies to compare systematically the effectiveness of an analytically oriented program with two other programs that emphasized a more structured and educational approach. These investigators found that, compared to the children in the structured treatment groups, the children in the psychodynamic treatment group made significantly less progress in areas such as speech, reading skills, and arithmetic skills and engaged in significantly more deviant behavior (e.g., self-stimulation).

The results of systematic studies are quite consistent. Summarizing the results of many years of research, a report by the National Institute of Mental Health (1975) concludes: "Psychotherapy with autistic children of the kind designed to provide insight has not proved effective and in the light of our knowledge about autism is unlikely to do so" (p. 207). Because of these findings one does not find these traditional psychotherapeutic interventions being used in many centers specializing in the treatment of autism.

Based on the perspective of today, approximately 30 years after the original application of the psychodynamic approach to treatment, it is not surprising that such treatment would not work. Given the inaccurate assumptions upon which it is based, there is no reason to expect otherwise. There is another issue related to this form of treatment that will always remain a tragic "side effect" of its existence. This is the needless blame and resulting guilt that the parents have suffered over the years. This parent-causation position has been a long time dying and is even now espoused by some. While this is an unfortunate legacy left by the psychodynamic model, one can see positive side effects as well. In reaction to the psychogenic hypothesis, parents and professionals dedicated to the understanding and treatment of autistic children founded the National Society for Autistic Children (now the Autism Society of America), which has been instrumental in fostering and disseminating information about the disorder. Also, the development of other treatments in some ways stems from both a dissatisfaction with the etiological assumptions of psychoanalysis and with the failure of treatments based on these assumptions. Interestingly, Bettelheim (1967) stated that ". . . the treatment of autistic children is by no means a closed chapter, but one that is just beginning to be written" (p. 10). One wonders whether he could have guessed just how prophetic this statement would become.

PSYCHOPHARMACOLOGICAL TREATMENTS

The use of psychopharmacological agents to treat autism has not led thus far to resounding success. Ideally, we would be able to identify a specific neurochemical aberration responsible for the etiology of the disorder and treat affected individuals with a specific drug that would cure autism. Unfortunately, as we have seen, no such specific cause has been identified for autism—or even a specific subgroup of autistic children. Furthermore, because there is no prescribed drug treatment for the disorder, clinicians and researchers have focused instead on assessing the effects of various drug agents on specific behaviors. The ultimate goal of these treatments is to utilize a minimal and safe dose of some drug to alleviate some of the more disruptive symptoms of autism, thereby enabling the children to better benefit from other environmental treatments (e.g., Campbell et al., 1978).

Towards this end, investigators have used a wide variety of drugs to treat autistic children. These treatments have involved stimulants, antidepressants, psychedelics, neuroleptics, thyroid hormones, lithium carbonate, amphetamines, and megavitamins. The results of most of this research are difficult to evaluate for several reasons. One problem relates to issues of medical dosage, such as high dosage over long periods of time, simultaneous multiple drug usage, no drug holidays (temporary cessation of medication to assess whether it is still necessary and to assess side effects), lack of appropriate drug monitoring, and the utilization of drugs such as sedatives that may interfere with learning, especially at high dosages (Campbell, 1979). Another problem is that when drug treatment is terminated, symptoms often reappear. Other problems in interpreting the results of many of the pharmacological studies with autistic children relate to experimental issues, such as poorly defined diagnostic groupings, heterogeneous populations, small sample sizes, lack of placebo controls, lack of adequate "blind" procedures, poor experimental designs, and lack of objective measurement of appropriate dependent variables. Only relatively recently have well-controlled and well-conducted studies appeared in the literature.

Amphetamines have sometimes proven useful in controlling hyperactive behaviors that are often associated with autism. These drugs may serve to improve the children's attention spans and lower their activity levels, thereby allowing them to benefit from educational interventions (Mesibov & Dawson, 1986). However, Campbell, Fish, Shapiro, Collins, and Koh (1972) indicate that despite the many clinical reports of the effectiveness of amphetamine treatment, the main published investigations of this treatment with autistic children suggest a worsening of behavior.

Neuroleptics, also known as antipsychotics and major tranquilizers, have been rather extensively researched and some conclusions may be drawn about the: effectiveness with this population. Chlorpromazine (Thorazine) is one of the most widely used neuroleptics. It tends to decrease autistic behaviors and calm the child (Korein, Fish, Shapiro, Gerner, & Levidow, 1971). It is known to diminish motor excitement and hyperactivity as well as alleviate agitation, tension, and anxiety (Levine, Brooks, & Schonkoff, 1980). It is also known to be epileptogenic and is thus contraindicated for individuals with seizure disorders. Nonetheless, there are many reports on the effectiveness of chlorpromazine and other neuroleptics, properly administered, in reducing hyperactivity, stereotypic behaviors, aggressiveness, temper tantrums, tics, and withdrawal. In young autistic children, however, chlorpromazine has been shown to be of limited effectiveness, and this result is associated with excessive sedation. On the other hand, trifluloperazine (Stelazine), a phenothiazine with a less sedative action than chlorpromazine has been shown to result in a decrease in withdrawal and an increase in alertness and verbal production in low-functioning autistic children (Campbell, Green, & Deutsch, 1985). It can be concluded that phenothiazines, under carefully controlled and monitored dosages, may be beneficial in reducing some of the behavioral excesses associated with autism and may make the child more susceptible to other, environmental, treatment interventions. However, intersubject variability, differential drug sensitivities, and potentially serious side effects associated with some of the drugs (e.g., lowered seizure threshold, tardive dyskenesia) limit their usefulness with all subjects. In addition, little is known of the long-term effects of phenothiazines, even though they are often prescribed over long periods of time.

Interestingly, another neuroleptic drug, *haloperidol* (Haldol), has recently shown promise as a means of improving the behavior of autistic children, especially in combination with behavioral treatments. In two studies that clearly represent this research direction, Campbell *et al.* (1978) compared haloperidol treatment to behavior therapy and the two in combination in terms of their effects on both behavioral symptoms and on imitative language acquisition in a group of 40 autistic children aged 2.6 to 7.2 years. The study employed a double-blind, between-groups design, included a placebo control, and utilized multiple independent raters on several rating scales of behavior. The results of this investigation revealed that haloperidol significantly reduced stereotypies (self-stimulation) and withdrawal in those subjects 4.5 years of age and older. Further, the combination of haloperidol and behavior therapy (contingent reinforcement for imitative language) was significantly superior to either treatment alone.

The results of this study lead to the question of exactly how the drug enhanced the efficacy of the behavior therapy. Was it because the haloperidol reduced stereotypy and withdrawal and thus removed two behaviors that could be expected to impede learning? Or did the drug somehow directly affect attentional mechanisms and thus facilitate learning? To address this question, a subsequent study (Anderson *et al.*, 1984) was conducted in which the effects of haloperidol were assessed in two situations—a highly structured experimental setting in which the children were trained on an automated operant discrimination task and an outside setting. Forty autistic children, aged 2.3 to 6.9 years, participated in the study, which utilized a within-subjects reversal design. The children were randomly assigned to one of two treatment schedules (haloperidol-placebo-haloperidol or placebo-haloperidol-placebo) with each treatment lasting for four weeks. The results indicated that outside the laboratory, the children showed significant decreases in ratings of stereotypies, withdrawal, hyperactivity, fidgetiness, abnormal object relationships, negativism, labile affect, and irritability during the haloperidol treatment. In the laboratory, discrimination learning increased significantly during the drug condition but there was no effect on behavioral symptoms during this condition. Thus, the investigators conclude that the effect of the drug on learning (in this study as well as the Campbell *et al.*, 1978 study) was not a function of its reducing symptoms, but rather that it probably directly affected attentional mechanisms. It was also noted that the autistic children sustained their gains on haloperidol maintenance therapy on a long-term basis (six months) but one week after termination of the drug, stereotypy, withdrawal, hyperactivity, fidgetiness, and abnormal object relations worsened significantly.

In another study Cohen *et al.* (1980) utilized objective rating scales and a double-blind, placebo-controlled, within-subjects reversal design to assess the therapeutic efficacy of haloperidol in a sample of 10 preschool-age autistic children. Haloperidol was found to decrease the percentage occurrence of stereotypy. This effect was more pronounced in older children and in those children who exhibited a high percentage of stereotypy during baseline. Another observed effect was that the drug facilitated the orienting reaction of the children to the request "Look at me," with this effect more pronounced in the older subjects and in those exhibiting a low percentage of orienting during the baseline phase. Stereotypy and orienting in baseline were negatively correlated.

Researchers working with haloperidol report minimal untoward effects with the drug and these effects are most commonly associated with excess dosages in children. These effects usually involve excessive sedation and worsening of pre-existing symptoms, plus hyperactivity, hypoactivity, irritability, apathy, decrease in verbal production, daze-like behavior, stereotypies, tics, and hallucinations (Campbell *et al.*, 1985). These authors point out that, as a general rule, neuroleptics should only be prescribed for moderately to severely disturbed children and for those for whom other treatments have failed. If the drug is effective, it should be given for a minimum of two to three months, with drug treatment discontinued after three to six months (for about one month) in order to assess whether further drug administration is required and whether withdrawal dyskinesias might develop.

It appears that of the neuroleptics, haloperidol has generated the most interest and the most provocative results. It appears that the drug yields significant decreases in behavioral symptoms in certain young autistic children. Campbell *et al.* (1985) conclude that haloperidol, when administered over a period of two to three months to hyper- or normo-active patients in a structured program, will enhance certain types of learning (e.g., imitative language, discrimination) without negative side effects if the dosage of the drug is individually titrated. While the parameters of the drug's effects and the mechanism by which it operates on specific behaviors remain to be determined, it is certain that this drug will continue to stimulate research interest.

Focusing on the *serotonergic and dopamine systems* as potentially fruitful sites for investigation, some investigators have attempted to relate levels of blood and brain serotonin (a neurotransmitter) to autistic behaviors. As noted earlier, it is known that concentrations of blood serotonin decrease with age and that high levels of serotonin past early childhood might be considered a sign of immaturity. Although clinically indistinguishable, it is also known that a subgroup of autistic children, perhaps as many as 40%, have elevated blood serotonin compared to sex- and age-matched controls (Geller, Ritvo, Freeman, & Yuwiler, 1982). This correlation between increased blood serotonin and autistic symptoms led to the hypothesis that if the concentration of serotonin were reduced, a concomitant decrease in autistic symptomatology might occur. To investigate this possibility, Ritvo *et al.* (1971) administered *L-dopa*, a known blood serotonin inhibitor, to see if blood concentrations of serotonin would be lowered in this population and if such a lowering was accompanied by any clinical and/or physiological changes. Four autistic children, 3 to 13 years old were hospitalized and given L-dopa after a 17-day placebo baseline. The results of the study indicated a significant decrease of blood serotonin in the three youngest children but no changes in the children's clinical status or other relevant behaviors. These authors later suggested several possible explanations for the finding that L-dopa was ineffective in reducing symptoms. First, perhaps serotonin metabolism may be normal in children with autism. Second, perhaps the serotonin was lowered after a critical phase and thus nothing at this point in time would have helped. Third, perhaps only blood and not brain serotonin may have been affected. Fourth, magnitude of blood and brain serotonin may have been insufficient to produce an effect. Fifth, the ameliorative effect of L-dopa in reducing serotonin levels may have been offset by the effects of L-dopa in increasing dopamine and/or norepinephrine (Ritvo, Freeman, Geller, & Yuwiler, 1983).

Because of the problems associated with L-dopa, these investigators turned to another known serotonin inhibitor and depletor, *fenfluramine* (Pondimine), which is an FDA-approved anorexigenic drug. While the effects of fenfluramine on human brain serotonin concentrations are unknown, it has been shown to produce marked, long-lasting, but reversible decreases in brain serotonin in animals. Again, the investigators were interested in assessing any clinical changes in autistic children correlated with reductions in serotonin. In an initial study, Geller *et al.* (1982) reported preliminary results suggesting that fenfluramine reduced the blood serotonin concentrations in three hyperserotonic autistic boys and that this reduction was accompanied by improvements in behavior and cognitive functioning. Dependent measures included performance on three IQ tests and scores on a symptom rating scale (which included assessments of motor behavior, social avoidance, affect, speech, object relations and sensory functioning). In addition, some of these positive effects were retained for several weeks after the drug had been terminated.

In an expanded study (Ritvo *et al.*, 1983) 14 autistic outpatients were studied in a double-blind crossover study which utilized a wide variety of dependent measures to assess the effects of fenfluramine on clinical features of autism. These assessments included serial observation scales, developmental profiles, intelligence scales, and parental interviews and diaries. During the study, the subjects were placed on placebo for one month, fenfluramine for four months, and return to placebo for two months. The effects of the drug on blood serotonin were rapid; serotonin concentration levels decreased an average of 51% after one month of medication and returned to baseline levels within one month after return to placebo. The reported changes in the dependent measures were most impressive. Parents reported no changes in their children's behavior during baseline placebo. During the drug trial they noticed decreased restlessness, motility disturbances, and sensory symptoms, improved sleep patterns, increased eye contact, and "more socialization". After four months on the drug, additional improvements were noted including increased spontaneity in use of language, decreased echolalia, more appropriate affect, and increased social awareness. Within two weeks after return to placebo the parents of some of the patients reported that motility, sensory disturbances and hyperactivity had reappeared. Significant increases on self-help, social, academic, communication, and IQ scales, as measured by the Alpern-Boll Developmental Profile, were also reported while the children were on the drug, followed by decreases when the placebo was reintroduced. Similarly, on a serial observation rating scale (Ritvo Freeman Real Life Rating Scale for Autism), all 14 subjects showed significant improvements on the specific scales designed to measure autistic behaviors (e.g., social, affect, motility disturbances) and worsened on return to the placebo condition. The Wechsler Intelligence Scale showed significant increases while the subjects were on fenfluramine and these increases were retained for two months on placebo. Other intelligence scales (Cattell/Stanford-Binet and Merrill-Palmer Preschool Performance Tests) yielded no significant changes.

In order to replicate the above effects with these subjects and also to determine if the effects could be sustained for twice as long, Ritvo et al. (1984) conducted another similar investigation. Basically, these investigators again found clinical improvement with these subjects; on some scales, gains after eight months on the drug exceeded those noted after only four months in the previous study. The authors concluded that patients of initially low blood serotonin values and high IQ respond best to fenfluramine. This may mean that patients with less central nervous system impairment, as reflected by higher IQ, have better cognitive resources, which can emerge when specific symptoms are reduced by medication.

Additional positive effects of fenfluramine were reported by Campbell, Deutsch, Perry, Wolsky, and Palij (1986). They sought to determine the effectiveness of the drug with a small sample of patients within a narrow age range. They studied 10 children, ranging in age from 3 to 5.75 years. Dependent measures included a series of clinical rating scales. They found increased relatedness and animated facial expressions, decreases in irritability, temper tantrums, aggression, self-injury, hyperactivity, and improved sleep patterns. Thus, this study replicates the positive effects noted by Ritvo and his colleagues.

As research on fenfluramine continues, more specific information on the nature and parameters of its effects are coming into focus. Beisler, Tsai, and Stiefel (1986) report that fenfluramine administration had no effect on measures of communication skills in their sample of six autistic children. Also, although Ritvo and his colleagues report negligible and only transient side effects with the drug, Piggott, Gdowski, Villanueva, Fischhoff, and Frohman (1986) report that four of their sample of eight autistic children suffered significant side effects including decreased appetite, drowsiness/ lethargy, irritability, nasal stuffiness and enuresis. One of the children showed severe regression. Piggot *et al.* conclude that these side effects are most likely dose-related and can be avoided by careful monitoring. However, Yarbrough, Santat, Perel, Webster and Lombardi (1987) report results of fenfluramine on 21 maladaptive behaviors in 20 autistic patients (age range 9 to 28 years) over a 9-month period using a well-controlled design. These investigators conclude that no significant reductions in maladaptive behaviors were effected and that this lack of positive effect, coupled with negative side effects (e.g., insomnia, tension, agitation), strongly indicate the need for caution in the use of fenfluramine.

There is no doubt that fenfluramine merits further study. Despite some hopeful initial results, it must be remembered that all results have not been positive, the parameters of its effects have not yet been identified, and the manner by which it acts to modify symptoms in autism is unknown. This drug may act via its known effects as a serotonin depletor or inhibitor of the dopamine system or by some other, as yet undetermined, means (Ritvo *et al.*, 1984). It is interesting to note, however, that the explanation of its effects in terms of reducing serotonin may be erroneous since some of the rather dramatic improvements reported in these studies have been with children who did not have elevated serotonin levels. It is apparent that, as with all psychopharmacological treatments, we have only just begun to fully evaluate the effects of fenfluramine.

Megavitamin treatment has also been investigated as a potentially useful intervention strategy for autistic children. Unfortunately, this area of study is hampered by a paucity of well-controlled experimental studies, with most of the reports consisting of individual case descriptions. Rimland (1973) has reported a preliminary study of 190 outpatient psychotic children receiving megadoses of vitamins over a 24-week period. Of this population, 37 were diagnosed as classically autistic and showed the most dramatic improvement. Rimland conservatively considered these results as only encouraging. Reviewing studies in this area, Mesibov and Dawson (1986) conclude that apparently some autistic children, though clearly not all and probably not even the majority, benefit from megavitamin treatment. More rigorous scientific investigations must be awaited before any firm conclusions can be drawn about the effectiveness of this regimen.

Only those psychopharmacological treatments that have received the most research and clinical attention have been described above. The effects of other agents, such as lithium carbonate and methylphenidate (Ritalin), have yielded conflicting results and these drugs are not commonly used with autistic children.

Evaluation

It is apparent that medication is a very lively area of research and one that will continue to provide challenges for researchers and clinicians. On the positive side, it is hoped that we will be able to identify specific psychopharmacological interventions that may serve to provide rapid effects on some of the more severe behavioral symptoms in autistic children and that these effects will allow for the administration of more effective environmental treatments. On the negative side is the realization that, although there have been some very recent breakthroughs, so far there are relatively few methodologically sound studies suggesting drug therapy is more effective than placebo or any other treatment. One must also be aware of potential negative side effects which may impair learning (e.g., sedation effects with neuroleptics). Thus, we are far from achieving consistent findings with any of the drugs used to date and we do not know enough about dosage, short- and long-term effects, side effects, parameters of effectiveness, and, importantly, the mechanisms by which many of these drugs produce their effects. These uncertainties, coupled with a highly heterogeneous and poorly defined population, make the goal of identifying any generalized psychopharmacological treatment a formidable one indeed, and one that is far from being realized.

BEHAVIORAL TREATMENT

One may conceptualize both the psychodynamic and organic models of treatment as based upon the idea that autism is due to a central process or "disease". Thus, the psychodynamicists view the disorder as symptomatic of an underlying problem caused by inadequate parenting (e.g., Bettelheims's "chronic autistic disease"). Individuals looking for an organic basis for autism are seeking to discover a neurophysiological origin of etiology and hence administer pharmacological agents that affect implicated areas of neurochemical functioning. In sharp contrast to these treatment models is the behavioral model. Its proponents posit that instead of treating the disease of "autism," it is more fruitful to view the syndrome as just that, a *syndrome* comprised of specific behaviors. The most appropriate approach to treatment therefore is to understand the child's behaviors in terms of their functional relationship to their environment. Once these relations are identified, one may change the behaviors by manipulating those aspects of the environment that affect them.

The behavioral model of autism and its treatment is certainly antithetical to the traditional psychodynamic model. It is perhaps ironic that behavioral treatment owes its existence to the failure of psychodynamic (or other disease-model) treatments. This is largely due to the fact that the psychodynamic model, despite years of dominating the treatment of autistic children, could not demonstrate its effectiveness. People then turned to the empirically based behavioral model. One behavioral psychologist has summarized the situation succinctly: "If the disease model had been a viable and effective model for treatment of autistic children, the behavioral model probably would not have seen the light of day" (Lovaas, 1979, p. 316).

Several problems with the disease model of autism have become apparent.

Some of these were briefly presented earlier in our discussion of behavioral assessment. Because there is still inadequate agreement regarding the diagnostic criteria for "autism" and since the existing criteria are unevenly applied, there is a tremendous heterogeneity in the population labeled autistic. A mute, retarded, self-injurious 12-year-old and an echolalic, nonretarded, compulsive 4-year-old may present very different clinical pictures, yet both carry the diagnosis of autism. The label "autism" tells us very little about the behavioral characteristics of an individual child. This heterogeneity leads to several other problems. First, one must begin to wonder if autism really is a specific unitary entity or merely a crossing of several continua of behaviors, each of which might have different etiologies. In other words, this heterogeneity might in fact reflect the existence of several independent disorders of varying etiologies. If this is the case, then the search for, or treatment of, a particular disease would be fruitless. A second problem resulting from the heterogeneity of this population is that the diagnosis of autism does not facilitate communication between professionals (Schreibman & Koegel, 1981). Different researchers may study autistic children but since the diagnosis is not behaviorally specific, they may in fact be studying very different populations and hence the results of their research may not be comparable. A third problem is that the diagnosis of "autism" *per se* does not suggest a treatment (Schreibman & Koegel, 1981). There is no consensus among professionals as to how to treat the disease of autism. While there may be agreement about the use of a treatment technique, the technique is usually for a specific symptom (e.g., SIB) and not for the whole syndrome. A fourth problem is that the term "autism" does not suggest a differential prognosis. We do know that without treatment most autistic children do not improve and thus their prognosis is very poor. However, a few autistic children do improve without treatment (Rutter, 1968). Furthermore, as some researchers have demonstrated, some autistic children improve remarkably with treatment, while others may improve minimally or not at all (Lovaas *et al.*, 1973). The term autism, by itself, does not specify which children will improve and which will not.

Approaching the formidable task of developing a treatment methodology for autistic children, behavioral psychologists have de-emphasized the importance of defining the entire syndrome at this time and have focused instead on assessing and understanding individual behaviors. (This is not meant to imply that the ultimate identification of a specific biological etiology for autism is not important—only that it is not useful to us at this time in the development of a treatment.) Following this approach, it is assumed that the individual behaviors manifested by children called autistic are each functionally related to their environment. Further, the relation of these behaviors to the environment is no different than the relation of any behavior to the environment. This means that identified psychological principles, particularly the laws of learning, can be used to understand these behaviors and that these behaviors are susceptible to the application of these same laws. This form of treatment is usually called "behavior modification" or "behavior therapy".

When addressing a cluster of behaviors, or "symptoms," the behavioral approach typically involves identifying behavioral "excesses" and "deficits". Behavioral excesses are behaviors that may be appropriate at some level but which occur at a level that is excessive (e.g., tantrums, compulsions, running, jumping) or behaviors that are inappropriate at any level (e.g., SIB, aggression). Behavioral deficits are those behaviors that in principle are desirable but that occur at an unacceptably low rate or not at all (e.g., appropriate speech, affection, toy play). By carefully specifying the nature of the behaviors we see in children diagnosed as autistic, we can address each of these behaviors in terms of their controlling variables in the environment. Once this information is in hand, we can apply the most appropriate treatment in our arsenal of treatments for specific behaviors. There are techniques that serve to reduce excessive behaviors and other techniques that serve to establish or strengthen deficient behaviors. By matching up the behavior with its controlling variables in the environment and then choosing the most likely effective treatment, the behavioral clinician has a focus of treatment. Each of these steps will be discussed in greater detail below, but let us first see how this behavioral approach to diagnosis and treatment helps to solve some of the problems mentioned above in relation to a disease model of autism.

By describing the behavioral characteristics of a child, or a group of children, the issue of heterogeneity is resolved. Since we are specifying the behavioral characteristics of the children one does not need to worry whether the children are very alike or very different—this will be apparent from the descriptions. By resolving the problem of heterogeneity in this way, several of the problems associated with heterogeneity of the autistic population are resolved. First, since we are describing the child in terms of the presence or absence of well-defined behaviors and since these behaviors will serve as the focus of treatment, a knowledge of any etiology (or etiologies) is unnecessary. Thus, a knowledge of the etiology of "autism" is not required for our study and treatment of children since we are describing the behaviors in the context of the child's current environment. Second, communication between professionals is enhanced since a professional can describe his/her population behaviorally and any other professional can readily determine if this population is like his. This will determine the comparability of research results, will assist in choosing populations for specific research questions, and allow for the determination of which behaviors may be associated with which research or treatment effects. Third, behavioral descriptions of the children suggest a treatment. Since we already have identified treatment techniques for specific behaviors found in the syndrome of autism, the treatment for any individual child would be dictated by the behavioral excesses and deficits manifested by this particular child. For example, if a child is mute, engages in self-stimulation, engages in SIB, and avoids social contact, the clinician would utilize those treatment techniques that are known to be effective in improving these behaviors. A child presenting a different configuration of behaviors would similarly have a treatment program designed for his/her specific needs. The behavioral description of the child would therefore indicate how treatment should proceed. Fourth, describing an individual child in terms of behaviors suggests a prognosis. Since some behaviors are presently better understood than others, it is reasonable to assume that a child who manifests behaviors that are well understood and for which we have effective treatments, would have a better prognosis than a child who manifests behaviors that are not as yet well understood and for which available treatments are not as effective. (These determinants of prognosis, of course, are additional to other known indicators, such as level of retardation and age of the child.)

Historically, the application of behavioral psychology to the treatment of autistic children can be traced to Charles Ferster's (1961) paper, discussed earlier, in which he argued that autism might be conceptualized as a failure of social stimuli (e.g., parents) to acquire rewarding properties for these children. While this original paper attempted to describe the social environment in which the autistic child's behaviors might develop, its lasting contribution has been a description of how environmental contingencies might affect the behaviors characteristic of autism. After Ferster's theoretical paper, he and DeMyer reported a series of experiments in which they demonstrated that the behavior of autistic children could be reliably brought under environmental control. Thus, they taught the children very simple behaviors, such as pulling levers, by providing food reinforcers (rewards) contingent upon these responses (Ferster & DeMyer, 1961, 1962). The importance of these early experiments is that they showed that the behavior of autistic children could be understood according to the established laws of learning, derived from experimental psychology, and that these children might be helped by that body of information (Lovaas, 1979). This early work stimulated a substantial amount of research in which investigators began using the methodology of experimental psychology to extend the behavioral model to other, more socially relevant, behaviors such as tantrums, aggression, and speech.

Evaluation

All of this research on the behavioral model of treatment, past and present, has the advantage of being based on a model well established in the literature on experimental psychology. The benefits of this model are precise description of behavior and controlling variables, careful delineation of intervention procedures, and the ability to replicate treatment effects in order to draw firm conclusions about the effectiveness of the methodology. This basis in experimental psychology, with its emphasis on replication and objective assessment of effectiveness, has allowed the field to move forward since effective procedures and ineffective procedures can be accurately determined. It is this adherence to scientific methodology, empirical verification, and a constant self-critical stance that has allowed the behavioral treatment of autism to continually evolve.

Once we have addressed some of the specifics of the implementation of the behavioral model to the treatment of autistic children (see Chapter Six), we will be in a better position to evaluate many aspects of this treatment approach. Suffice it to say for now that while the behavioral model is the only treatment method empirically demonstrated to be effective with this population, certain limitations prevent us from saying we have all the answers. Yet the underlying model of this approach, with its reliance upon the principles of experimental psychology, allows us to treat these limitations as challenges to be approached and met. One of the main strengths of this model is that it allows for the identification of specific areas where our knowledge is not yet sufficient and where our efforts need to be channeled. Again, this allows for the continual evolution and refinement of treatment techniques.

Criticisms often levelled against the behavioral model of treatment are that the model is "simplistic" or "reductionist" and does not take into account complex behaviors and behavioral interactions. However, a look at the evolution of the work in this area demonstrates an expansion in scope with a focus on generalization, training of "pivotal" behaviors (behaviors that have an impact on a wide range of other behaviors) and maintenance. Again, the basis in experimental psychology allows for this positive evolution in direction and scope.

SUMMARY

Three main models of treatment have been applied to autistic children. The most well-known, the psychodynamic model of treatment, which follows from the psychogenic hypothesis of etiology, involves removing the child from the pathological environment provided by the parents and placing him/her in an environment that is more conducive (according to the theory) to normal growth. Thus, the child is provided with an environment within which he/she is allowed to express feelings and activities with no fear of the frustration and pressures that characterized the home environment. Within the permissive treatment environment the child is able to express growing autonomy and develop a trust in others. Through this trust and the growing sense of autonomy cognitive areas such as language are able to develop. The child no longer has a need to defend itself against reality and can fully participate in the world. Arguments against this treatment model include the lack of any empirically derived data implicating the parents in the cause of autism, the lack of empirical data to support the effectiveness of such treatments, and a substantial body of data indicating the ineffectiveness of this treatment approach.

A second model involves the use of psychopharmacological treatments. Since we have not yet identified a specific neurochemical aberration responsible for the etiology of autism, researchers and clinicians have not had a strong lead as to a specific pharmacological treatment regimen. Accordingly, these professionals have instead focused on assessing the effects of various drug agents on specific behaviors. Those pharmacological agents receiving the greatest attention include amphetamines, neuroleptics (e.g., chlorpromazine, trifluloperazine, haloperidol), serotonin inhibitors (L-dopa, fenfluramine), and megavitamins. While the results of this research have been provocative in some areas, there have been disappointments as well. To date, no specific treatment has been adequately substantiated as the treatment of choice for autistic children and many have potential negative side effects. While some pharmacological agents might have some helpful effect on a limited range of behaviors exhibited by autistic chidren, there is as yet no evidence that any of these agents treat "autism" nor that they are more effective than other treatments.

In contrast to both the psychodynamic and organic models of treatment is the behavioral model. Thus, while the psychodynamic and organic models view autism as a "disease" in that it is due to some central process, the behavioral model views autism as a syndrome of behaviors that are best understood in terms of their functional relation to the environment. Once these relations are identified, treatment proceeds by manipulating those aspects of the environment that affect them. This form of treatment, called "behavior modification" or "behavior therapy" utilizes identified psychological principles, particularly the laws of learning, to change behavior. Treatment proceeds by first specifying the behavioral excesses and deficits exhibited by a particular child. Then procedures from the available arsenal of behavioral techniques can be applied to increase deficient behaviors and decrease excess behaviors. Literature documenting the effectiveness of the treatment model is quite extensive.

6

SPECIFICS OF
BEHAVIORAL TREATMENT

Now that we have a basic understanding of the behavioral model for treating autistic children, it is appropriate to describe *how* this approach is implemented. One can conceptualize the design of a behavioral treatment as consisting of three main steps (Dunlap *et al.*, 1985). First, one must carefully and precisely define the behaviors targeted for change. Second, the behavior must be accurately measured. Third, based upon the first two steps, a treatment intervention is designed and implemented.

Defining the target behaviors typically involves a description of the topography of the response, its relative frequency of occurrence, its duration, and its occasion for occurrence. To illustrate, if we decide to target "self-stimulation," then we must behaviorally define that behavior for the specific child we wish to treat. This is because while self-stimulatory responses show some common features across individuals (e.g., it is repetitive, stereotypic), any one child will show a specific, perhaps idiosyncratic set of responses. Thus, we may define Jan's self-stimulatory behavior in these terms: Flapping hands at wrists, twisting hair with fingers, waving fingers in front of eyes, mouthing of objects, and head-weaving (moving head from side to side). Each of these behaviors must occur for a continuous period of 15 seconds before it is considered self-stimulatory. We might also determine that these behaviors are likely to occur when Jan is not occupied with another task, while in the presence of other children, and/or at bedtime. With this information, we have a rather clear picture of the behavior we have targeted for change.

Much of the accuracy of our definitions of target behaviors depends upon our measurement of the behavior. Accurate measurement allows for the quantification of the initial severity of the behavior, identification of environmental controlling variables (e.g., in what situations is the behavior most likely to occur), and for the continuous assessment of treatment effects. Discrete events, such as isolated vocalizations or SIB acts, can be tallied to provide a frequency count. Behaviors that occur on variable duration or an intermittent basis, such as self-stimulation and play, can be quantified on an interval or time-sampling basis. Other measurement procedures, such as trial-by-trial recordings and measurement of permanent products (e.g., number of math problems completed), can also be used to quantify changes in behavior (Dunlap *et al.*, 1985). The main objective is to employ assessment procedures that will allow for the objective, observable, accurate record of the behavior(s) of interest.

As mentioned above, the behavioral approach dictates that each child's "autism" be expressed as a group of specific behaviors (excesses and deficits). Indeed, the careful definition of target behaviors and the use of precise assessments allows the clinician to decide on the particular treatment procedures that would be most appropriate for these target behaviors. The accumulation of these procedures comprises the child's treatment program. However, the clinician's task does not stop here. It is essential that continuous assessments be used to provide an ongoing evaluation of the effectiveness of the procedures. If a treatment is ineffective, then a new treatment is designed and implemented based on the information culled from the initial assessments and the additional information that might be gleaned from the failure of the previous treatment. This process allows for the treatment to evolve and be most appropriate for the child. Let us look more closely at how the identification of treatment procedures occurs.

Once the identified target behaviors are defined and appropriate assessments are established, the clinician now attempts to relate the occurrence of the behaviors to those environmental conditions which support them. The next step is to manipulate the environment to alter the behavior in the desired direction (Schreibman & Koegel, 1981). Fortunately, we already have an extensive existing literature for many of the behaviors seen in autism and the therapist can use this knowledge to identify potentially successful treatments. For example, we now have a rather good understanding of the variables controlling SIB (e.g., Carr, 1977). The clinician can use this existing knowledge and relate it to the specific case at hand. Thus treatment procedures that have already been identified and developed can be utilized. Unfortunately, it is sometimes the case that the literature has not isolated the variables controlling a behavior or perhaps multiple variables are functional. In these instances, the clinician will attempt to identify the controlling variables. The usual approach to this problem is to observe events immediately preceding the behavior (antecedents) and events immediately following the behavior (consequences) and seek a pattern. For example, the therapist might notice that when a teacher asks the child a question, the child engages in SIB, which results in the teacher ceasing the demands. If this is a pattern, the therapist might speculate that the teacher's demands are a cue for the child to hit herself and this SIB is reinforced by a cessation of the demands. This would be an example of negative reinforcement of SIB. That is, the SIB allows the child to escape an aversive situation. An understanding of this relationship then suggests certain treatments. In this example, the therapist might so arrange the environment that the child's SIB does not lead to a cessation of the demands, thus removing the reinforcer that has been maintaining the behavior.

The identification of controlling variables may allow for the development of more efficient treatments. As environmental influences on an increasing number and variety of individual behaviors are understood, those behaviors that have similar controlling variables may be grouped together and manipulation of these variables may affect multiple behaviors. These functional relationships are very important for the behavioral clinician as they allow treatments to result in the modification of large aspects of the child's functioning in a reduced amount of time (Dunlap *et al.*, 1985).

An extensive discussion of the principles of behavior modification or of the tremendous body of literature on treatment of autistic behaviors will not be attempted here. What follows is a rather brief summary of some of the major developments to date in the behavioral treatment of autistic children. This section is divided into discussions of the specific behavioral excesses and deficits characteristic of these children.

BEHAVIORAL EXCESSES

Self-Injurious Behavior

Few behaviors are as demanding of immediate remediation as SIB. As discussed earlier, this behavior can be life threatening at worse and disruptive at best. Historically, this has been one of the most difficult behaviors to treat and earlier conceptualizations of SIB as due to some intrapsychic conflicts (e.g., the child is punishing himself) have not led to effective treatments. Indeed, reassurance, affection, attention, and acceptance have been shown to actually lead to an increase in the behavior (e.g., Lovaas, Freitag, Gold, & Kassorla, 1965). Further, treatments involving drugs have been effective in sedating the child but have not been shown effective in remediating the behavior when the child is not on medication. It is perhaps because of both the serious nature of this behavior and the failure of other treatments to be effective that the utilization of behavioral techniques was welcomed.

Lovaas *et al.* (1965) focused on SIB as an operant behavior and demonstrated that it was under stimulus control. That is, these investigators demonstrated that a child's SIB was lawfully related to environmental events. It was evoked by particular circumstances (e.g., withdrawal of social attention) and maintained by another set of circumstances (e.g., social attention). In a subsequent study Lovaas and Simmons (1969) demonstrated that SIB in three retarded children satisfied three of the requirements necessary for a behavior to be considered operant: it was reduced when followed by contingent electric shock (punishment), it was reduced when maintaining social reinforcers were no longer provided contingent upon the behavior (extinction), and it could be strengthened when social attention was presented contingent upon SIB episodes (positive reinforcement). These investigators showed how focusing on the environmental determinants of this specific behavior and manipulating these determinants led to changes in the behavior. This investigation stimulated a substantial amount of research into understanding the nature of SIB and, importantly, methods of affecting a rapid and effective remediation.

Perhaps one of the most important papers in the literature on SIB was presented by Carr (1977), who reviewed the rather extensive literature on the subject and presented three motivations that seem to be related to SIB in developmentally disabled (including autistic) individuals. In some cases, the behavior seems to be motivated by the positive consequences it provides.

Thus the child may self-injure in order to obtain social attention, a desired activity, or some other positive event. This is the case when the child indicates some desire (e.g., a cookie) and the parent says "no". The child may throw a tantrum and in the course of the tantrum engage in SIB. The parent, eager to stop the SIB, says "OK. Don't hit yourself. Here is the cookie." The child has learned that self-injury is an effective means of obtaining reinforcement. SIB maintained by such consequences is said to be motivated by *positive reinforcement*. However, in other instances the behavior is motivated by the desire to avoid or escape an aversive situation. Carr, Newsom and Binkoff (1976) provide an excellent example of this situation. They reported the case of a boy, Tim, whose SIB was particularly severe when his teacher worked with him. The teacher, not wanting to provide attention for the SIB when it occurred, turned away and ceased interacting with him. However, despite the teacher's good intentions, this procedure actually led to an increase in the SIB. Carr and co-authors' (1976) systematic analysis found that Tim's self-injury was maintained by the escape and avoidance of the teacher's instructional demands, events that were aversive to him. When behavior is motivated by the desire to avoid or escape an event, it is said to be maintained by *negative reinforcement*. A third motivation reported by Carr (1977) is *self-stimulation*. In these instances, it is apparent that the SIB does not lead to any extrinsic change in the environment and the maintaining reinforcement is internal. The individual enjoys engaging in the behavior for its own sake (see discussion of self-stimulation below). Carr's (1977) careful analysis makes clear several important points. First, it is useful to view SIB as a behavior that can have multiple motivations; an effective treatment can only be derived if the therapist is careful to assess the behavior and identify the motivation in a particular case. Second, one must realize that the same behavior may have multiple motivations in any one individual. Thus, Denise's SIB might be maintained by positive reinforcement in some conditions and by negative reinforcement in others. Or, perhaps, multiple SIBs in one child have multiple motivations. Third, in analyzing SIB in this way, it is not necessary to know the etiology of the behavior. We may not know how the relationship between the self-injury and particular events originated; what is important is understanding this relationship now.

Let us now look at some specific behavioral treatments that have been developed for the treatment of SIB. Treatments that focus on modifying the environmental consequences of SIB can be divided into three main approaches—extinction, punishment, and differential reinforcement of other behaviors (DRO). In addition, altering the stimulus control, or antecedents of the behavior, have recently come under investigation with promising results.

Extinction refers to a behavioral procedure in which the environmental event that maintains the behavior is removed. In one of the earliest demonstrations of the effectiveness of extinction for children for whom social attention maintained the behavior, Lovaas and Simmons (1969) placed a self-injurious child in a room by himself where the SIB was allowed to occur and no attention was provided. These researchers reported that over several such

90-minute sessions the child ceased the SIB. This effect has been replicated numerous times and extinction is a popular and effective technique for treating SIB in instances where it is maintained by positive reinforcement. Similarly, the same technique is effective when the behavior is maintained by negative reinforcement. In the case of Tim (Carr et al., 1977) cited above, it is clear that the appropriate extinction procedure would be for the teacher to continue interacting with Tim so that the maintaining consequence (escape from demands) was no longer forthcoming in response to the self-injury. Under these conditions, one would expect that Tim would cease to self-injure since the behavior would no longer "pay off".

There is one important caveat that must be remembered when considering the use of extinction for SIB. During the extinction procedure the child will engage in SIB for a period of time, and during the initial stage of the procedure there will be a temporary increase in intensity (the extinction "burst"). Therefore, if a child's SIB is particularly intense, extinction would probably not be the treatment of choice since the child might inflict severe damage before the treatment is completed.

Punishment is a treatment alternative to be considered in cases where the self-injury is intense and must be stopped quickly. Punishment, the contingent application of an aversive stimulus, has the advantage of providing relatively rapid results (if an effective punisher is used). Lovaas and Simmons (1969) demonstrated the effectiveness of a localized contingent electric shock, delivered to the arm or leg by a hand-held inductorium, in stopping SIB in three children who had long histories of such behavior. In the majority of the cases, only a few such shocks were necessary to reduce the behavior to zero levels. In another example, Tanner and Zeiler (1975) used aromatic ammonia in a punishment paradigm to successfully eliminate SIB in an autistic woman.

Since the use of electric shock or other applications of physical aversives (e.g., a spank) are understandably unpopular with many practitioners and do indeed hold the potential for abuse, other punishment procedures have been identified. One such procedure that has proven effective in treating SIB is "overcorrection". Briefly, this procedure involves having the child engage in effortful behavior (an aversive stimulus) contingent upon an SIB response. For example, Azrin, Gottlieb, Hughart, Wesolowski and Rahn (1975) report the successful use of an overcorrection procedure for reducing SIB. Treatment included a combination of procedures including: (a) positive reinforcement of incompatible behaviors (e.g., playing ball); (b) "required relaxation" where, contingent upon SIB, the client was required to "rest" in bed for two hours while maintaining his arms in an extended downward position next to the legs (a position incompatible for striking the head); (c) requiring the client to spend 20 minutes practicing holding his hands away from his body in several positions whenever an SIB occurred; and (d) requiring the client to do other things with his hands such as clasp them behind his back or hold onto armrests.

While this procedure has the advantage of avoiding the use of more directly and intensely painful stimuli, it also has the disadvantage of being cost-intensive in terms of staff time. In certain treatment environments it may not be feasible for staff to supervise the application of overcorrection. Here again, a therapist must weigh the pros and cons of using a particular procedure.

In using any punishment procedure one must be aware of certain general concerns. First, punishment serves only to suppress, not eliminate, a behavior since removal of the punisher is typically followed by return of the behavior (see Church, 1963). It is thus important to teach the child another behavior to replace the SIB in order to maintain the suppression initially accomplished via punishment. For example, if a child has been engaging in SIB for the positive attention it provides, one might consider using punishment to temporarily suppress the behavior and during this period teach the child another, more appropriate, behavior for attention (e.g., talking, play). Second, in recent years the emphasis has been on the promotion of non-aversive interventions in treatment of autistic and other handicapped people. It is important to remember when considering punishment procedures that there is nothing inherent in the definition of punishment that denotes pain. Punishers may range from mild (e.g., a frown) to severe (e.g., a spank) and the least intrusive effective treatment should be employed. Thus one needs to respect the dignity of the client and choose procedures that will facilitate the individual's integration into society, as opposed to segregating him/her either by instituting an aversive procedure that serves to stigmatize or to reduce opportunities to participate in society. Third, while punishment has been shown to be effective, the issues relating to the use of such procedures in community settings has not been adequately addressed. The coming years will certainly illuminate this important area.

Another treatment for SIB that is used either alone or in conjunction with a punishment procedure is differential reinforcement of other behavior (DRO). DRO involves systematically providing reinforcement when the child is *not* engaged in SIB. Typically, reinforcement is presented contingent upon longer and longer periods of refraining from SIB (e.g., Favell, McGimsey, & Jones, 1978). This procedure strengthens other behaviors and, by exclusion, weakens SIB. The therapist might need to punish the SIB in order to obtain periods of non-SIB during which reinforcement is presented, but the subsequent elimination of the punishment should not lead to resumption of the self-injury since the child will hopefully have learned another behavior in its place.

Touchette, MacDonald, and Langer (1985) investigated another approach to treating self-injury that involves manipulating the *antecedent* conditions for the behavior rather than altering the consequences. These authors point out that SIB occurs under some stimulus conditions but not under others. One might observe, for example, that a child hits herself whenever demands are placed upon her. In contrast, she almost never hits herself when she is watching television, eating meals, or taking a bath. Touchette and his colleagues propose that certain stimulus conditions become discriminative for SIB and others do not. Given this information, the therapist can ensure that the child's day is programmed such that only those conditions that do not lead to SIB occur while conditions that might precipitate an SIB episode are eliminated. In our example, the child would spend most of the day watching television, taking baths, and eating meals, with no demands placed upon her. Such a program should lead to long periods of no SIB. Situations that once led to self-injury (e.g., demands) are then gradually reintroduced in such a way that they no longer evoke the behavior. Touchette *et al*. (1985) propose the use of a "scatter plot" assessment whereby the therapist can determine which times of the day and during which activities the SIB is likely, or unlikely, to occur and use this information to reprogram the day as described above for treatment. The obvious advantage of this treatment approach is that it may be possible to immediately reduce the frequency of the behavior without the use of a contingent aversive stimulus. The only potential limitation to this treatment is that it may not always be feasible to reprogram all the situations in a child's day to the extent required. However, it is likely that the therapeutic use of manipulating the stimulus control of SIB will be a technique receiving much research and clinical attention in the future.

Self-Stimulatory Behavior

Self-stimulation (e.g., body-rocking, hand- or arm-flapping, repetitive vocalizing) is observed in many children diagnosed as autistic. Besides appearing bizarre and thus stigmatizing the child, such behavior severely impairs the child's ability to respond to his/her learning environment (e.g., Koegel & Covert, 1972; Lovaas, Litrownik, & Mann, 1971). Lovaas *et al*. (1971) demonstrated that responding to previously functional auditory cues was disrupted when the cues were presented while the child was engaged in self-stimulation. Similarly, Koegel and Covert (1972) found that autistic children with high rates of self-stimulation did not learn a simple discrimination task (i.e., press a lever when a compound auditory-visual stimulus was presented). Suppression of the self-stimulation, however, resulted in the children's acquisition of the discrimination. These results clearly show that self-stimulation interfered with the children's learning. This apparent inverse relationship between self-stimulatory behavior and the acquisition and performance of new appropriate behaviors has been repeatedly demonstrated (e.g., Epstein, Doke, Sajwaj, Sorrell, & Rimmer, 1974; Foxx & Azrin, 1973; Koegel *et al*., 1974; Lovaas *et al*., 1987; Risley, 1968). It is therefore apparent that self-stimulation is a behavior that cannot be allowed to continue if we hope to teach the child more appropriate behaviors.

The behavioral interventions that have been applied to self-stimulation have been quite varied. DRO has been used with moderate success. Mulhern and Baumeister (1969) attempted to reduce rocking behavior in two retarded children by reinforcing them for sitting still (a behavior incompatible with body-rocking). This technique resulted in a reduction of the behavior by about one-third. Other investigators have also reported substantial reductions in self-stimulation using DRO (e.g., Dietz & Repp, 1973; Herendeen, Jeffrey, & Graham, 1974). While apparently helpful in reducing the level of the behavior, DRO has not, however, proven effective in completely suppressing self-stimulation. Indeed, not all investigators found it effective in reducing the behavior significantly (e.g., Foxx & Azrin, 1973).

Probably the most commonly used behavioral technique for reducing self-stimulation has been forms of punishment. This has typically been the case because, until recently, functional analyses of the behavior were unable to identify a maintaining environmental stimulus that could be removed, thereby allowing for the use of extinction. In the past, contingent punishers applied to self-stimulation have included localized electric shock (Lovaas, Schaeffer, & Simmons, 1965; Risley, 1968), contingent slaps on the hand or thigh (Bucher & Lovaas, 1968; Foxx & Azrin, 1973; Koegel & Covert, 1972) and contingent restraint (Koegel et al., 1974). These studies have been consistent in demonstrating that contingent presentation of a physical aversive stimulus is highly effective for suppressing self-stimulation.

Another punishment procedure that has been successfully applied to self-stimulation is overcorrection (Azrin, Kaplan & Foxx, 1973). This procedure involves stopping the child's ongoing self-stimulation and then requiring the child to engage in incompatible behavior for a period of time. For example, if a child engages in repetitive arm-flapping, a "positive practice" overcorrection procedure might involve having the child perform other movements with his arms, such as moving them up, then out, then forward, then up, etc. for an extended period of time (e.g., 10 minutes). This is called "positive practice" in that it allows the child to practice appropriate (not flapping) arm movements. It is, of course, also aversive in that the child is forced (first by physical prompts and later by verbal instructions) to repeat these movements over and over (Schreibman et al., 1983). This aversive component makes this technically a punishment procedure. Foxx and Azrin (1973) compared positive practice overcorrection with other techniques used to suppress self-stimulation (including punishment with a slap and DRO) and concluded that the only procedure that eliminated self-stimulatory behavior was the positive practice overcorrection. Other investigators have replicated and extended these results (Azrin et al., 1973; Epstein et al., 1974; Harris & Wolchik, 1979; Herendeen et al., 1974). There are some problems associated with overcorrection for self-stimulation. One is that not everyone has reported success with the procedure, and the precise functional elements of the package have not been clearly identified. The other problem, alluded to earlier in the discussion of SIB, is that while overcorrection offers an alternative to intense physical punishment, its practicality in applied settings may be limited due to its demand on staff time and energy.

Unfortunately, enthusiasm about the success of the above procedures must be tempered by the realization that self-stimulatory behaviors, as a rule, are often only temporarily suppressed and generalization of the suppression is limited at best. Thus, the goal of a generalized, durable elimination of the behavior has yet to be achieved (Rincover & Koegel, 1977b). This has probably been due in no small part to the failure of behavioral investigators to clearly identify and delineate those environmental events that maintain the behavior. It has recently been established that one of the reasons for this difficulty in identifying maintaining variables in the past is that the variables are probably internal. We now know that self-stimulation may be conceptualized as operant behavior maintained by its sensory consequences (Lovaas et al., 1987; Rincover, Newsom, Lovaas, & Koegel, 1977). For example, self-stimulatory body-rocking might be reinforced by the proprioceptive feedback the behavior provides. This view of self-stimulation as behavior maintained by sensory (auditory, visual, or proprioceptive) events has led to the development of a relatively new treatment for the behavior and one that allows for the use of extinction. The procedure is termed "sensory extinction" and is based on the notion that if the sensory reinforcing consequences of self-stimulation are removed, the behavior should extinguish. Rincover (1978) empirically validated this notion with a study wherein he removed, or allowed access to, the sensory consequences of self-stimulation. The rate of the behavior decreased or increased accordingly. He also found, not surprisingly, that self-stimulatory behaviors for individual children were idiosyncratic and thus the specific maintaining sensory reinforcement had to be identified for each child's behaviors. This necessitated different sensory extinction procedures for different behaviors. To illustrate, for one child a blindfold was used to eliminate the visual feedback produced by the self-stimulatory behavior of spinning objects, while for another child, a carpeted table was used to mask the auditory feedback produced by plate-spinning.

While the results of this research and the identification of sensory consequences as maintaining events for self-stimulation are intriguing, a nonaversive, readily available and easy-to-implement set of treatment procedures have yet to be developed. In most clinical situations it is very difficult to set up circumstances that would allow for the identification of maintaining sensory consequences for each self-stimulatory behavior of each autistic child. Further, the prevention of this sensory feedback might be difficult or impossible to obtain. A promising first step is provided by Rincover, Cook, Peoples and Packard (1979), who have shown how one might identify a child's preferred sensory consequence and use this consequence to maintain appropriate, competing behaviors such as toy play. Thus, if a child engages in self-stimulatory behaviors for visual feedback (e.g., waving fingers in front of the eyes), then a similar form of visual feedback might be provided by appropriately playing with a visual toy.

As is probably apparent, self-stimulation is a very complicated and treatment-resistent behavior. Continued behavioral investigations into environmental determinants and effective treatments will undoubtedly become available as researchers continue their efforts in this area. As of now, the most common treatment utilized is some form of punishment. However, the identification of the importance of sensory consequences promises to provide alternatives that will allow us to achieve durable and generalized control of these behaviors using nonaversive interventions.

In contrast to the foregoing discussion about procedures to reduce self-stimulation, other investigators have looked instead at the possibility that any behavior that is so important to autistic children might be used as a positive reinforcer to strengthen appropriate behaviors. Thus, Hung (1978), Charlop and Greenberg (1985a, b), and Charlop and Kurtz (1987) have reported studies wherein autistic children could gain access to a specified period of self-stimulation contingent upon the performance of an appropriate behavior. For example, Charlop and Greenberg (1985a, b) compared the effectiveness of food reinforcers versus the opportunity to engage in self-stimulation as consequences for correct responses on a discrimination task. They found that self-stimulation proved to be a more powerful reinforcer as indicated by the children's superior performance during self-stimulation-as-reinforcement condition. Importantly, they did not observe concomitant increases in the children's self-stimulation in other situations. Future research into the possibility of incorporating this behavior into treatment may provide some very helpful ways of using behavior the children already seem to have for improving their future behavior.

Disruptive Behaviors

Included in this category are aggression, tantrums, compulsive rituals, and destruction of property. These behaviors in autistic children seem to operate in the same manner that they do in other children and so there are no treatments specifically designed for autistic children. Four frequently used treatment alternatives for eliminating various forms of disruptive behavior are extinction, punishment, time-out, and overcorrection.

During extinction, the therapist withholds a reinforcer (e.g., social attention) contingent upon a behavior. Since many children throw tantrums in an attempt to gain attention or to get adults to "give in" to demands, withdrawal of attention and noncompliance with the child's demands are often very effective in eliminating the disruptive behavior. In such cases, if a child frequently cries and screams because he wants his mother to get off the telephone and give him a cookie, the mother might successfully treat the behavior by ignoring the child's tantrum and remaining on the telephone until he has ceased. While extinction is often successful when used in this manner, a therapist must be aware of several factors in choosing extinction as a treatment. First, there is usually a gradual reduction rather than a sharp decrease in the behavior. This means that extinction would not be the treatment of choice if the behavior was so severe as to require immediate cessation (see "punishment" below). One cannot necessarily afford to allow a child to engage in severely aggressive behavior while an extinction procedure is being implemented since he/she might inflict damage before the behavior extinguished. Second, there is usually a temporary increase in the strength of the behavior when extinction is first initiated (the extinction "burst"). The therapist must anticipate the increase and determine whether this would pose a problem. Third, extinction will only be effective if the therapist has correctly identified the controlling consequence for the disruptive behavior. If a child is throwing a tantrum in order to avoid complying with some request ("Give me the ball") and the therapist ignores the tantrum and leaves the child alone, chances are that the tantrum behavior will increase since the behavior was successful in securing for the child what he wanted (to keep the ball). Since the tantrum behavior was not maintained by social attention, removing the attention would not lead to a decrease in the disruptive behavior.

As discussed earlier, punishment is a general term describing a procedure in which an operant behavior is weakened by the contingent application of an aversive stimulus. Punishment has been demonstrated as an effective procedure for decreasing a wide range of disruptive behaviors in autistic children, just as it has with other populations including normal children. Punishment alone merely suppresses the behavior, which can be expected to recur once the punisher is removed. This means that the procedure cannot be used in isolation but must instead be used in conjunction with educative procedures to teach the individual another, alternative behavior. To give an example, if a child is hitting other children in an attempt to force them to leave him alone, the therapist might punish the aggressive behavior (e.g., a loud "No!"), while simultaneously prompting the child to say "Go away". If "Go away" is effective in deterring the other children, the aggressive child would be less likely to return to the physical aggression. The effective, sensitive and prudent use of punishment with autistic and other severely handicapped individuals requires training in the principles involved. In many settings such trained personnel are not always available. Although the use of severe punishers, such as contingent electric shock (as discussed above with SIB) has been shown to be effective and even to produce positive "side effects" (Lichstein & Schreibman, 1976), such punishers are inappropriate for use in some settings and hold the potential for abuse (Schopler, 1986). The search for alternative decelerative procedures has led to the identification of other effective treatments.

"Time-out" is an effective, but relatively mild, punishment technique for dealing with disruptive behavior. White, Nielsen, and Johnson (1972) have defined time-out as a situation in which the occurrence of a response is followed by a period of time during which a variety of reinforcers are no longer available. Thus, contingent upon a behavior, the child does not have the opportunity to obtain reinforcement. A common example with a normal child would be that he is "sent to his room" contingent upon a disruptive behavior. This prevents his access to a variety of potential reinforcers such as parental attention, television, perhaps dinner, etc. Wolf, Risley, and Mees (1964) presented one of the first empirical demonstrations of the effectiveness of time-out with an autistic child. They used the procedure with a child who manifested tantrum and self-injurious behaviors. These behaviors were effectively reduced by placing the child alone in a room each time the behavior occurred.

There is no consensus as to the optimal duration of time-out, but some parameters have been identified. Time-out intervals ranging from two minutes (Bostow & Bailey, 1969) to three hours (Burchard & Tyler, 1965) have been used with success. White et al. (1972) noted that the majority of investigators have reported success with durations in the range of 5 to 20 minutes and indeed most therapists use intervals within this range.

While the duration of time-out is undoubtedly an important determinant of its effectiveness, perhaps a more important factor relates to the differences between the time-out and the "time-in" setting (the setting from which the child is removed). As Solnick, Rincover and Peterson (1977) demonstrated, time-out is only likely to be effective if the time-in setting is more reinforcing than the time-out setting. They found that for one child, time-out for tantrums actually led to an increase in the tantrum behavior since the child could engage in self-stimulatory behavior while in the time-out setting. Since self-stimulation was more reinforcing to the child than the ongoing time-in activity, these results are not surprising. It is apparent, then, that a therapist wishing to maximize the effectiveness of time-out should ensure that the time-in setting is highly reinforcing while the time-out setting is minimally so. In addition, the therapist can negatively reinforce "quiet" behavior by terminating time-out contingent upon the nonoccurrence of the punished behavior.

"Overcorrection," as we have seen in the context of SIB, is another form of punishment that can be quite effective in reducing disruptive behaviors and avoids the necessity of presenting strong contingent aversives. In this situation, overcorrection has two objectives: (1) to overcorrect the environmental effects of a disruptive behavior; and (2) to require the disruptor to thoroughly practice overly correct forms of appropriate behavior. The first objective is achieved through the use of restitutional overcorrection. Here the individual is required to repair the disrupted scene to a state even better than it had been before. So if a child throws paint materials on the floor during a tantrum, he might be required to wipe up the paint and wash and wax the floor. The second objective is achieved through positive practice overcorrection and, as we have seen, requires the individual to practice appropriate behavior. In our example, the little boy might be required to properly put away the paint materials, take them out, put them away, take them out, etc. If the disruptive behavior does not result in environmental disruption, only positive practice is used. As is apparent, overcorrection is a punishment procedure, since it involves following the behavior with an aversive consequences. However, as Foxx and Azrin (1972) note, it may minimize some of the negative properties of other punishment procedures. It does not involve the use of strong physical aversive stimuli and it incorporates training in alternative, appropriate behaviors. While some of the specific parameters and mechanisms for the effectiveness of overcorrection are as yet controversial (e.g., Axelrod, Branter, & Meddock, 1978), few deny that it can be a very effective procedure for reducing disruptive behavior in autistic and other handicapped populations.

BEHAVIORAL DEFICITS

Speech and Language

Needless to say, deficits in language behavior comprise perhaps the most serious problem in treating autistic children. No one would argue that the failure to use language to communicate constitutes a profound deficit and one which has serious and pervasive ramifications for other areas of development. This would, of course, include difficulties in social behavior since language is so important in our dealings with our social environment. Thus, while some see autism as primarily a deficit in social behavior, others view it primarily as a communication disorder. To further emphasize the importance of language, follow-up studies have indicated that individuals who develop some language and communicative facility early in life (i.e., by the age of five years) have a much better clinical prognosis then those who do not (Eisenberg & Kanner, 1956; Rutter, 1968). Given this information, it is certainly understandable that a substantial proportion of the experimental work in the treatment of autism has focused on language. While this literature is certainly too extensive to be covered in this book, a general overview of the behavioral analysis and treatment will be provided.

Approximately 50% of autistic children are functionally mute, lacking expressive as well as receptive language (Rimland, 1964; Rutter, 1966a). Prior to the 1960s no one had achieved systematic success in teaching speech to these children, until a paper by Lovaas, Berberich, Perloff, and Schaeffer (1966) provided the first empirically derived, replicable, effective program for teaching vocal speech. These investigators, after first trying to produce speech in the children by shaping individual vocal responses through the method of successive approximations, developed a more effective and efficient method based on imitation training. Through a series of systematic steps the child's vocal responses were reinforced when they matched those of the therapist and were not reinforced if they did not. Once established, this imitation served as the cornerstone in building more complex language functions, such as semantics and syntax (Lovaas, 1966, 1977; Risley & Wolf, 1967). For example, once a child has learned to say "Cookie" imitatively, procedures can begin to teach the child the "meaning" of the word "Cookie". This is done for both receptive and expressive labeling. To teach receptive labeling, for instance, the therapist might have a cookie and one or two other objects placed in front of the child. The therapist says "Cookie" and prompts the child's response by guiding the child's hand to the cookie. This is repeated over many trials with the therapist gradually fading out the prompt (e.g., providing less physical guidance) until the child reliably points to the correct referent when the therapist says "cookie". To teach the expressive label, the therapist might hold up a cookie and say "What is this?" and prompt the child by saying "cookie" which the child would imitate. Gradually, over a series of trials, the therapist would repeat the process while gradually withdrawing the prompt (perhaps whispering "cookie" or saying "co—," etc.) until the child responded with "cookie" when shown the cookie and asked "What is this?"

While teaching the children basic speech and language forms is a necessary step in their training, such skills do not constitute a complete intervention program. Questions remain as to just how far one can go with operant procedures in teaching more complex language skills. There is some evidence to suggest that these children have particular difficulty in learning language skills involving abstract concepts (e.g., Hermelin & O'Connor, 1970; Rutter, 1968). Can operant techniques be successful in teaching such concepts? There are many demonstrations in the literature that indeed such techniques can be used effectively to teach a variety of abstract concepts. For example, Lovaas (1977) demonstrated how these behavioral techniques could be used to teach abstractions involving prepositions, pronouns, concepts of time, and other concepts such as yes/no and same/different. Research in this area continues to demonstrate how behavioral training can establish complex linguistic functions and forms in these children. While an exhaustive discussion and description of behavioral techniques of language intervention with autistic children cannot be presented here, the interested reader is referred to Lovaas (1977) and Fay and Schuler (1980) for more detailed information.

Despite the successful training of speech to previously mute, or nonverbal, autistic children, it has been noted that these children are often not spontaneous in their use of their speech. They may be quite skillful at answering questions such as "What's your name?", "What did you do at school today?", and "Where's the ball?" but will seldom speak unless asked. In other words, their speech remains under the control of the verbal behavior of others, rather than under the control of the nonverbal stimulus environment (Charlop, Schreibman, & Thibodeau, 1985). In an attempt to teach autistic children to spontaneously request items from their environment, Charlop *et al.* (1985) utilized a procedure in which stimulus control of an appropriate response (i.e., "I want cookie") was gradually transferred from the therapist's model "I want cookie" to the presentation of the object (i.e., a cookie). Thus, the children learned to make requests without verbal cues. Further research, in which stimulus control of verbal responses is transferred from the object (i.e., cookie) to the general situation or environment (i.e., kitchen), has suggested that these children can be taught to speak spontaneously in appropriate situations (Schreibman, Charlop, & Tryon, 1981).

Unfortunately, even with extensive use of available treatment methods, some mute children remain without functional speech. The failure of this subgroup of mute autistic children to acquire spoken language has prompted researchers to explore the use of sign language as an alternative communication system (Creedon, 1973; Konstantareas, Oxman, & Webster, 1977). As noted by Carr (1979), although considerable empirical work addressing sign language has been done, little of it involved systematic experimentation designed to identify the variables that are functional in bringing about sign acquisition. (As pointed out earlier, the behavioral approach to treatment focuses heavily on the identification of such functional variables.) Carr and his colleagues thus embarked on a series of investigations to study the factors that facilitate the acquisition of both expressive and receptive sign labels (Carr & Kologinsky, 1983), simple sentences (Carr, Kologinsky, & Leff-Simon, 1987), and abstractions (Carr, 1982a, 1982b). It has also been found that some children are able to profit from sign training while some can profit from speech training.

Teaching speech to echolalic autistic children differs from procedures described to teach mute children. Echolalic children already know how to imitate. In fact, they imitate too much and this behavior can not only be socially stigmatizing but also interfere with the acquisition of normal functional language. With these children, speech training consists of teaching the child to use speech in appropriate contexts. Since they already know how to speak, speech training with echolalic children consists of teaching the child to discriminate between appropriate and inappropriate (echolalic) utterances (Fay & Schuler, 1980).

Behavioral technology has provided a variety of successful procedures for reducing or eliminating echolalic speech. Prompting procedures have been employed to teach autistic children appropriate speech (e.g., Lovaas *et al.*, 1973; Risley & Wolf, 1967). Using such a procedure the therapist might present a picture of a car, say "That's a car," and wait for the child to echo "That's a car". Then, control of the response would be gradually shifted from the therapist's verbal prompt to the picture of a car. For example, during the fading of the prompt the therapist might hold up the picture of the car and say "That's a c—" and allow the child to finish the response. Finally, upon presentation of the picture, the therapist would be silent and the child would say "That's a car". In an interesting variation of such a procedure, Freeman, Ritvo and Miller (1975) designed a procedure in which echolalia was prevented through the reinforcement of appropriate responses. The answers to questions were provided *before* the question. The child's echolalic response was interrupted with reinforcement after the echo of the answer. To illustrate, the therapist might say "Running. What is the girl doing?". If the child starts to echo, he/she is reinforced after saying "running" but before he can echo the question. Other investigators (e.g., Fay & Schuler, 1980; Lovaas, 1977) have successfully employed procedures incorporating suppression of echolalia by punishment procedures or instructions such as "Don't echo" in conjunction with reinforcement of appropriate speech.

While these procedures have proved helpful for decreasing instances of echolalic speech and thereby increasing appropriate speech, the fact remains that until the 1970s we still did not yet understand the environmental variables responsible for the speech anomaly called immediate echolalia. The generalized, durable suppression of the behavior required an analysis of these variables. Carr *et al.* (1975) conducted an analysis of echolalia to determine what factors might be most prominent in controlling this behavior. These investigators demonstrated that echolalic children would echo novel verbal stimuli (nonsense phrases the children had never heard before) but would respond appropriately to discriminative stimuli (verbal stimuli for which they had a response). Therefore, it seemed that one variable affecting the occurrence of immediate echolalia (but not the only one, as noted by Prizant & Duchan, 1981) was the "comprehensibility" of the verbal stimulus. To substantiate this conclusion, Carr *et al.* (1975) demonstrated that when the children were taught appropriate responses to the novel verbal stimuli, their echolalia ceased. However, the children still echoed the novel verbal stimuli to which specific responses had not been trained. Since it would be tedious (and virtually impossible) to achieve a generalized reduction of echolalia by teaching appropriate responses to every novel stimulus the child might encounter, Schreibman and Carr (1978) taught echolalic children a generalized verbal response that would be functional in any situation where they were asked a question for which they had no response. These researchers taught the children to say "I don't know" to previously echoed questions. This facilitated an appropriate verbal response common in normal children. By saying "I don't know" the children sounded more "normal" and also indicated to the speaker that they could not respond, thus signaling the need for the speaker to teach the response. This line of research provides an illustration of the contributions of rigorous behavior analysis to the development of successful intervention strategies.

Other lines of research have chosen to view echolalia not necessarily as a completely inappropriate behavior to be suppressed, but rather one that might be useful in building other forms of more appropriate communication. In an attempt to use echolalic speech to promote, rather than hinder, language acquisition, Charlop (1983) designed a procedure in which echolalia was used to teach receptive labels (e.g., "Ball") to autistic children. No attempt was made to discourage echolalia. To the contrary, the children were allowed to echo the object's label as a means of providing their own verbal discriminative stimulus (cue) before manually responding. This procedure facilitated generalization of the appropriate response as well as acquisition. This study demonstrated that, at least under these circumstances, echolalia might be a useful tool in subsequent language training.

It should be pointed out here that the research reported above has dealt with immediate echolalia. It is likely that the variables controlling the occurrence of delayed echolalia and other similar speech anomalies are different. We anticipate that future systematic analyses of these other speech deficits will follow a similar progression from identification of controlling variables to development of appropriate treatments.

In a particularly imaginative analysis and conceptualization, Carr and his colleagues have continued to look at echolalia, and other aberrant behavior, in terms of the communicative function that such behavior may serve for severely language-impaired individuals. Some children apparently use echolalia to communicate the notion that they do not understand what is being said to them (see Carr *et al.*, 1975). A recent focus on the area of communication or, more technically, pragmatics, has become a major focus of language research in recent years (Carr & Kologinsky, 1983; Halle, Marshall, & Spradlin, 1979; Hart, 1980; Koegel, O'Dell, & Koegel, 1987; McGee, Krantz, & McClannahan, 1985). Apparently there are a number of ways in which an individual can communicate needs and desires and only some of these involve language as we normally consider it. Carr and Durand (1985a) suggest that there is a relationship between behavior problems and communicative competence. These investigators posit that it may be useful to view behavior problems as a primitive form of communication and, following a functional analysis of the problem, proceed to teach verbal skills designed to replace the behavior problem. As mentioned above, Schreibman and Carr (1978) taught children a verbal skill (saying "I don't know") to replace the problem behavior of echolalia. Similarly, in a particularly impressive demonstration, Carr and Durand (1985b) demonstrated that an autistic child's aggressive behavior could be conceptualized as the child's means of communicating that he did not want to engage in an activity, that the activity was too difficult, and so forth. By teaching the child a verbal response such as "Help me," the child's communicative intent was achieved in a more appropriate manner and the reinforcement he received for this behavior maintained it.

The research described in this section represents the technology that behaviorists have employed to analyze language deficits, develop language skills, and remediate language disorders. The fact that these procedures can be, and are, quite effective lends support to the argument that behavioral conceptualizations can play a critical role in language remediation strategies.

Attentional Deficits

How one uses information from the environment is an important determinant of how well one may adapt to that environment. The problems autistic children have in responding to, and learning from, their physical and social environments are legend. As discussed earlier, many of these children have early histories of suspected blindness or deafness because of their failure to notice salient aspects of their surroundings. Similarly, they may not typically pick up behaviors that are modeled in their social environment. It stands to reason that a failure to effectively utilize environmental stimulation would have a profound and devastating effect on an individual's ability to learn new behaviors. This seems to be the case with children diagnosed as autistic.

Since a behavioral model of treatment emphasizes the identification of environmental variables controlling behavior, it was natural for behavioral investigators to utilize the principles of experimental psychology, particularly discrimination learning, to identify the specifics of this deviant attentional pattern. Identification and description of this attentional deficit would then allow for the study of effective treatments. If effective procedures for altering, or normalizing, these children's attention could be identified, then one could predict that widespread areas of their functioning would be affected. Indeed, this is exactly what has been accomplished.

In our discussion of the behavioral characteristics associated with autism (Chapter 2) we noted that a substantial body of behavioral research has identified a particular pattern of attention wherein many autistic children, when presented with a learning situation requiring response to simultaneous multiple cues, characteristically respond to a very restricted number of the available cues (see Lovaas et al., 1979 for a review of much of this research). This pattern of attention has been labeled "stimulus overselectivity" to suggest that the children are overrestrictive in their use of available cues in a learning situation. The first investigations in this area focused on identifying the parameters of the overselectivity. For example, the initial study in this line of research (Lovaas, Schreibman, Koegel, & Rehm, 1971) presented autistic, retarded, and normal children with a discrimination task in which they were taught to press a lever when presented with a complex cue consisting of a visual cue (red floodlight), an auditory cue (white noise from a speaker), and a tactile cue (slight pressure to the leg). When each of these three component cues was subsequently presented in isolation to determine how much control it had acquired over the children's responses a fascinating pattern emerged. The autistic children typically responded to only one of the three component stimuli that was contained in the trained complex stimulus. Some of the autistic children responded to the auditory cue and some to the visual; none responded to the tactile cue. In contrast, the normal children characteristically responded to all three cues and the retarded responded at a level in between these two extremes so that, on the average, they responded to two of the cues. It was further demonstrated that the problem for the autistic children was not one of being unable to respond to a sensory modality since subsequent training on the previously nonfunctional cues indicated that the children could learn to respond to them. Rather, the problem was with responding to the cues in the context of other cues. This initial study led to a series of investigations and we now know that stimulus overselectivity: (a) occurs when simultaneous cues fall across different modalities (e.g., Lovaas et al., 1971; Lovaas & Schreibman, 1971), (b) occurs when the cues fall within a single modality (e.g., Koegel & Wilhelm, 1973; Reynolds et al.,

1974; Rincover, 1978; Schreibman, 1975; Schreibman, Kohlenberg, & Britten, 1986), and (c) may be more a function of low mental age than of autism *per se* (e.g., Wilhelm & Lovaas, 1976).

The implications of stimulus overselectivity for the functioning of these youngsters become apparent when one considers the number of learning situations that require response to multiple cues. Since most learning situations require the contiguous or near-contiguous association of cues, it stands to reason that someone who has difficulty in such situations is going to be at a severe disadvantage in learning situations. Also, as noted previously, stimulus overselectivity has been implicated as a variable influencing language acquisition, social behavior, observational learning, and the use of prompts. Another, particularly serious, implication of overselectivity is its adverse effects on the generalization of learned behaviors. Rincover and Koegel (1975) provided a dramatic demonstration of this phenomenon. They had therapists teach autistic children simple tasks such as touching body parts when asked. Several of the children failed to demonstrate this newly learned behavior when asked by a different therapist (i.e., the behavior did not generalize). It was subsequently determined that these children's responding had come under the control not of the verbal request but rather under the control of an irrelevant cue such as a therapist's idiosyncratic hand movement. Since these irrelevant cues were not present in the generalization setting, the behavior did not occur in these settings. Obviously, an important aspect of designing effective treatment procedures for autistic children is developing strategies for ameliorating the effects of this attentional deficit. Behavioral psychologists have approached this task along two lines. The first approach has involved attempting to directly remediate the overselectivity by teaching the children to respond to multiple cues. The other approach has involved developing teaching strategies that allow the child to learn despite the overselective pattern of attention.

The question of whether or not overselective autistic children could indeed learn to respond to simultaneous multiple cues is an important one and has deservedly received attention. Since the overselectivity research had revealed that under some conditions the overselectivity effect disappeared (e.g., Schreibman, Koegel, & Craig, 1977), it seemed hopeful that this abnormal attentional pattern could be changed. In research directly addressing this issue, Koegel and Schreibman (1977) and Schreibman, Charlop, and Koegel (1982) demonstrated that overselective autistic children can learn to respond to multiple cues if trained on a conditional discrimination. A conditional discrimination is one in which the discrimination task must be solved by responding to multiple features. For example, the child might be presented with a red toothbrush, a blue toothbrush, and a blue pencil. If the correct (i.e., reinforced) choice is blue toothbrush, the discrimination can only be performed correctly if *both* color (blue) and object (toothbrush) are attended to. Further, it was demonstrated that not only can these children learn such a conditional discrimination, but if presented with a series of such discriminations, they will learn a "set" to respond to multiple cues and thus approach new conditional discriminations without showing the overselectivity pattern. While this finding is certainly encouraging in that it shows that the abnormal, overrestrictive attentional pattern is amenable to treatment, even more encouraging is the possibility that other, widespread, positive changes in the children's behavior might be anticipated with the reduction in over-selectivity.

The effects of reducing overselective responding were addressed by Schreibman, Charlop, and Koegel (1982). This study demonstrated that while overselective autistic children failed to learn a difficult discrimination task when provided with a pointing prompt (therapist pointing at the correct choice and then fading this assistance), these same children learned from such a prompt after training on successive conditional discriminations. Figure 6.1 presents the conditional discriminations used in this study. Mastery of each training discrimination, shown on the left in the figure, was followed by a test conditional discrimination, shown on the right in the figure. Performance on the test discrimination indicated whether the training discrimination had been learned on the basis of only one cue (i.e., in an overselective manner). If so, training continued on the test discrimination until it was mastered, indicating that the child was now responding to multiple cues. At this point training began on the next discrimination, and so on, until the child had learned two consecutive training discriminations without demonstrating overselectivity. Presumably, before the conditional discrimination training the children had "overselected" to the pointing prompt and did not attend to the training materials. However, after the training they responded to both the prompt and training materials and thus were able to benefit from the prompting procedure. It thus appears that many of these children can learn to respond to the environment in a manner more similar to normal children and, therefore, they may be in a better position to benefit from the teaching strategies commonly used in classrooms as well as from their social environment.

In another demonstration Burke and Koegel (in preparation) found that after overselective attention was reduced via training on successive conditional discriminations, autistic children demonstrated both increased social responsiveness and increased utilization of incidental language cues. Again, reduction of overselectivity led to positive collateral changes in behavior.

While the above approach is certainly encouraging in that it suggests a treatment for overselectivity, for some autistic children these procedures fail and the children remain overselective. To allow these children to benefit from treatment, special techniques have been developed that involve designing the educational situation in such a way that the child can learn even though he/she is overselective. As described above, many teachers use "prompts" to assist learners with new discriminations. These prompts often involve providing an added cue ("extra-stimulus" prompt) such as pointing to the correct answer, underlining, using different colors, etc. Such prompts are commonly used and are gradually faded until the child responds correctly without the prompt. Unfortunately, the total removal of a prompt can be problematic in the case of overselective autistic children in that the child may respond only to the prompt and fail to attend to the training stimulus.

However, since prompt fading is such a useful technique for bringing about correct responding, it is a tool the therapist can ill do without. To address this problem some investigators (e.g., Rincover, 1978; Schreibman, 1975) have

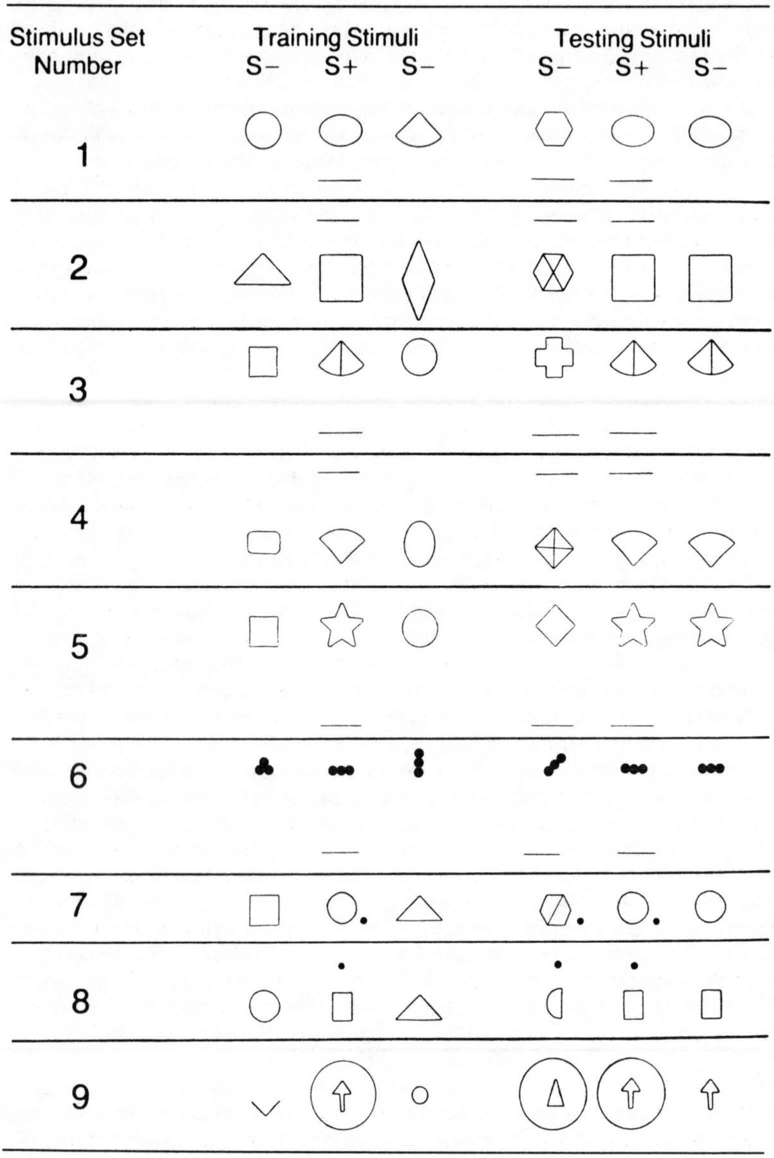

Figure 6.1 Conditioned Discrimination Task Stimuli

sought to develop prompts that allow an overselective autistic child to be overselective, yet still benefit from a prompting procedure. Basically, these prompts involve exaggerating the relevant component of a stimulus and after the child reliably responds to this component, gradually fading the exaggeration until the component is in its normal state. This procedure is called "within-stimulus" prompting since the assistance is provided by changing the relevant component of a discrimination and the child need only attend to this component and not to multiple cues (e.g., an extra-stimulus prompt and a training stimulus). Figure 6.2 presents a within-stimulus prompt fading sequence for teaching the discrimination between ·X· and Ẋ. The only reliable cue for the discrimination of these two stimuli is vertical versus horizontal dots. The X is redundant. The first step in within-stimulus prompting involves pretraining an exaggerated presentation of the S+(correct stimulus) relevant component—the horizontal dots (Figure 6.2, Part A, Step 1). In this step only the horizontal dots are presented, ensuring that the child can only respond on the basis of this cue. Once the child learns this step, the S−(incorrect stimulus) component (vertical dots) are slowly faded in (Steps 2 to 5). The child is now reliably discriminating S+ from S−. The exaggerated size of the dots is now gradually faded to their normal size (Part B of Figure 2). At this point (Part C, Steps 1 to 5), the redundant component of the discrimination (X) is faded in.

Schreibman (1975) found that using this prompt procedure, autistic children learned difficult discriminations that they previously did not learn without a prompt, or with an extra-stimulus (therapist pointing) prompt. The strength of this procedure is that the child is never required to attend to simultaneous multiple cues and the initial steps of the procedure ensure responding to the relevant feature of the discrimination. Rincover (1978) elaborated on these findings and demonstrated the importance of exaggerating the "distinctive feature" of the discrimination.

The results of these, and other, lines of research on remediating attentional deficits in autistic children are most encouraging. The identification of a procedure (training on successive conditional discriminations) to reduce or eliminate overselective responding seems to hold potential to normalize the attention of these children. However, for some children this may not be achieved and within-stimulus prompts, while limited in the scope of their potential use and potentially difficult to program, may allow these children to learn behaviors previously impossible for them. One can only be positive about the outlook for more significant work in this area and for the potential for affecting widespread areas of the children's functioning by eliminating their unusual, and maladaptive, pattern of responding to their environment.

Social Behavior

It is unfortunate that although severe deficits in social attachment and behavior are among the hallmark features of autism, our understanding of this behavioral characteristic is as yet limited. A number of investigators (e.g., Ferster, 1961; Lovaas, Schaeffer, & Simmons, 1965; Lovaas & Newsom, 1976) have noted the difficulty involved in establishing meaningful social reinforcers for many autistic children. These investigators, and others,

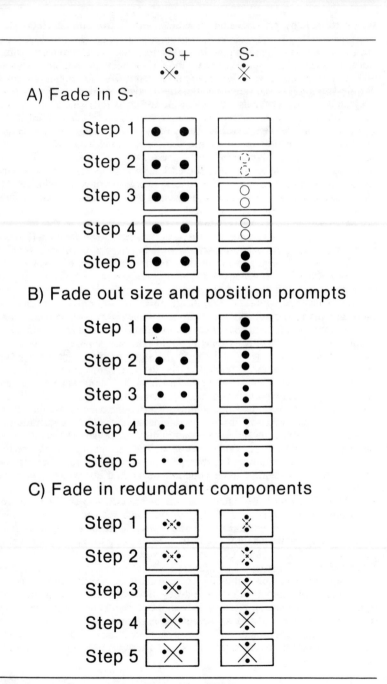

Figure 6.2 Example of Within-Stimulus Prompt Fading

have viewed the failure of people to become meaningful to these youngsters as a problem in the acquisition of secondary reinforcers (in this case, social reinforcers). Something has gone very wrong and the mechanism that allows normal (and other nonautistic) children to become dependent on social reinforcers, such as praise and approval, does not work for autistic children. From a behavioral perspective, the failure to acquire social reinforcers is seen as crucial to overall development since events such as praise, hugs, and approval appear to support so much behavior in normal individuals. One need only consider the behavior of young normal children to realize how much they "value" and respond to the social consequences provided by important adults in their life.

While lack of responsiveness to social stimuli typically makes these stimuli ineffective as reinforcers, two early studies used methodology established in the animal laboratory to successfully establish social stimuli as reinforcers for these children. Lovaas, Freitag, et al. (1966) established the word "good" as a social reinforcer by first establishing it as a discriminative stimulus ("cue") for the acquisition of a primary reinforcer (food). After "good" was established as a functional discriminative stimulus, it became functional as a secondary reinforcer, as demonstrated by its ability to maintain another learned response upon which it was contingent. This procedure was effective in establishing the word "good" as a social reinforcer after another procedure, pairing the word "good" with a primary reinforcer, food, had failed. (It is interesting to speculate that perhaps the first procedure was unsuccessful because the children may have overselected to the food and thus never attended to the word being paired with it.) In another study, Lovaas, Schaeffer, and Simmons (1965) used a negative reinforcement paradigm in which an appropriate approach response to a therapist's verbal request, "come here," was required to terminate an aversive stimulus (mild electric shock to the feet). The results of this investigation demonstrated that autistic children could be taught to respond to social stimuli.

Although the results of this early research demonstrated that social reinforcers could be established for autistic children in a carefully controlled laboratory situation, the procedures used were difficult to implement, impractical, unacceptable in the natural environment, and most importantly did not yield durable or generalized responsiveness to social reinforcers. More recent research has focused on utilizing more naturalistic situations to teach behaviors that may lead to more social responsiveness, and thus the potential for the establishment of social reinforcers. For example, Koegel, Dyer, and Bell (1987) reduced the social avoidance so often seen in autistic children by allowing the children to engage in child-preferred activities in educational settings. The authors suggested that by being able to direct the social situation, increased success in this situation was experienced and social approach behavior was therefore reinforced. Thus, by maximizing the child's chances of success, motivation to engage in social approach behavior was heightened and, since this behavior was reinforced, the generalization and maintenance of the behavior increased. These results are significant in that the child's social approach behavior was maintained by natural reinforcement contingencies, an important variable for the continued maintenance of the behavior.

Another area of investigation that is receiving considerable attention is that of directly increasing the social interaction of autistic children with their normal (or handicapped) peers. Perhaps the most important work in this area has been conducted by Strain and his colleagues who have explored various procedures for assessing specific deficit play and social interaction skills and for increasing social initiations and responses in these children (e.g., Fox *et al.*, 1984; Odom & Strain, 1986; Ragland, Kerr, & Strain, 1978; Strain, 1980; Strain, Kerr, & Ragland, 1979).

While there have been numerous investigations documenting variables that both describe the parameters of autistic children's social withdrawal/avoidance and suggest procedures to improve social responsiveness, the fact remains that this behavior is by far the strongest challenge for the behavior (or any) therapist. We still know relatively little about this very basic deficit. It is perhaps prophetic that the behavior characteristic which most uniquely defines autism, is also the one that has proven the most difficult to understand and treat.

Play

Another area in which social involvement is apparent in nonautistic children is through play. Play can be very simple or quite sophisticated, but in many ways it is a behavior that children engage in because they are socially involved. A normal child might "play house" or use toys to act out a trip to the auto mechanic. As might be expected, autistic children typically have extremely impoverished play repertoires. They typically ignore toys or, if they interact with them, it is in an inappropriate, compulsive, or self-stimulatory manner (e.g., Schreibman & Mills, 1983). Such a child might ignore a toy truck, or throw it, or turn it over and spin the wheels in a self-stimulatory manner. Or the child might spend hours lining up toy cars by color, size, etc. Perhaps one of the most relevant investigations into toy play was conducted by Koegel *et al.* (1974). They studied the relationship between appropriate toy play and self-stimulation. They found that the toys made available to their autistic subjects were ignored; instead, the children engaged in self-stimulatory activities such as gazing, repetitive vocalizations and finger manipulations. This was the case even though the children had been previously trained to play appropriately with the toys (e.g., drop blocks into a toy mailbox). In subsequent sessions, the investigators suppressed the children's self-stimulation and, when this was done, the children began to engage spontaneously in appropriate play with the toys. This research serves to demonstrate that self-stimulation and appropriate interaction with toys were inversely related.

In an interesting follow-up to the Koegel *et al.* (1974) study, Rincover *et al.* (1979) proposed identifying the sensory reinforcers for a child's self-stimulation and teaching the child to play with those toys that provide that particular mode of stimulation. For example, if a child's preferred self-stimulatory behavior provides visual stimulation (e.g., waving extended fingers in front of eyes while staring at a light), perhaps a toy that provides varied visual stimuli (e.g., video games) will reinforce appropriate play. Thus, it is hoped that the sensory events resulting from toy play would serve to maintain the appropriate play in the natural environment.

Appropriate play in normal children is also probably maintained by self-stimulatory behavior but in this case the stimulation received is considered appropriate. For autistic children the dependence on self-stimulatory input is deviant and so are the means of acquiring it. In other words, they are more likely to wave their fingers in front of their eyes than to play appropriately with a toy that provides visual input. More research will determine how we might best normalize the play and therefore the acquisition of sensory input in these children.

Motivation

One of the most frustrating experiences reported by therapists working with autistic children is that they seldom show any motivation to learn. Unlike nonautistic children, who seem to enjoy learning new behaviors and strive to succeed in educational endeavors, autistic youngsters do not seem to find any intrinsic reinforcement in academic achievements and indeed may resort to other behaviors in order to avoid learning situations. It seems that these children are motivated to learn only by primary reinforcers, such as food or avoidance of pain, rather than by reinforcers such as praise, achievement, and so forth. In the past, in a rather desperate effort to motivate these children to learn, therapists have typically resorted to food, drink, or even pain as motivators. However, there are obvious limitations to the utility of these sorts of reinforcers.

As Lovaas and Newsom (1976) discuss, these primary reinforcers may become artificial for older children since they exist only in limited settings such as clinic environments. Dependence on food also leads to limited generalization of treatment effects since these reinforcers are seldom available in extra-therapy (generalization) environments. Another problem is that a therapist using food as reinforcement must be concerned about the child becoming satiated and ceasing to work. These issues represent severe difficulties for a therapist attempting to teach and motivate these children and have led to investigations of methods to increase motivation.

One approach to this problem has been to identify ways in which the effectiveness of food reinforcers could be enhanced by preventing or considerably delaying satiation. Since we know that novelty is a variable known to maintain behavior (e.g., Berlyne, 1950, 1955, 1960; Cantor & Cantor, 1964a, b; Hutt, 1975; Young, 1969), it has been studied as a means of increasing reinforcer effectiveness. Egel (1981), for example, sought to determine if the rapid satiation typically found when using food reinforcers with autistic children could be reduced if the reinforcer was varied as opposed to held constant over learning trials. The effectiveness of two training procedures were compared. In one situation the children worked on a bar-pressing task and the same food reinforcer was presented after each response; in the other situation the reinforcer was varied (after approximately every third response a different edible reinforcer was delivered). The results indicated that children satiated more rapidly when the reinforcers were held constant than when they were varied. In addition, the response latencies were shorter when the reinforcer presentation was varied. These results suggest that clinicians can sustain a relatively high level of motivation in autistic children by merely varying the presentation of previously functional, edible reinforcers. This relationship between reinforcer effectiveness and performance was further investigated by Litt and Schreibman (1981) who found that in addition to varying the reinforcer, it was even more effective if a particular reinforcer was tied to correct responding to a particular training stimulus. Thus, for example, in teaching the discrimination between ball and car, correct responses to "Point to the ball" would always be reinforced with a piece of cookie and correct responses to "Point to the car" would always be reinforced with a raisin (with both cookie and raisin, of course, being established as reinforcers for the child). This is called *stimulus-specific* reinforcement and it involves both reinforcer variation and pairing the stimulus with a specific reinforcer.

In another experiment along these lines, Koegel and Williams (1980) found that if a reinforcer was obtained as a natural part of the correct response sequence, it was more effective than if it was presented in an independent manner. To illustrate, if a child is being taught the concept of "in" versus "under," the therapist could put the reinforcer (e.g., candy) inside a box for the stimulus "in" and under the box for the stimulus "under". In this way the correct response (reaching in or under) leads directly to acquisition of the reinforcer. These investigators found that this *direct response-reinforcer* relationship resulted in faster learning than a situation in which the correct "in" or "under" responses were reinforced with an indirect reinforcer, such as the therapist placing a piece of candy in the child's mouth.

While these investigations have addressed ways of increasing motivation by enhancing the effectiveness of food reinforcers, other investigations have involved attempts to develop new reinforcers. As discussed in relation to self-stimulation, the sensory events this behavior provides undoubtedly have powerful reinforcing properties since autistic children characteristically spend so much time engaged in such behavior. Rincover *et al.* (1977) studied the reinforcing properties of sensory stimulation for these children. First, preferred sensory stimuli were identified for each child and then this sensory stimulation was provided as reinforcement for responding on a learning task. For example, brief presentations of the child's preferred sensory event (e.g., music) were presented contingent upon correct responses. The results demonstrated that sensory stimulation when used as reinforcement produced high levels of responding that were quite durable over time; the children did not seem to become satiated in the general area of their preferred sensory stimulation. Rincover and Koegel (1977b) have pointed out that sensory reinforcers have two main advantages. First, they are relatively easy to identify and provide. Second, their use may facilitate generalization of treatment effects since such reinforcers are not necessarily limited to a particular setting. To this may be added a third advantage, that such sensory reinforcers are more "natural" in that they occur in the natural environment and indeed serve to maintain so much behavior in normal individuals.

Looking at other aspects of the motivation problem, a number of researchers have suggested that motivation may be depressed, performance impaired, and task avoidance increased by repeated failure experiences (Clark & Rutter, 1979; MacMillan, 1971; Rodda, 1977). This is particularly pertinent to the autistic population, as the severity of their handicap may result in their repeated exposure to failure. In addition, pathological failure in autistic and schizophrenic children has been found to increase dramatically during exposure to failure (Churchill, 1971). It has also been noted that as autistic youngsters frequently respond incorrectly when attempting a task, unusual accidental contingencies of reinforcement may be created and the attempts the child may make may either go unrewarded or be minimally rewarded (Koegel & Egel, 1979; Koegel & Mentis, 1985). These conditions may therefore function to further decrease motivation. It is thus apparent that failure may be a significant factor involved in the deficient motivation observed in these children. Addressing this issue, Koegel and Egel (1979) have provided a fascinating study that investigated the influence of correct task completion upon motivation to respond in learning situations. The results are particularly interesting in that they indicate that autistic children responded in a manner similar to normal children. When the children worked at tasks on which they were typically unsuccessful (many incorrect responses), their overall attempts to respond (i.e., motivation) to these tasks generally decreased. However, when the treatment procedures were designed to maximize correct responses, and thus amount of reinforcers, the child's attempts to respond on these tasks increased. In an extension of this line of research, the positive influence of success on motivation was clearly demonstrated (O'Dell, Dunlap, & Koegel, 1983). The investigators found that all the children who participated in this study achieved higher percentages of correct verbal responding and progressed more rapidly when their observable attempts to verbalize were reinforced, than when a more narrowly defined shaping contingency (under which only very strictly defined successive approximations to a target verbalization were reinforced) was used. When the child's attempts were reinforced, all the children were judged (by independent raters) not only to have more appropriate speech, but to be happier, more enthusiastic, more interested, and better behaved. In other words, they were motivated.

In a related area of investigation, it has been demonstrated that autistic children's motivation to respond can be enhanced by allowing them to have some control over the learning situation. It has been suggested that by giving autistic and other children some control over the choice of topic of conversation, the materials to be used or the activities to be engaged in, an increased level of interest and motivation in the activity may be achieved (Koegel et al., 1987; O'Dell & Koegel, 1981; Turner, 1978). This is an important consideration as it has been reported that the major type of interaction between adults and autistic youngsters seems to be adult-directed demands and requests (Bernard-Opitz, 1982; Duchan, 1983). Several recent studies suggest that providing the child with a nondirective environment (where the adult does not exert total control of the activities) results in less avoidance and more spontaneous communication by the autistic children (Bernard-Opitz, 1982; Koegel et al., 1987; Wetherby, 1982). For example, Koegel et al. (1987) reported that a condition of "shared control and turn-taking" wherein the child and therapist both chose activities, as opposed to a situation wherein the child was "drilled" by the therapist, led to decreased social avoidance and higher ratings of interest and involvement in the interaction. These studies suggest that the low motivation demonstrated by autistic children can be increased in a setting in which the control is shared by the child and clinician and in which the child is given a choice regarding the selection of materials, activities, and topics.

GENERALIZATION AND MAINTENANCE OF TREATMENT EFFECTS

In this chapter we have discussed the application of effective behavioral intervention procedures for autistic children. While the development and application of these techniques represents a substantial step forward in the treatment of this severely handicapped population, one very important criterion for evaluating the effectiveness of a treatment is the extent to which treatment effects *generalize*. A behavior may be said to have generalized if it proves durable over time (maintenance), appears in a variety of possible environments and settings or in the presence of different people (stimulus generalization), or spreads to a wide variety of related behaviors (response generalization). For example, the improvement of a child's language skills in a clinic setting will have generality if it endures in the future, after the termination of clinic visits; if the improved speech is evidenced in nontraining settings (e.g., school and home); and if related language behaviors, not specifically trained, also improve. Unfortunately, the early enthusiasm of behavior therapists working with autistic children has been somewhat tempered by the oft-observed failure of the treatment gains to generalize. As pointed out by Stokes and Baer (1977), generalization does not automatically occur simply because a behavior change has been accomplished. It seems then that a truly successful treatment program must be concerned not only with producing a therapeutic behavior change, but also with promoting the generalization of that behavior change. Consequently, behavioral researchers have increasingly addressed this issue by investigating variables that might facilitate generalization.

The difficulties autistic children have with generalization are well known. Anyone who has had the opportunity to work with these youngsters is well aware that learned behaviors may not generalize to new settings or people. Many a parent has been surprised to discover that the behavior he/she has tried so hard to teach at home had actually been mastered at school weeks or months earlier. While anecdotal accounts of lack of generalization abound, systematic assessment of maintenance and generalization of treatment effects have similarly indicated that effective treatment of autistic children requires a greater understanding of how to ensure that generalization will occur (e.g., Koegel, Schreibman, Britten, Burke, & O'Neill, 1982; Lovaas *et al.*, 1973; Rincover & Koegel, 1975).

Most issues relating to generalization are not unique to autism and, in fact, have been raised in relation to a wide variety of behaviors and populations. Research has illuminated a number of strategies that can be adopted to promote the three basic types of generalization (stimulus generalization, response generalization, maintenance) and these have been described in detail (e.g., Carr, 1980; Horner, Dunlap, & Koegel, in press; Stokes & Baer, 1977). While no attempt to detail these procedures will be made here, a brief description of them will aid the reader's understanding of the direction of this work.

To enhance *temporal generalization* (maintenance) several procedures have proved very helpful:

1. Intermittent reinforcement, although not an efficient method for establishing a behavior change, can be an effective procedure for maintaining behavior. Stokes and Baer (1977) suggested that intermittent reinforcement may promote generalization because the contingencies are unpredictable. For example, if a teacher were training a child to label simple objects (e.g., toys, food items), initially the child should be reinforced for every correct response. As the child masters the task, the therapist should gradually fade the child from a continuous to an intermittent schedule of reinforcement, thus making the contingencies at least partly indiscriminable. Several investigators (e.g., Koegel & Rincover, 1974; Koegel & Rincover, 1977; Rincover & Koegel, 1977a; Schreibman, 1988) have reported increased maintenance of behavior change if the consequences of the behavior are presented intermittently. It is suggested that the durability of treatment gains is due to reducing the discriminability of the reinforcement schedules used in therapy and extra-therapy settings. In such a case, the child would not be able to tell the difference between a treatment environment, in which the contingencies can be expected, and an extra-therapy environment, in which the contingencies are not in effect. If a light schedule of reinforcement is used during treatment, it is possible that naturally occurring intermittent reinforcers in extra-therapy settings may serve to maintain the behavior in the future.

2. In addition to intermittency of reinforcement, recent research suggests that administration of delayed rewards may promote the maintenance of behavioral changes (Dunlap, Koegel, Johnson, & O'Neill, 1987). These investigators demonstrated that by gradually lengthening the time between a behavior and the relevant consequence, they were able to establish longer and longer periods of appropriate responding. The children were eventually able to receive the appropriate consequences (positive or negative) delivered at the end of the day, perhaps several hours after the occurrence of the target behavior.

3. Another strategy for promoting temporal generality is to teach the children behaviors that are likely to be reinforced in the natural environment. This can be helpful since if the child performs the behavior in the natural environment and the behavior is rewarded, the child has essentially been reinforced for generalizing. For example, Carr (1980) used sign language to teach autistic children to request items that were likely to be found outside the training setting. These items included, for example, preferred food items and toys and were of functional significance to the children. In addition, these items were present in the natural environment (e.g., school, home). Therefore, it is likely that the child's spontaneous use of a sign for food would be reinforced by acquiring the food. In contrast, teaching a child to label common objects (e.g., chair, horse) will be of little use to the child outside the treatment setting and will probably not be maintained since these labels

have little functional significance. Obviously, if a child spontaneously signed for boat, it is less likely that a reward would be forthcoming. Another behavior that will normally meet maintaining reinforcement after teaching is toy play (Baer & Wolf, 1970; Buell, Stoddard, Harris & Baer, 1968; Hall & Broden, 1967; Rincover et al., 1979). This behavior seems to be maintained by reinforcers inherent to playing with toys. While much of this research has addressed nonautistic populations, it would be important to determine which behaviors result in natural contingencies that operate in the environment of severely handicapped populations, such as autistic children.

4. Another strategy for achieving maintenance of treatment effects is to provide ongoing treatment for the child. This is usually achieved by training others (parents, teachers, siblings) in the child's environment to continue the treatment when they are with the child. Several studies suggest that parent (see Berkowitz & Graziano, 1972; Forehand & Atkeson, 1977; Johnson & Katz, 1973; O'Dell, 1974) and teacher training (e.g., Koegel, Russo & Rincover, 1977; Russo & Koegel, 1977) can be structured to facilitate temporal generality. By training others to provide appropriate contingencies, the therapist is creating an environment in which treatment remains in effect. We will discuss the training of parents and teachers in the next chapter, which deals with extra-therapy treatment.

Several additional strategies have been employed to enhance the *stimulus generalization* of treatment effects. These can be categorized under four headings.

1. Sequential modification (Stokes & Baer, 1977) is a procedure in which generalization is programed in every nongeneralized condition, e.g., settings or people. Thus, if a therapist wanted a trained behavior (e.g., language) to generalize across settings (e.g., home and school) and people (e.g., teachers, parents, siblings), then he/she would train the behavior in each of the desired settings. For example, Nordquist and Wahler (1973) trained the parents of an autistic child in a clinic setting to modify compliance and to teach imitative skills. Once treatment gains were established, the parents implemented the same treatment program at home. Treatment gains generalized from the clinic to the home. Similarly, Russo and Koegel (1977) wished to integrate an autistic child into two normal public school classes. To do so, it proved necessary to train *both* teachers since treatment gains made with one teacher did not generalize to the other teacher. It is obvious that sequential modification may require a great deal of time and effort as a means of promoting generalization and for that reason it may not be the most popular choice. However, while it may not necessarily be efficient, it is an almost sure means of promoting generalized treatment effects for those children whose generalization problems cannot be remediated in other ways.

2. With another strategy, training of sufficient exemplars, generalization to untrained stimulus conditions and to untrained responses is achieved

by training more than one exemplar of each stimulus condition and/or response. Rather than training in every setting or training every response (as in sequential modification discussed above), this strategy involves training in enough settings or across sufficient behavioral examples until the behavior generalizes across all settings and all relevant behaviors. Schreibman and Carr (1978) taught echolalic children to respond to a set of previously echoed questions with the sentence "I don't know". The children were trained on multiple examples of the appropriate situation (e.g., when presented with a question to which the child had no response, such as "Where is Cincinnati?") until they generalized the "I don't know" response to a broad set of untrained questions that had formerly been echoed. Since it would obviously be impossible to teach the children to answer "I don't know" to any and all stimuli they might encounter, the strategy of teaching with sufficient exemplars was most appropriate.

3. Programming common stimuli refers to a procedure in which common stimuli are present in both the training and generalization settings. This ensures that the environmental stimuli that control the behavior are in the settings in which one wishes the behavior to occur. To illustrate, Koegel and Rincover (1974) found that the transfer of appropriate responding in autistic children from one-to-one sessions in an experimental setting to a classroom were minimal. In order to facilitate generalization of appropriate responding to the classroom, a few children at a time were gradually faded into the experimental setting until a classroom-sized group was formed. Thus, the one-to-one stimulus situation (i.e., the experimental setting) was made to resemble the classroom stimulus situation (i.e., the generalization) by gradually decreasing the teacher-to-student ratio. As a result, there was increased performance on previously learned and new behaviors in the classroom.

4. Mediated generalization refers to establishing a response in a treatment setting that is likely to be used in extra-therapy settings. The most common such mediator is, of course, language. Language is something the individual can take with him into any setting and use to control behavior. In a study by Charlop (1983), described earlier, echolalia served as a verbal mediator. Six autistic children, three echolalia and three nonverbal, were taught two receptive labeling tasks. For one task, the children were given the opportunity to echo the label, after the experimenter said it, before manually handing the object to the experimenter. In the other condition, the children were not given the opportunity to echo the label of the object before handing it to the experimenter. The results indicated that the children learned the labeling tasks in fewer trials when they echoed the experimenter's label, compared to when they were not given the opportunity to do so. Echolalia facilitated generalized treatment gains across unfamiliar settings and persons for the echolalic children but not for the nonverbal children. Charlop suggested that the mediation of generalization for the echolalic children may have occurred because, unlike their nonverbal compatriots, the echolalic children provided their own self-imposed discriminative

stimulus (the echo of the label) in the generalization setting. The mediation of generalization is also exemplified in the research on self-management procedures. These procedures, which usually involve self-recording and self-reinforcement, can be taught as part of an intervention procedure and function to promote generalization. While most of child self-management research has involved disruptive children (Drabman, Spitalnik, & O'Leary, 1973; Holman & Baer, 1979; Turkewitz, O'Leary & Ironsmith, 1975), Koegel and his colleagues have been successful in employing these techniques with autistic children (Koegel & Koegel, 1986; Koegel & Koegel, in press; Koegel, Koegel, & Ingham, 1986). These investigators have adapted the self-management procedures to the autistic population in an attempt to enhance generalization. Using this procedure, these investigators first prepare for the training of self-monitoring by specifically defining both appropriate and inappropriate target behaviors. Functional rewards, chosen by the child, are identified and an appropriate period of time or unit of behavior small enough to result in success on the child's part is determined. Second, the therapist begins training the child to self-monitor. The child is taught to discriminate between correct *vs.* incorrect behavior. This may be accomplished via modeling, or if the child is more severely handicapped, it may be possible to begin with simply prompting the child to engage in the appropriate behavior. Third, the child is taught to self-observe, self-evaluate, and then record the fact that a unit of behavior has taken place. After the child has demonstrated he/she is able to perform the activities at a criterion level in the training setting, he/she is prompted to perform the self-monitoring activities under appropriate natural stimulus conditions. Once this step is completed, the fourth step, fading the formal self-monitoring activities, is implemented.

Response generalization refers to collateral changes in behaviors that are not targeted during the treatment. Although one or two behaviors are usually selected for modification, it would be cost-effective for therapists and beneficial for children if nontargeted behaviors also changed in the desired direction. There are some strategies that have proven helpful in achieving response generalization.

1. Teaching toy play seems to be an effective strategy for achieving behavioral generality. As discussed earlier, decreasing self-stimulatory behavior was accompanied by a concomitant increase in appropriate play (Epstein *et al.*, 1974; Koegel *et al.*, 1974). However, Koegel *et al.* (1974) pointed out that self-stimulation increased over time, and appropriate toy play decreased, indicating that the behavioral gains were not maintained over time. Rincover *et al.* (1979), in a study discussed earlier, used sensory extinction (Rincover, 1978) to program multiple treatment gains in self-stimulation and spontaneous play. One child's self-stimulation involved spinning plates. It was determined that the auditory feedback provided by the plate spinning on the floor maintained this behavior. Having identified the sensory reinforcer as an auditory stimulus, the investigators taught the child to play with a toy that also

produced auditory stimulation—a music box. The use of sensory extinction during toy-play training resulted in the elimination of the self-stimulation. Because the experimental contingencies were applied only to toy play, and not to self-stimulatory behavior, behavioral generalization was demonstrated. It was also demonstrated that the appropriate play was maintained without using external reinforcers. Thus it seems that teaching toy play to autistic children can result in more than one type of generalization. Further, since we know that reduction of some inappropriate behaviors (e.g., self-stimulation) is correlated to increases in appropriate behaviors (e.g., toy play, discrimination learning), it is apparent that these interrelationships have implications for programming lawful and predictable behavior changes that may result in generalized treatment gains.

2. A second strategy effective in promoting behavior generalization is observational learning. Several investigations have suggested that developmentally disabled children can learn nonverbal imitation from models, which, in turn, facilitates widespread behavior change (Baer, Peterson, & Sherman, 1967; Lovaas, Freitag, Nelson, & Whalen, 1967; Metz, 1965). In other words, children can learn to imitate specific modeled behaviors. It was subsequently determined that this imitation generalized to similar, but relatively new, tasks on which no training had been given. It has also been shown that observational learning can facilitate temporal (Egel, Richman, & Koegel, 1981) and stimulus generalization (Charlop, Schreibman, & Tryon, 1983). Egel et al. (1981) assessed whether autistic children's correct responding would be maintained after learning visual discriminations through observing normal peer models. They found that the autistic children maintained their high levels of correct performance in the absence of these peer models. In an extension of this work, Charlop et al. (1983) demonstrated that autistic children also learned visual discriminations through observation of autistic peer models. In addition, these investigators found that generalization of the newly acquired skill to an unfamiliar setting and person was superior, compared to a trial-and-error procedure without a peer model. These investigations in observational learning appear to demonstrate that the ability to learn from observing the behavior of others may be an effective treatment strategy for facilitating learning and generalization in this population.

While these generalization strategies, and others commonly used (see Stokes & Baer, 1977), have improved the generalization of treatment effects with autistic children, a relatively new approach may hold promise for much more extensive and effective generalization. Specifically, some investigators are evaluating the generalized effects of teaching "pivotal" behaviors. These are called "pivotal" because changes in such behaviors seem to affect widespread changes in other areas of the child's functioning. In recent research, two central behaviors have been implicated in the failure of behavioral gains to be generalized. These two behaviors are *motivation* and *responsivity*. While we have addressed both these issues before, in a somewhat different context, let us look at them again in relation to achieving generalized treatment effects.

As discussed above, problems with motivation seem to lie behind many of the autistic youngster's learning difficulties, as evidenced by the fact that learning and performance improve when motivation is increased. It therefore seems that incorporating procedures known to enhance motivation would lead to a broad range of collateral behavioral improvements. Similarly, we have discussed how an overselective attention pattern may affect, and be responsible for, several areas of behavioral deficits. It stands to reason, then, that a treatment package comprising procedures previously identified as effective in increasing motivation and procedures shown to normalize responsivity, might indeed lead to widespread generalization and maintenance of treatment effects.

In a recent demonstration indicating that indeed this approach to generalization may be effective, Koegel et al. (1987) devised a language-training program for nonverbal autistic children. This program incorporated several of the specific motivation-enhancing procedures including shared-control of activities, task variation, direct response-reinforcer relationships, reinforcer variation, and reinforcement of child's attempts. These investigators found that this "natural language" training paradigm was superior to a structured, repetitive-practice, language training in several dimensions of generalization, including increased use of appropriate, spontaneous, and generalized speech and language. The results of this research and of related research on incidental teaching (see Hart & Risley, 1980; McGee, Krantz, Mason, & McClannahan, 1983; McGee et al., 1985; Neef, Walters, & Egel, 1984) suggest that a "natural language paradigm" may be a useful treatment program since it increases the child's interest and motivation to learn and facilitates generalization of acquired skills. Generalization is further enhanced since the program utilizes stimulus events and contingencies which more closely approximate the child's natural environment. Similarly, it appears that responsivity to multiple cues can be increased and that this augmented responsivity leads to positive collateral behavior changes, such as the ability to learn from traditional (previously ineffective) teaching modalities for example, prompts (e.g., Schreibman et al., 1982) and incidental learning (Burke and Koegel, in preparation).

Science is a cumulative process and we progress by building on prior knowledge. Perhaps nowhere in the literature on the behavioral treatment of autistic children is this so apparent as in the area of generalization. As we have seen, the experimental analysis and treatment of this population has evolved from rather simple demonstrations of behavior change (e.g., increasing imitation of vocal speech) to extremely sophisticated and complex demonstrations of behavioral interactions (e.g., motivation and generalization). Hindsight is twenty-twenty and we cannot go back and reassess the treatment we have provided these children in the past to see how the emphasis on repetitive practice, carefully controlled instructions, consistent and artificial reinforcers, highly structured and simple training environments, and so forth, might have actually worked against our efforts to achieve generalized treatment effects. Yet it would be very wrong to conclude that all our prior efforts were misguided or "wasted". Indeed, it is precisely *because* of these earlier efforts and our analysis of their effects that we have been able to allow our treatments to evolve. It is highly unlikely that we would be where we are in understanding generalization if it were not for the earlier building blocks of research that allowed us to establish our early inroads in dealing with this most difficult population of children.

SUMMARY

The application of the behavioral model to treatment intervention can be conceptualized as involving three distinct steps. First, the therapist carefully and precisely defines the behaviors to be targeted for treatment. Second, these behaviors must be accurately measured. Third, based on the first two steps, treatment interventions are designed and implemented. Once these steps are carried out, the clinician can evaluate the effects of treatment.

Typically, when designing a treatment program, the behavior therapist will consider which specific behavioral excesses and deficits are exhibited by the individual. Next, the therapist draws from a rather extensive arsenal of treatment techniques which have been identified as effective for specific behaviors under particular environmental circumstances. By matching the behavior with the environmental factors serving to maintain it, the therapist constructs an intervention plan.

One behavioral excess that has attracted much attention is self-injury. This is certainly not surprising considering the very serious nature of this behavior. Relatively recent work has suggested that SIB may be considered an operant behavior maintained by its environmental consequences. Specifically, the behavior may be maintained by positive reinforcement (e.g., attention), negative reinforcement (e.g., escape from demands), or by reinforcement provided by self-stimulation (e.g., sensory reinforcement). Treatment techniques for decreasing SIB have involved manipulation of environmental consequences, such as when one uses extinction, punishment, or differential reinforcement of other behaviors. Manipulation of the antecedents of SIB have also shown recent promise for the control of this behavior.

Self-stimulation is another behavioral excess which has received considerable attention. Besides the often bizarre and stigmatizing appearance of this behavior, it has been shown to interfere with the autistic child's responsiveness to the environment and to interfere with the acquisition of new behavior. Intervention strategies have included differential reinforcement of other behavior, punishment (including overcorrection), and sensory extinction.

Other excessive behaviors often seen in this population are disruptive behaviors, such as tantrums, aggression, compulsive rituals and destruction of property. These behaviors are viewed as operant behaviors maintained by environmental consequences, and the same learning principles which apply to other operant responses have been successfully applied to these behaviors.

Behavioral deficits pose the opposite problem for therapists in that rather than involving an excess of responding, they involve behaviors that are either not performed at all or are performed at inadequate levels. One behavioral deficit that is considered a hallmark of autism is language. Consequently, a large body of work has addressed remediating language deficits in autistic individuals. This work has included both work on establishing speech in mute autistic children, beginning with early work on vocal imitation and more recently emphasizing the teaching of more complex language skills, spontaneity, and nonvocal language (e.g., signs). Additional work has focused on remediating the inaccurate language of echolalic children and on understanding the communicative properties of pathological behaviors such as echolalia and disruptive behaviors.

Research focusing on the attentional deficits of autistic children has identified a particular attentional pattern—stimulus overselectivity—which may greatly influence wide areas of these youngsters' functioning. Two approaches have led to improved learning in children who exhibit an overselectivity pattern. One approach is to remediate the attentional pattern by training on successive conditional discriminations. A second approach has been to design learning environments (e.g., within-stimulus prompts) in such a way that the child can learn even though he/she is responding in an overselective manner.

Research on social deficits in autism have ranged from very early work attempting to use learning principles to establish conditioned social reinforcers to more recent work focusing on directly training social interactions. Additional research has focused on assessing collateral changes in social behavior associated with specific treatment interventions, such as allowing the child access to preferred activities. In a related field of treatment research, appropriate play has been studied with particular reference to its relation to self-stimulatory behavior.

Motivation has long been a behavior known to be deficient in the autistic population and we are now developing strategies designed to increase motivation. Some of these strategies include frequent task variation, direct response-reinforcer relations, stimulus-specific reinforcement, reinforcing attempts to respond, and the identification of new reinforcers.

The focus on generalization and maintenance of treatment effects well illustrates the behavior therapist's attention to treatment evaluation results. While early behavioral interventions focused on fairly small units of behavior, it has become apparent that a more global approach is necessary to achieve treatment results that could be considered truly effective. Thus, attention to generalization and maintenance issues and strategies has allowed for broader based treatments which address the often complex interactions involved in sophisticated behaviors.

7

EXTENDED TREATMENT ENVIRONMENTS

In an attempt to maximize the effectiveness of behavioral treatment for autistic children, extensions of clinic treatment have been investigated and implemented. The rationale for extending the treatment is to enhance generalization and maintenance of treatment effects and to allow the child to benefit from the treatment environments most functional for normal children—the home and the classroom. Correspondingly, such treatment research has focused mainly on parent-training programs, classroom programs, and programs incorporating combinations of these environments. It is important to emphasize here that the specific nature of the treatment for the child is based upon the behavioral principles discussed in the last chapter. What characterizes parent training and classroom applications of the treatment is who provides the treatment and the setting involved.

The impetus for broadening treatment delivery to non-clinic environments can be traced to three main factors. First, as discussed above, the issue of limited generalization with only clinic treatment was an important motivating factor. Second, clinic treatment of autistic children can be extremely costly in terms of staff time and funding. There are few clinics that provide such treatment and many of these are affiliated with research programs at universities. Thus appropriate clinic treatment is not very available to most autistic children. Third, related to the issue of expense, the present emphasis on decentralization of mental health care has served to prompt the use of resources in the community since centralized services, such as state-sponsored institutions, are being phased out.

PARENT TRAINING

Training parents to provide treatment for their children is a technology with a relatively long history. Early reports took the form of case reports and single family studies and appeared in the late 1960s and early 1970s. Much of this early work addressed individual target behaviors such as noncompliance and tantrums and involved children with behavior problems rather than children with developmental disabilities. Wetzel, Baker, Roney, and Martin

(1966) provided the first report on training parents to cope with their autistic child's behavior, albeit Wolf, Risley, and Mees (1964) presented a now-classic report of a comprehensive program (including parent training) for the behavior problems of an autistic boy. The literature on training for parents of autistic children is now rather extensive and a comprehensive coverage of it does not fall within the scope of this volume. For reviews of this field, the interested reader is referred to Altman and Mira (1983), Baker (1984), Dangel and Polster (1984), Gordon and Davidson (1981), Graziano (1977), Moreland, Schwebel, Beck, and Wells (1982), O'Dell (1985), and Sanders and James (1983).

It is interesting to speculate on why parent-training programs for autistic children arose only after training parents was established in the literature for nonautistic populations. Perhaps the severity of the behavior problems of this population discouraged clinicians from involving parents. While conduct-disordered children demonstrate relatively circumscribed, isolated behavior problems, such as noncompliance or tantrums, the autistic child presents a very different challenge. The range and severity of autistic behaviors requires that the parents learn a variety of procedures to increase some behaviors and to decrease others. This is a formidable task indeed. Another possible reason why parent training for autistic children has been somewhat delayed may relate to some of the early conceptions of the etiology of the disorder. Since the psychogenic hypothesis of etiology implicated the parents as causative factors in the development of autism, it is obvious that parents would not be the psychoanalyst's first choice as treatment agents. However, with the decline of the parent-causation hypothesis and the demonstration that parents can be excellent therapists for their children, clinicians from a variety of theoretical orientations are now advocating parent-training programs and making use of an excellent clinical resource. In fact, in recent years there has been an increasing emphasis on training the parents of autistic children to implement the principles and procedures of behavioral intervention (e.g., Freeman & Ritvo, 1976; Harris, Wolchik, & Milch, 1983; Harris, Wolchik, & Weitz, 1981; Kazdin & Moyer, 1976; Koegel, Egel, & Dunlap, 1980; Koegel, Glahn, & Nieminen, 1978; Koegel & Rincover, 1974; Koegel, Schreibman, Britten, Burke, & O'Neill, 1982; Kozloff, 1973, 1974; Lovaas et al., 1973; Nordquist & Wahler, 1973; Schopler & Reichler, 1971; Watson, 1973; Wing, 1972).

As pointed out by Schreibman, Koegel, Mills and Burke (1984) parent training has several obvious advantages. First, the parent is around the child more than anyone else and thus has the potential to provide the child with an around-the-clock treatment environment. This is in contrast to teachers and clinicians, who are with the child for only a limited amount of time on a daily basis. Also, compared with clinics and schools, which focus heavily on remediating academic deficiencies, the home treatment environment can be amenable for treatment of other aspects of the child's behavior (e.g., tantrums, compulsive behavior, enuresis). Second, since we know that autistic children may not generalize treatment gains across environments and people, it has been suggested that generalization of gains might be facilitated by involving the parents (e.g., Rincover & Koegel, 1975; Wahler, 1969). In addition, the parents can work in conjunction with the child's therapist as well as teacher to assure continuity in the child's programs across settings. Third, schools and clinics specializing in the treatment of autistic children are relatively scarce and might not be conveniently available to families who live in rural or isolated areas. In such situations, the parents can travel to the closest clinic or school and receive training, and then return home and become their child's therapist. This greatly increases the availability of treatment. Fourth, training programs that emphasize general treatment procedures may allow the parent to handle any new problem behaviors that arise, alleviating the need for additional, and costly, professional intervention. Fifth, training parents to be therapists for their children enables them to take an active role in their child's development. This is particularly important for parents who have felt excluded from their child's education.

As apparent as these rather obvious advantages are, there is an even more compelling reason why parents of autistic children need to be trained to provide the treatment. It is now known that parent training is an essential component of the child's treatment. This was dramatically demonstrated by Lovaas *et al.* (1973), who conducted a follow-up study of 20 autistic children in behavior therapy. The investigators assessed these children during one year of behavior therapy treatment. Although appropriate behaviors were increased and inappropriate behaviors were decreased during the original treatment, prognosis for the children at follow-up (up to four years after treatment) depended on the posttreatment environment. Those children whose parents had not been trained in the behavior modification treatment, or those who had been institutionalized, had lost their previously acquired skills. In contrast, those children whose parents had been trained to provide the treatment either maintained the gains originally established during treatment or continued to improve. This study proved a landmark in the research on treatment of autistic children in demonstrating that parent training is not only intuitively a good idea but essential.

Knowing that parent training is essential led clinicians to pursue this avenue with increased enthusiasm. It now became important to determine *what* the parents should be taught, *how* they should be taught, and how to ensure that the training would have a positive, rather than negative, impact on the parents and the entire family unit. No matter how effective a parent-training program may be, if the parents perceive it as too effortful, too stressful on family life, or ineffective, they will be disinclined to use it.

What the parents should be taught, or the content of parent-training programs, has evolved as our understanding of both the children and their parents has progressed. As mentioned above, the range and severity of the problems presented by an autistic child require that the parent learn a curriculum including contingency management and operant training procedures. This is because the parents have to teach self-care, communication, and play skills to children who do not seem to respond to the child-rearing practices used in homes with normal children (Twardosz & Nordquist, 1987).

It is now apparent that for parents to learn generalized skills to teach their children, they need to learn the basic procedural rules of behavior modification as opposed to learning specific strategies for teaching individual target behaviors. Investigators have demonstrated the need to teach general behavioral principles in order to generalize parenting skills to the home and/or to handle a wide range of behaviors (Baker & Heifetz, 1976; Glogower & Sloop, 1976; Koegel, Glahn, & Nieminen, 1978; McMahon, Forehand, & Griest, 1981). Koegel *et al.* (1978) compared the effects on parents of autistic children of training general rules of behavior modification with various training procedures not including such training. Included in the general rules of behavior modification were teaching the parents how to present antecedent stimuli (questions or instructions), how to present consequences, how to use shaping, and so forth. These investigators found that a brief demonstration (modeling) of how to teach an autistic child new behaviors was sufficient for parents to learn how to teach those behaviors to their children. However, there was essentially no generalization to new, unmodeled, child tasks. Thus, a parent who observed a trained therapist teach a child to tie his shoe became capable of teaching that specific behavior, but was not enabled thereby to teach the child another skill, such as "say Mama". In contrast, parents who had received training in the general rules of behavior modification were able to teach a variety of behaviors. The training procedure was therefore effective in teaching a general set of skills that could be applied across multiple children and target behaviors. It is also interesting that these same general principles were taught to siblings of autistic children (Schreibman, Oke, Mills, & Ploog, 1986; Schreibman, O'Neill, & Koegel, 1983) with similar positive results.

Several parent-training modalities have been employed to teach parents to work with their own children. These have included lectures, written instruction, live and videotape modeling, direct prompting, shaping, behavioral rehearsal, feedback from the parent trainer, and telephone contacts (see Schreibman & Britten, 1984; Schreibman *et al.*, 1984; Twardosz & Nordquist, 1987). Most programs have utilized a combination of these procedures. O'Dell, Krug, Patterson, and Faustman (1980) compared the effectiveness of several parent-training programs (e.g., modeling, lectures, role-playing) to teach parents how to effectively use time-out procedures and found no significant difference between groups when the parent's behavior was measured in the home. In addition, parent training has been conducted with families individually as well as in groups. O'Dell (1985) concluded that the different training methods do not account for a large portion of the variance in the outcome of parent-training programs. Thus one cannot conclude that any set of training materials or procedures is better than another—as long as one is certain to include training in basic behavioral principles.

As discussed earlier, one crucial area of study involves an evaluation of how these parent-training programs affect not only the autistic child, but also the parents and the rest of the family. Many professionals have focused on this concern (e.g., Harris, 1984, 1986; Helm & Kozloff, 1986; Koegel, Schreibman, Britten, Burke, & O'Neill, 1982). While this area is relatively new and receiving a good deal of attention at this time, there have been some investigations addressing specific questions about the impact of behavioral parent-training programs on families with autistic children. There is no doubt that having an autistic, or other severely handicapped child, can be a stressful and very disruptive influence on the parents and family. Although Koegel, Schreibman, O'Neill, and Burke (1983) demonstrated that families of autistic children do not exhibit higher rates of psychopathology than other families, other studies suggest that the stress level may be higher among these families (e.g., DeMyer, 1979). In addition, the mothers of children with autism or other developmental disabilities have been described as experiencing more anger, fatigue, tension and depression than mothers who do not have children with these handicapping conditions (DeMyer, 1979; Holroyd, 1974).

Programs aimed at utilizing parents as delivery agents must be acceptable to the parents and must have a positive impact on the entire family. In addition to the direct effects on the target child, the acceptability of a program to consumers (e.g., parents, teachers, society at large) is important. In addition to analyzing treatment gains made by the children as a result of training their parents, it is crucial to determine the effects of such a program on other family members as well. While collateral effects of behavior modification have been investigated in terms of the target subject (e.g., Sajwaj, Twardosz, & Burke, 1972; Wahler, Sperling, Thomas, Teeter, & Luper, 1970; Buell et al., 1968; Risley, 1968), little has been reported relating to the collateral effects of parent training.

As an example of this line of research looking at treatment effects on a wide range of child and family behaviors, Koegel et al. (1982) conducted a study directed at obtaining information about the effects of parent training on the entire family as well as on the child. Families with autistic children were divided on a random basis into two groups. For one group, the children received behavior modification therapy provided by trained clinicians while the parents received no training in the treatment procedures. For the other group, the parents were trained in the procedural rules of behavior modification and subsequently provided the treatment to their own child. No in-clinic treatment was given to this second group. The investigators gathered two sets of dependent measures to determine any differential effects of the two treatment modalities (clinic versus parent training). One set of measures focused on changes in the children's behavior and included: (1) measures of changes in psychotic and appropriate behaviors; (2) measures of durability and generalization of these changes; and (3) measures of social maturity. The other set of measures focused on potential changes in the family. These measures were deemed particularly important since the effect of parent training on the family had never been assessed before. One could hope that the training would make life for the parents and family easier and thus have a positive effect, but still argue that potential problems might arise from the training. One might speculate, for example, that the parents' marriage would suffer if the husband perceived the wife as spending too much time with the autistic youngster and not enough with him, or perhaps the training demands would be too stressful and the parents' psychological adjustment would suffer, or perhaps the siblings of the affected child would be "jealous" of the attention the autistic sibling received, which might lead to discord in the family unit, and so forth. To assess these possible effects, potential changes in the family were measured in these specific areas: (1) parent psychological and marital adjustment; (2) the family environment; (3) parental time allocation for daily activities; and (4) family members' interactions.

After initial assessment, each family received the assigned treatment. Families in the parent-training group received training in the same type of treatment as was used in the clinic-treatment group. Briefly, this training consisted of the use of clear antecedents (questions and instructions), use of prompts, use of shaping and chaining, and use of consequences. The difference between the clinic-treatment and parent-training groups was that in the parent-training group the child's treatment was conducted by the parents instead of a clinician, with the clinician serving essentially as a parent trainer and consultant. The basic goals, sequence, and content of the treatment were the same for both groups. The parents were taught via written training materials, videotape demonstration, and practice with feedback.

The research yielded some very interesting findings (Koegel, Schreibman, Britten, Burke, & O'Neill, 1982). Looking at the effects on the children, the investigators found that on almost every individual measure there was as much initial improvement and more durable improvement with 25 to 50 hours of parent training as compared with 225 hours of direct treatment in the clinic. Also, the children whose parents were trained showed greater generalization of behavior gains than did their clinic-trained peers. This is undoubtedly due to the fact that the parents are present in many different settings and situations, while a clinician is not. However, it appeared that problems in generalization still existed since the children did not tend to generalize their gains in the absence of the parent (i.e., with a stranger). These results served to replicate the Lovaas *et al.* (1973) findings that parent training was superior to clinic treatment in terms of generalization, but extended the findings to suggest that the increased generalization was still limited.

The findings relating to the family were likewise interesting. The measures of psychological and marital adjustment revealed that the parents scored well within the normal range and did not appear to be significantly affected by either type of treatment. On measures of daily activity of the parents and family, the results showed essentially no change for the families in the clinic group but substantial changes for the parent-training group. The parents who were trained reported spending significantly more time than the clinic parents in outside recreation, quiet leisure at home, and social activities. This was deemed as particularly significant given the fact that parents of autistic children often describe feelings of being "chained to their child" because other aspects of their lives seem to be limited by the demands of caring for the child. In a related finding, the parents who were trained reported that after training they spent more time in educational activities, and less time in custodial activities, with their children. This was in contrast to the clinic-group parents who reported no such changes (Koegel, Schreibman, Johnson, O'Neill, & Dunlap, 1984).

While the results of the Koegel *et al.* (1982) research seem to make the superiority of parent-training treatment over clinic-only treatment obvious, the enthusiasm must be tempered with another finding: Before and after treatment, the parents of both groups were asked to fill out questionnaires asking about their confidence in working with their child, how much they felt they could teach their child, and how much they liked the training. Some families who participated in both programs (one at a time) were asked which they preferred. While the objective results of the study clearly showed that both the children and families benefited more from the parent-training treatment than from the clinic treatment, the parent-training program was rated less preferred and the parents felt neither competent nor confident in their abilities to help their child (Schreibman, 1983). These results suggest that simply identifying programs which are effective may not be enough. We need to develop programs that the parents can enjoy and readily accept and perceive as effective.

One set of procedures that holds promise for alleviating the generalization problem with parent training cited above may be those discussed earlier in relation to increasing generalization in clinic settings. These procedures, relating to enhancing motivation, are those of the "natural language paradigm" strategies employed by Koegel *et al.* (1987). Responding to the limitations noted by others in the area of research in training parents of autistic children, Laski, Charlop, and Schreibman (in press) implemented a parent training package consisting of the language-training procedures described by Koegel *et al.* (1987), such as shared control, reinforcing attempts to speak, frequent task variation, and direct reponse-related reinforcement (e.g., access to toy or activity). Parents of four nonverbal and four verbal/echolalic autistic children were instructed in this program and treatment effects were assessed in three nontreatment locations—a clinic playroom, a home free-play setting, and a clinic waiting room. Three categories of behaviors were measured: (a) the frequency with which parents requested that their child perform a verbal behavior (e.g., "What do you want?"); (b) the level of child vocalizations, including imitation, answers, and spontaneous speech; and (c) the level of echolalia exhibited by the children. The results were noteworthy in that the training resulted in a rather dramatic change in both the children's and the parents' behaviors. Following the training, all parents increased the frequency with which they modeled appropriate words and phrases for their child to imitate, prompted verbal responses, and required the child to respond verbally. Assessing the changes in the children's verbal behavior, the results were especially encouraging. Verbal imitation increased for all children, as did answers to questions and spontaneous speech. These data suggest, therefore, that parents can learn these generalization-enhancing teaching procedures and that their use produced generalization speech gains in their children. Importantly, these results also suggest that parent training with these procedures may have the positive effect of changing the way parents verbally interact with their autistic children.

While these investigators did not gather consumer-satisfaction information from these parents, it is interesting to speculate whether such a program might not be more readily acceptable to parents. The incorporation of these generalization-enhancing procedures basically means the incorporation of more "naturalistic" interactions between parent and child, compared to the highly structured discrete-trial procedures used in the earlier research (e.g., Koegel, Schreibman, Britten, Burke, & O'Neill, 1982). It remains to be seen whether such a parent-training package may be easier for parents to learn and utilize, and thus be more acceptable to them.

That parents may, in fact, have a particular acumen regarding treatment effects and acceptability of treatment targets has documentation in the literature. In a social validation assessment of treatment effectiveness, Runco and Schreibman (1983) asked parents of both autistic and normal children to view videotapes of autistic children before and after behavior therapy. The parents were asked to rate the children on a variety of appropriate and inappropriate behaviors, as well as to indicate their willingness to be close to or interact with the children. Consistent with other social validation assessments of behavior therapy efficacy with autistic children (Runco & Schreibman, in press; Schreibman, Koegel, Mills & Burke, 1981; Schreibman, Runco, Mills & Koegel, 1982), both groups of parents judged the children as significantly improved after treatment, and also indicated more willingness to interact with the children after treatment than before treatment. In a subsequent investigation (Runco & Schreibman, 1987) of the importance of various behaviors as targets of treatment, it was found that parents differed from teachers in those behaviors they viewed as most important to change. For example, they did not consider aberrant speech to be a very important focus of treatment compared to other behaviors. Yet we know that language skill is highly correlated with treatment prognosis. Perhaps we need to educate the parents about the importance of certain behaviors. Since we wish parents to be motivated to work with their children (i.e., see the treatment targets as significant) and we want to affect the most extensive treatment gains in the children, perhaps it is necessary to educate the parents about some of the known relationships between specific behaviors and treatment outcome. This might help to ensure that parents are satisfied with the treatment while increasing the chances that the child will receive the maximum benefit from the treatment.

The research described in this chapter is certainly not exhaustive of the work that has been conducted in training parents of autistic and other developmentally disabled children. The extension of the child's treatment to the parents and the home is definitely an important component of the child's treatment. It is apparent, however, that we are still in the process of developing programs that will address all the issues raised so far in the area of parent training.

CLASSROOM INSTRUCTION

Another important treatment extension of a clinic setting is the child's school. School programs for the autistic student are at least as important as programs for the nonhandicapped child, perhaps even more important because of the serious deficits many of these children exhibit. Sadly, until the mid-1970s the educational system was not very responsive to the needs of these children. Prior to this time, many autistic children were denied access to public-school programs and the results were predictable. Many of these children were placed in private schools which varied in quality and often were not specifically geared to the needs of autistic student (i.e., many were for the retarded or otherwise handicapped). Many of the parents could not afford private programs, and being unable to handle the child in the home were forced to place him/her out of the home in residential (e.g., institutional) environments. Thus, until the 1970s, many autistic children were placed in institutions before they reached adolescence.

Two main events changed this situation. First, the Autism Society of America (then called the National Society for Autistic Children) actively led the legal challenges that advocated the rights of these children to an appropriate public education. Second, the passage of Public Law 94–142, the Education for All Handicapped Children's Act, in 1975 provided a federal mandate for such education and further stipulated that autistic and other handicapped children had the right to be educated in the "least restrictive" environment possible. Things were definitely looking up for the education of the autistic child.

The requirement that these children be educated in public-school settings and in appropriate classrooms provided a challenge to those involved in the treatment of autistic children. This, in turn, led to an intensive research effort directed toward the development of effective procedures for educating autistic children in the classroom. While many of the major issues and results of this work will be briefly discussed here, the interested reader is referred for more extensive coverage to Horner *et al.* (1986); Koegel, Rincover and Egel (1982); and Wilcox and Thompson (1980).

Over the last 10 to 15 years, research and practice in educating autistic children has focused on a number of important areas. What follows is an attempt to acquaint the reader with those issues that have been identified as important in the education of all handicapped children, but the emphasis of this discussion will be on the autistic individual. Also, since the behavioral approach is typically considered the treatment of choice for autistic children, the majority of the work in this area is behavioral in nature.

One very important consideration in the development of educational programs that fulfill the spirit and letter of PL94-142 is the curriculum to be taught. Many have advocated that the curriculum for autistic children must be comprehensive, encompassing programming in communication, cognitive and social areas (Handleman, 1986). A truly profound impact on school programming has been the identification and development of "functional" curricula (Brown, Branston, *et al.*, 1979; Brown, Branston-McClean, *et al.*, 1979; Brown, Nietupski, & Hamre-Nietupski, 1976; Dunlap, Koegel, & Egel, 1979; Halle, 1982). Basically, a functional curriculum includes behaviors that are frequently required in the individual's everyday environments (e.g., home, school, community, vocational), are longitudinal, and are age-appropriate (Donnellan & Neel, 1986; Johnson & Koegel, 1982). This curriculum requires the educator to assess the behaviors and the environment of the individual and to target for instruction those behaviors that will be the most useful (and thus reinforced) in the individual's environment. Examples of these behaviors might include learning how to use public transportation, vending machines, kitchen appliances, and playing sports. A nonfunctional curriculum item might be learning how to sort colored pencils into matching-colored holes in a box. Chances are good that this individual will never need to sort pencils in the natural environment he/she normally encounters. A functional curriculum also emphasizes teaching skills that are age-appropriate.

Since many of these children function at a lower age level, the tendency has been to work on tasks that would be appropriate for that younger age. Thus, a severely retarded autistic 18-year-old might be taught to sort knives and forks. While sorting silverware may be useful in the everyday environment, it would likely be very stigmatizing for an 18-year-old to focus on this task. A child that age would be more likely to sort tools or sports equipment. A functional curriculum should also be longitudinal in that the specific skills taught should be ones for which the form and content can be shifted as the student ages, but for which the basic skill required will remain relatively the same (Donnellan & Neel, 1986). An example of a longitudinal skill is the use of a videotape recorder. A younger child might use the skill to access tapes of Disney movies, Sesame Street, or cartoons; an older child might use the same basic skill to access tapes of music videos, television dramas, or age-appropriate movies. The emphasis on development and implementation of functional curricula has had a strong impact on the educational planning of autistic and other handicapped individuals and, undoubtedly, has contributed to the participation of these individuals in integrated classrooms and to the generalization and maintenance of acquired skills.

Another area that has received intensive research attention relates to the type of classroom best suited for the autistic child and how these classrooms should be structured. Many autistic children, especially those with the most severe impairments, are placed in autism classes within the public school system. These classes typically comprised only autistic children or may include children with similar educational needs. It is now known that teachers need to have specific skills for this population of children. For example, Koegel, Russo, Rincover and Schreibman (1982) make the point that when autistic children fail to do well in school they, and not the teachers' skills, are often blamed (i.e., the children "cannot learn"). In other words, no one assesses whether or not the teacher is implementing those techniques known to facilitate learning in autistic children. Specifically, Koegel et al. (1977) systematically addressed this issue and found that when teachers failed to correctly use the behavior modification procedures known to be effective with autistic children (e.g., presentation of instructions, prompts, consequences, use of shaping and chaining), the children showed no measurable improvement on educational tasks. Conversely, when the teachers showed consistently high proficiency in the use of the behavioral procedures, their teaching was effective in producing gains in the children's responding.

Another important area of research has provided an analysis of the skills necessary for autistic children to be successful in a classroom and a set of procedures for teaching those skills. Koegel and his colleagues (Koegel & Rincover, 1974; Rincover & Koegel, 1977a; Rincover, Koegel, & Russo, 1978) identified two main skills that must be taught if autistic children are to benefit from a classroom situation. These skills are: (1) the child must be able to learn while in a large group, and (2) the child must be able to work on individualized tasks without constant teacher supervision.

It has long been reported that handicapped children may acquire behaviors in a one-to-one teaching situation only to have the behaviors fail to generalize to a larger group setting (Bijou, 1972; Koegel & Rincover, 1974; Peterson, Cox &

Bijou, 1971). Koegel and Rincover (1974) found that when eight autistic children were individually taught some basic classroom tasks, the performance of these behaviors by any one child was greatly reduced by the introduction of only one additional child (i.e., in a group of two). These investigators determined that in a classroom of eight autistic children, no new learning occurred even after several weeks of instruction. The necessity of developing a procedure to teach these youngsters to learn in a group was quite apparent. Koegel and Rincover (1974) developed such a procedure. First the children were taught in 1:1 training sessions in which the schedule of reinforcement was thinned from a continuous schedule (where every correct response was reinforced) to one in which every other correct response was reinforced (FR2). Then, when each child performed two responses for only one reinforcer, two children were brought together with one teacher and two aides. The aides alternately reinforced one child on one trial and then the other child on the next trial. When these two children were proficient during these sessions, the schedule of reinforcement was thinned to FR4 (every fourth response was reinforced). At this point, two additional children (who had undergone the same training) were brought together to form a group of four. These procedures were continued until the children could respond correctly in a group of eight. Particularly encouraging was the finding that not only did the children perform the individually taught behaviors when in a group but they also continued to learn new behaviors when instruction was presented by one teacher to the entire group. Thus they could now learn in a regular classroom format, something they did not do before the specialized training procedure.

While learning in a group situation is important, individualized needs and abilities of the children require that some tasks be taught on an individual basis. In such a situation, each child will work on a specific task designed for him/her and work at his/her own pace. Koegel and Rincover (1977) demonstrated how autistic students could be taught to work on an individualized basis without constant teacher supervision. The children were taught to work on long sequences of behavior (preacademic readiness tasks) after teacher instruction. This was done by using a shaping procedure wherein the child was reinforced by the teacher after only one response. The response requirement was then increased to two, then three, and so forth, until the child could complete an entire task on his/her own. A child who has learned both these prerequisite skills, attending in a large group and working on an individualized task, is in a much better position to benefit from the typical classroom environment that is provided for most children.

The development of strategies for classrooms of autistic children has been a major accomplishment in the success of these youngsters in the public-school system. However, the goal is to serve their educational needs within as normal a classroom situation as possible. This, too, is in keeping with the intent of PL 94–142 in that the children have a right to education in the least restrictive (i.e., most "normal") environment in which they can effectively function. Thus, after intensive educational programming many autistic children can make the transition into a less structured setting such as a classroom that is integrated with normal and/or other nonautistic students or, better yet, into a mainstreamed situation in a classroom populated entirely with normal children. Some youngsters may be able to go directly into less restrictive classrooms without prior placement in an autism classroom.

The importance of placement in classrooms with normal children cannot be overstated. As Koegel, Rincover and Russo (1982) point out, special classrooms for the autistic child can be designed to be effective but they still present a potential problem—they provide their own kind of segregation in that they usually comprise solely autistic children. Thus these children are denied the several benefits associated with the nonautistic curriculum taught in regular classrooms and, perhaps more importantly, from the appropriate role models provided by normal children. It seems reasonable that the feasibility of integrating some autistic children into classrooms would be increased if it could be demonstrated that the autistic students can learn from observing the correct responding of their nonhandicapped peers. In fact, it has been demonstrated that autistic children do benefit from role models of normal peers. Egel et al. (1981) demonstrated that autistic students could learn from observing nonhandicapped peers model correct responses. These investigators studied the acquisition of discrimination tasks for four autistic children. After the children failed to learn the tasks with the standard reinforcement and prompt-fading techniques, the children were exposed to normal peers who modeled the correct response. After the model performed the correct response and was reinforced by the teacher, the same instruction and materials were presented to the autistic student. The results indicated that whereas the no-modeling condition did not produce successful learning of the discriminations, each of the children did learn the tasks after the modeling condition was presented. This study is particularly encouraging in that it serves to strengthen the argument that some autistic children will greatly benefit from the opportunity to observe their nonhandicapped peers. It has further been demonstrated that at least some autistic children can also learn from observing the correct responding of other autistic students (Charlop et al., 1983).

Not surprisingly, the focus on integrating autistic children into less restrictive and mainstreamed environments has necessitated research into transitional services to prepare these special students for entry into such classrooms. Many studies in this area have focused on classroom management procedures, preparatory skills to be taught to the autistic students, and the preparation of teachers to facilitate the transition (e.g., Dunlap et al., 1979; Egel, Richman, & Button, 1982; Koegel et al., 1980; Koegel, Rincover, & Russo, 1982; Koegel, Russo, Rincover, & Schreibman, 1982; Koegel & Rincover, 1974; Koegel et al., 1977; Lovaas & Newsom, 1976; Rincover & Koegel, 1977a, b; Rincover et al., 1978; Russo & Koegel, 1977; Sasso, Simpson, & Novak, 1985; Strain, 1983; Voeltz, 1984). Basically, these procedures include teaching the autistic students to work in classroom environments (e.g., learning in groups, working independently on tasks), improving their social skills and responsiveness to peers, teaching teachers the behavioral principles necessary to be effective in programing the transition, and programing for generalization and maintenance.

Other components of a successful educational experience for autistic children include the involvement of the family (e.g., parent training), other support services such as respite care, and the provision of a full-day, year-round program. These components are desirable and even necessary, given the results of research that demonstrate that a clinic or classroom setting alone may be insufficient to provide generalized and maintained treatment gains (e.g., Lovaas et al., 1972) and that some autistic children may regress during prolonged vacations from their school programs (Handleman & Harris, 1984).

In order to meet the complex needs of the autistic child, some programs provide a combination of services including classroom education, parent training, and other support services. Perhaps the most widely known of these programs is the TEACCH program in North Carolina. Founded in 1972 by Eric Schopler, TEACCH (Treatment and Education of Autistic and related Communication handicapped CHildren) provides a broad range of services to autistic and other severely handicapped children and adolescents. Included in these services are comprehensive diagnostic evaluations, individualized treatment, special education, school and other agency consultations, parent training and counseling, and facilitation of parent group activities (Schopler & Olley, 1982; TEACCH Annual Report, 1985–86). The treatment model used in this program is rather eclectic, focusing on developmental and inter-actional influences of the child and the child's social environment (e.g., Reichler & Schopler, 1976). TEACCH personnel feel that the professional overspecialization of many programs leads to treatment centers that are too narrowly focused and thus unable to address the multiple and complex needs of the family. To counteract this the TEACCH program employs staff of varying backgrounds and emphasizes a variety of involvements for the family as well as individualization of treatment programs for the children. Based on its own research evaluation, the program presents documentation of the overall effectiveness of the TEACCH model and on the contributions of individual components. Consonant with much of the research discussed in this book, this research supports the appropriateness of structured and be-haviorally oriented programing in the educational setting (Lansing & Schopler, 1978; Schopler, Brehm, Kinsbourne, & Reichler, 1971; Schopler, Mesibov, & Baker, 1982) and on the positive effects of training parents as co-therapists for their children (Marcus, Lansing, Andrews, & Schopler, 1978; Schopler et al., 1982; Schopler, Mesibov, Shigley, & Bashford, 1984; Schopler & Reichler, 1971; Short, 1984).

Another very important area of recent attention is provision of services to autistic adolescents and adults via other community-based service models. This work is responsive to the different needs of older autistic individuals and to the realities and opportunities afforded in the community. Not only has there been an emphasis on functional curricula (including vocational training, social skills development, independent living skills, and so forth) but de-velopment of effective treatment-delivery models has become a vital part of comprehensive treatment planning. Included here is research on improved residential programs (including improvement of staff performance), the design of effective group homes, the design of programs specifically for adult clients, and programs to facilitate transition to less restrictive environments.

This emphasis on a wide spectrum of community-based services has greatly expanded the resources available to this population. For more extensive discussions of work in this area the reader is referred to Anderson, Christian, and Luce (1986); Christian, Hannah, and Glahn (1984); and Schopler and Mesibov (1983).

The parent-advocacy movement, legislative action, and research into the design and implementation of appropriate classroom interventions, community-based programs and ancillary services—all these have contributed to the brightened picture for the education of autistic children and adults. As the push towards normalization and mainstreaming continues and our skills in facilitating the effectiveness of these programs increase, the picture should be even brighter. These factors as well as the greater availability of respite care and community-based group homes signal the continuation of community participation and the avoidance of institutionalization (e.g., Christian et al., 1984).

SUMMARY

The emphasis on extending the treatment environments of autistic individuals can be traced to three events. First, the finding that limited generalization of treatment effects may occur if intervention is conducted in only one (e.g., clinic) environment. Second, specialized treatment in clinics is costly in terms of both staff time and funding. Third, the recent emphasis on decentralization of treatment services has moved interventions into the community.

One major direction of change for the treatment of autistic children is the inclusion of parents in the treatment program. Parent training has evolved from the early work with parents of nonautistic children and the focus on relatively circumscribed behaviors, to a more recent emphasis on training parents of autistic children in the skills necessary to address the wide variety of behaviors necessary to provide treatment to their handicapped children. There are several advantages to teaching parents to be therapists for their children but perhaps the most important one suggested by research is that clinic treatment effects will likely not be generalized or maintained if the parents are not trained to conduct treatment.

Research on the conduct of parent training has indicated the importance of teaching parents the procedural rules of behavior modification as opposed to teaching them how to achieve specific target behaviors. Armed with the knowledge of general rules, the parents are able to use these skills in working on a variety of child behaviors. Parents have been taught these rules via written materials such as manuals and books, in vivo feedback, videotape models, and lectures.

One major concern that has received attention is the effects of parent training on the entire family. Obviously, if a parent-training program has deleterious effects on the family, it will not be implemented. Work in this area suggests that parent training is likely to have a positive effect on the family, although we still need to develop ways to increase parental satisfaction and confidence. Recent research suggests that we may be making progress in this area.

Classroom instruction for autistic children has advanced considerably since various legal challenges and political actions have forced the educational system to address the needs of this population. Acknowledgment of the importance of providing functional curricula, teacher training for the special needs of autistic student, research into the design of autism classrooms (including teaching the children to learn in groups and to work on independent tasks), and transition of the child to less restrictive classroom environments, have all been extremely important in the current design of educational programs.

In addition to parent training or classroom treatment, some programs have incorporated a combination of services including parent training, classrooms, and other support services in a comprehensive treatment effort. A further extension of treatment environments includes the development of programs for the adolescent and adult autistic individual. Such programs include group homes, transition homes, and other community-based resources.

8

AUTISM:
PROGNOSIS AND
FUTURE OUTLOOK

In 1964 Bernard Rimland concluded that the prognosis for autistic children was extremely poor. "Chances of recovery are slight . . . and the great majority of the victims of infantile autism live out their years in empty hopelessness at home or in institutions" (p. 1). In 1985 Schwartz and Johnson concluded that although recent findings "demonstrate that some autistic children have a more favorable future than others, it should be kept in mind that the majority are destined for lives of little hope" (p. 126). The pessimism reflected in these statements, made 21 years apart, suggests that we have not progressed very far in improving the outlook for victims of autism. While it is only realistic to accept the fact that we have as yet no cure for autism, and that the large majority of these children will remain handicapped to some degree throughout their lives, perhaps we can find grounds for optimism in recent research. Several lines of research are providing needed information both about the nature of the disability as well as the design of effective treatments.

There is little doubt that prior investigations have indicated that without effective treatments autistic children do very poorly. DeMyer *et al.* (1973) reported a follow-up study of 85 autistic boys and 34 autistic girls, as well as a control group of 36 children. The children were reassessed seven years after initial assessment and the results indicated that only a few of the autistic children used speech more complex than that required to make simple requests. The autistic subjects were also found to have significant social problems in that they tended to be loners and remained seriously detached from their social environment. These investigators also reported that the autistic children were functioning below the educable level of mental retardation and that those children who were not using functional language by the age of five had the poorest prognosis. Consonant with these findings are those reported by Ornitz and Ritvo (1976), who reviewed several studies and found that approximately 75% of autistic children are likely to be assessed as mentally retarded throughout life and that between 7 and 28% of these children develop seizures before the age of 18. Like DeMyer *et al.* (1973), Ornitz and Ritvo found that even those autistic children who showed improvement continued to exhibit severe social and interpersonal problems. DeMyer, Hingtgen, and Jackson (1981) summarized the results of six longitudinal studies including both autistic and other severely handicapped children. The studies followed the children into adolescence and adulthood. Looking at the overall outcome, 5 to 19% of the children were reported to have a "good" outcome as suggested by their description as borderline normal, 16 to 27% were reported as "fair," and 55 to 74% as "poor." (These numerical values represent the range reported across the different studies).

One important and potentially useful way to address the issue of prognosis is to determine which characteristics of the children are indicative of future functioning. It is widely accepted that the single most important prognostic indicator (for autistic and other handicapped children) is language ability. As noted above, the presence of functional (i.e., useful) language by the age of five years is commonly considered an important indicator of prognosis; those children who do speak by that age have a significantly better prognosis than those who do not (e.g., DeMyer *et al.*, 1973; Eisenberg, 1956; Lotter, 1974; Rutter, 1968, 1978a, b). In fact, the general correlation between language ability and future level of functioning in a variety of areas has been widely assessed (e.g., Bender, 1973; Rutter, Greenfield, & Lockyer, 1967). Several investigators have broken the issue down to the point of suggesting that particular features of language (e.g., forms of echolalia) are relevant to prognosis (Shapiro, Roberts, & Fish, 1970; Wolff & Chess, 1965; Fay, 1967). Others have focused on identifying the specific areas of functioning related to language ability. For example, Ruttenberg and Wolf (1967) concluded that level of language may be correlated with eventual progress in establishing relationships with other people, while Fish, Shapiro, Campbell and Wile (1968) have suggested that language ability may be correlated with eventual progress on drug or placebo treatment. In addition, since language ability and general cognitive functioning are so closely related, some investigators (e.g., Rutter *et al.*, 1967) have emphasized that IQ may be a more relevant predictor of long-term prognosis than language *per se*. Indeed, higher scores on IQ tests, as well as communicative speech and appropriate play, are considered favorable prognostic indicators (Lotter, 1967).

It is perhaps useful to look at two sets of prognostic indicators. Those that are immutable, at least for the present, and those that relate to treatment effectiveness. In the first category we have seen that these children vary in intellectual and cognitive abilities, genetic endowment, and neurological impairment. We have also seen that research efforts in these areas have focused on potential subgroupings of the autistic population, with the intent of better specifying the precise nature of the impairment(s) involved. Such research holds the potential for isolating factors that will allow us to better identify etiological factors and offering some predictive power that might help clinicians to begin effective treatments much earlier than is presently the case.

The efforts aimed at the development of treatment strategies is another promising line of research. In previous chapters we have discussed the development and advantages of the behavioral approach to treating autistic children and the fact that, to date, this form of treatment is the only one to have been empirically demonstrated as effective for this population. One main advantage of this model is the continuous refinement of techniques, striving for the most comprehensive and generalizable gains possible with the most precise treatment procedures.

As one looks at the almost 30 years of behavioral work with autistic children, one can see that there are certain characteristics of the children and the treatment that have suggested a better treatment outcome. One of these, as also suggested by the studies discussed above, relates to the level and nature of language the child brings with him or her at the start of therapy. A child who has no language has a poorer prognosis for treatment outcome than another child who has some degree of language competence. Thus an echolalic child who may use speech in a limited but communicative manner would be expected to do better than a child who is mute. Another factor seems to be the age of the child. Children who receive treatment at a very young age tend to benefit more from treatment than a child who is older (all else being equal). Not surprisingly, level of intellectual functioning has also been reported to be important in that the more retardation present, the poorer the prognosis in treatment (e.g., Lovaas et al., 1973; Rutter, 1966b). Consistent with the behavioral model of treatment, as discussed in Chapter 6, the presence of behaviors that are well understood would suggest a better prognosis than the presence of behaviors more poorly understood. Hence severe social withdrawal, bizarre attachments, and high rates of self-stimulatory behavior are not the behaviors most welcomed by behavior therapists (nor any clinician). While the cause of autism is undoubtedly organic, the question remains whether or not nonorganic treatments can lead to the profound changes that one might characterize as a "cure" for autism. Basically, can these children be made normal by treatment?

The idea that behavior therapy treatment might allow for some autistic children to become "normal" is advanced by Lovaas (1987), who reported the results of an intensive, comprehensive behavior therapy program for young (under 46 months at start of treatment) autistic children. Two groups of children participated in this study. One group (n = 19) received intensive behavior therapy amounting to more than 40 hours of one-to-one treatment per week. The treatment was provided by trained student therapists who worked with the children in their home, school, and community. Systematically applied contingent aversives were presented for seriously disruptive behaviors. In addition, the parents were also trained and worked with their children as part of the treatment intervention. One control group (n = 19) was presented with the same behavioral treatment except with lesser intensity (less than 10 hours of one-to-one treatment per week) and without the use of systematic physical aversives. A second control group did not receive the behavioral treatment and were included to guard against a sampling or referral bias. All groups received a minimum of two years of treatment. The results of this investigation indicated that 47% of the children receiving the intensive, long-term experimental treatment achieved normal intellectual and educational functioning, with normal-range IQ scores and successful first-grade performance in a regular public school classroom. Another 40% scored in the mildly retarded range and were assigned to special classes for the language delayed, while 10% were profoundly retarded and assigned to classes for the autistic or retarded. In contrast, only 2% of the children in the control groups achieved normal educational and intellectual functioning; 45% scored in the mildly retarded range and were placed in classes for the language delayed; and 53% scored in the severely retarded range and were placed in autism/retardation classes. The enthusiasm for this investigation must be tempered by the existence of certain methodological and interpretive questions. It should also be pointed out that this investigation did not include those autistic children with the lowest levels of functioning at intake and that the results need to be replicated. Yet the results of this investigation suggest that autistic children may indeed achieve more progress in treatment than previously thought possible. Future research along these lines will undoubtedly address the specifics of child characteristics and treatment procedures and elucidate the complex relationships that underly treatment and prognosis.

With the advancements in identification of subgroups of the autistic population, understanding of the nature of the psychopathology, and the development of effective treatments, one can only be more optimistic about the future of these children. It seems as though every facet of the professional community is working and continuously extending our knowledge of this severe disorder. It seems reasonable to believe that we are very close to important answers.

REFERENCES

Altman, K., & Mira, M. (1983). Training parents of developmentally disabled children. In J. L. Matson & F. Andrasik (Eds.), *Treatment issues and innovations in mental retardation*. New York: Plenum.

American Psychiatric Association (1980). *Diagnostic and statistical manual of mental disorders* (3rd ed.). Washington, D.C.

American Psychiatric Association (1987). *Diagnostic and statistical manual of mental disorders* (3rd Edition, Revised). Washington, D.C.

Anderson, L. T., Campbell, M., Grega, D. M., Perry, R., Small, A. M., & Green, W. H. (1984). Haloperidol in infantile autism: Effects on learning and behavioral symptoms. *American Journal of Psychiatry, 141,* 1195-1202.

Anderson, S. R., Christian, W. P., & Luce, S. C. (1986). Transitional residential programming for autistic individuals. *The Behavior Therapist, 9,* 205–211.

Ando, H., & Tsuda, K. (1975). Intrafamilial incidence of autism, cerebral palsy, and mongolism. *Journal of Autism and Childhood Schizophrenia, 5,* 267–274.

Anthony, E. J. (1958). An experimental approach to the psychopathology of childhood autism. *British Journal of Medical Psychology, 31,* 211–225.

Applebaum, E., Egel, A. L., Koegel, R. L., & Imhoff, B. (1979). Measuring musical abilities of autistic children. *Journal of Autism and Developmental Disorders, 9,* 279–285.

August, G. J., & Lockhart, L. H. (1984). Familial autism and the fragile-X chromosome. *Journal of Autism and Developmental Disorders, 14,* 197–204.

August, G. J., Stewart, M. A., & Tsai, L. Y. (1981). The incidence of cognitive disabilities in the siblings of autistic children. *British Journal of Psychiatry, 138,* 416–422.

Axelrod, S., Brantner, J. P., & Meddock, T. D. (1978). Overcorrection: A review and critical analysis. *Journal of Special Education, 12,* 367–391.

Azrin, N. J., Gottlieb, L., Hughart, L., Wesolowski, M. D., & Rahn, T. (1975). Eliminating self-injurious behavior by educative procedures. *Behavior Research and Therapy, 13,* 101–111.

Azrin, N. J., Kaplan, S. J., & Foxx, R. M. (1973). Autism reversal: Eliminating stereotyped self-stimulation of retarded individuals. *American Journal of Mental Deficiency, 18,* 241–248.

Bachman, J. A. (1972). Self-injurious behavior: A behavioral analysis. *Journal of Abnormal Psychology, 80,* 211–224.

Baer, D. M., Peterson, R. F., & Sherman, J. A. (1967). The development of imitation by reinforcing behavior similarity to a model. *Journal of the Experimental Analysis of Behavior, 10,* 405–416.

Baer, D. M., & Wolf, M. M. (1970). The entry into natural communities of reinforcement. In R. Ulrich, T. Stachnik, and J. Mabry (Eds.), *Control of human behavior (vol. 2)*, Glenview, IL: Scott, Foresman.

Baker, B. L. (1984). Intervention with families with young, severely handicapped children. In J. Blacher (Ed.), *Severely handicapped young children and their families: Research in review*. Orlando, FL: Academic Press.

Baker, B. L., & Heifetz, L. J. (1976). The READ Project: Teaching manuals for parents of retarded children. In T. D. Tjossem (Ed.), *Intervention strategies for high risk infants and young children*. Baltimore: University Park Press.

Ball, J. (1978). *A pragmatic analysis of autistic children's language with respect to aphasic and normal language development*. Unpublished doctoral dissertation, Melbourne University.

Baltaxe, C. A. (1977). Pragmatic deficits in the language of autistic adolescents. *Journal of Pediatric Psychology, 2*, 176–180.

Baltaxe, C. A. (1981). Acoustic characteristics of prosody in autism. In P. Mittler (Ed.), *Frontiers of knowledge in mental retardation*. Baltimore: University Park Press.

Baltaxe, C. A. (1984). Use of contrastive stress in normal, aphasic, and autistic children. *Journal of Speech and Hearing Research, 27*, 97–105.

Baltaxe, C. A., & Simmons, J. Q. (1975). Language in childhood psychosis: A review. *Journal of Speech and Hearing Disorders, 30*, 439–458.

Bartak, L., Bartolucci, G., & Pierce, S. J. (1977). A preliminary comparison of phonological development in autistic, normal, and mentally retarded subjects. *British Journal of Disorders of Communication, 12*, 137–147.

Bartak, L., & Rutter, M. (1973). Special educational treatment of autistic children: A comparative study. I. Design of study and characteristics of units. *Journal of Child Psychology and Psychiatry, 14*, 151–179.

Bartak, L., & Rutter, M. (1974). The use of personal pronouns by autistic children. *Journal of Autism and Childhood Schizophrenia, 4*, 217–222.

Bartak, L., & Rutter, M. (1976). Differences between mentally retarded and normally intelligent autistic children. *Journal of Autism and Childhood Schizophrenia, 6*, 109–120.

Bartak, L., Rutter, M., & Cox, A. (1975). A comparative study of infantile autism and specific developmental receptive language disorder. I. The children. *British Journal of Psychiatry, 126*, 127–145.

Bartolucci, G., Pierce, S. J., Streiner, D., & Eppel, P. T. (1976). Phonological investigation of verbal autistic and mentally retarded subjects. *Journal of Autism and Childhood Schizophrenia, 6*, 303–316.

Bauman, M. L., & Kemper, T. L. (1985). Histo-anatomic observations of the brain in early infantile autism. *Neurology, 35*, 866–874.

Beisler, J. M., Tsai, L. Y., & Stiefel, B. (1986). Brief report: The effects of fenfluramine on communication skills in autistic children. *Journal of Autism and Developmental Disorders, 16*, 227–233.

Bell, R. Q. (1968). A reinterpretation of the direction of effects in studies of socialization. *Psychological Review, 75*, 81–95.

Bell, R. Q. (1971). Stimulus control of parent or caretaker behavior by offspring. *Developmental Psychology, 4*, 63–72.

Bender, L. (1947). Childhood schizophrenia, clinical study of one hundred schizophrenic children. *American Journal of Orthopsychiatry, 17*, 40–56.

Bender, L. (1973). The life course of children with schizophrenia. *American Journal of Psychiatry, 130*, 783–786.

Berkowitz, B. P., & Graziano, A. M. (1972). Training parents as behavior therapists: A review. *Behaviour Research and Therapy, 10*, 297–317.

Berlyne, D. E. (1950). Novelty and curiosity as determinants of exploratory behavior. *British Journal of Psychology, 41*, 68–80.

Berlyne, D. E. (1955). The arousal and satiation of perceptual curiosity in the rat. *Journal of Comparative and Physiological Psychology, 48*, 238–246.

Berlyne, D. E. (1960). *Conflict, arousal and curiosity*. New York: McGraw-Hill.

Bernard-Optiz, V. (1982). Pragmatic analysis of the communicative behavior of an autistic child. *Journal of Speech and Hearing Disorders, 47*, 99–109.

Bettelheim, B. (1967). *The empty fortress*. New York: Free Press.

Bettelheim, B. (1974). *A home for the heart*. New York: Knopf.

Bijou, S. W. (1972). The technology of teaching young handicapped children. In S. W. Bijou & E. Ribes-Inesta (Eds.), *Behavior modification: Issues and extensions*. New York: Academic Press.

Blackstock, E. G. (1978). Cerebral asymmetry and the development of infantile autism. *Journal of Autism and Childhood Schizophrenia, 8*, 339–353.

Bleuler, E. (1919). *Das Autistische—Undisziplinierte Denken in der Mediziin und seine Überwindung*. Berlin: Springer.

Bleuler, E. (1950). *Dementia praecox or the group of schizophrenias*. Translated by J. Zinkin. New York: International Universities Press.

Bostow, D. E., & Bailey, J. B. (1969). Modification of severe disruptive and aggressive behavior using brief timeout and reinforcement procedures. *Journal of Applied Behavior Analysis, 2*, 31–38.

Brask, B. H. (1970). A prevalence investigation of childhood psychosis. Paper presented at the 16th Scandinavian Congress of Psychiatry, 1970. Cited by L. Wing, (1976). *Early childhood autism*. Oxford: Pergamon Press.

Bronfenbrenner, U. (1979). *The ecology of human development*. Cambridge, MA: Harvard University Press.

Brown, L., Branston-McClean, M. B., Baumgart, D., Vincent, L., Falvey, M., & Schroeder, J. (1979). Utilizing the characteristics of a variety of current and subsequent least restrictive environments as factors in the development of curricular content for severely handicapped students. *AAESPH Review, 4*, 407–424.

Brown, L., Branston, M. B., Hamre-Nietupski, S., Pumpian, I., Certo, N., & Gruenewald, L. (1979). A strategy for developing chronological age appropriate and functional curricular content for severely handicapped adolescents and young adults. *Journal of Special Education, 13*, 81–90.

Brown, L., Nietupski, J., & Hamre-Nietupski, S. (1976). The criterion of ultimate functioning and public school services for severely handicapped students. In L. Brown, N. Certo, & T. Crowner (Eds.), *Papers and programs related to public school services for secondary-age severely handicapped students* (Vol. VI). Madison, WI: Madison Metropolitan School District.

Bucher, B., & Lovaas, O. I. (1968). Use of aversive stimulation in behavior modification. In M. R. Jones (Ed.), Miami symposium on the prediction of behavior, 1967: Aversive stimulation. Coral Gables, FL: University of Miami Press.

Buell, J., Stoddard, P., Harris, F. R., & Baer, D. M. (1968). Collateral social development accompanying reinforcement of outdoor play in a preschool child. *Journal of Applied Behavior Analysis, 1*, 167–173.

Burchard, J. D., & Tyler, V. O., Jr. (1965). The modification of delinquent behavior through operant conditioning. *Behaviour Research and Therapy, 2*, 245–250.

Burke, J. C., & Koegel, R. L. (in preparation). Stimulus overselectivity and autistic children's social responsiveness and incidental learning. University of California, Santa Barbara.

Campbell, M. (1979). Pharmacotherapy. In M. Rutter & E. Schopler (Eds.), *Autism: A reappraisal of concepts and treatment*. New York: Plenum.

Campbell, M., Anderson, L. T., Meier, M., Cohen, I. L., Small, A. M., Samit, C., & Sachar, E. J. (1978). A comparison of haloperidol and behavior therapy and their interaction in autistic children. *Journal of the American Academy of Child Psychiatry, 17*, 640–655.

Campbell, M., Deutsch, S. I., Perry, R., Wolsky, B. B., & Palij, M. (1986). Short-term efficacy and safety of fenfluramine in hospitalized preschool-age autistic children: An open study. *Psychopharmacology Bulletin, 22*, 141–147.

Campbell, M., Fish, B., David, R., Shapiro, T., Collins, P., & Koh, C. (1972). Response to triiodothyronine and dextroamphetamine: A study of preschool schizophrenic children. *Journal of Autism and Childhood Schizophrenia, 2*, 343–358.

Campbell, M., Green, W. H., & Deutsch, S. I. (1985). *Child and adolescent psychopharmacology*. Beverly Hills: Sage Publications.

Campbell, M., Small, A. M., Collins, P., Friedman, E., David, R., & Genieser, N. (1976). Levodopa and levoamphetamine: A crossover study in young schizophrenic children. *Current Therapeutic Research, 19*, 70–86.

Cantor, J. H., & Cantor, G. M. (1964a). Children's observing behavior as related to amount and recency of stimulus familiarization. *Journal of Experimental Child Psychology, 1*, 241–247.

Cantor, J. H., & Cantor, G. M. (1964b). Observing behavior in children as a function of stimulus novelty. *Child Development, 35*, 119–128.

Cantwell, D. P., Baker, B. L., & Rutter, M. (1978). Family factors. In M. Rutter and E. Schopler (Eds.), *Autism: A reappraisal of concepts and treatment*. New York: Plenum Press.

Carr, E. G. (1977). The motivation of self-injurious behavior: A review of some hypotheses. *Psychological Bulletin, 84*, 800–816.

Carr, E. G. (1979). Teaching autistic children to use sign language: Some research issues. *Journal of Autism and Developmental Disorders, 9*, 345–359.

Carr, E. G. (1980). Generalization of treatment effects following educational intervention with autistic children and youth. In B. Wilcox & A. Thompson (Eds.), *Critical issues in educating autistic children and youth*. U.S. Department of Education, Office of Special Education, November.

Carr, E. G. (1982a). *How to teach sign language to developmentally disabled children*. Lawrence, KS: H & H Enterprises.

Carr, E. G. (1982b). Sign language. In R. L. Koegel, A. Rincover, & A. L. Egel (Eds.), *Educating and understanding autistic children*. San Diego: College-Hill Press.

Carr, E. G., Binkoff, J. A., Kologinsky, E., & Eddy, M. (1978). Acquisition of sign language by autistic children. I. Expressive labeling. *Journal of Applied Behavior Analysis, 11*, 489–501.

Carr, E. G., & Durand, V. M. (1985a). The social-communicative basis of severe behavior problems in children. In S. Reiss & R. Bootzin (Eds.), *Theoretical issues in behavior therapy*. New York: Academic Press.

Carr, E. G., & Durand, V. M. (1985b). Reducing behavior problems through functional communication training. *Journal of Applied Behavior Analysis, 18*, 111–126.

Carr, E. G., & Kologinsky, E. (1983). Acquisition of sign language by autistic
children. II. Spontaneity and generalization effects. *Journal of Applied Behavior
Analysis, 16*, 297–314.

Carr, E. G., Kologinsky, E., & Leff-Simon, S. (1987). Acquisition of sign language by
autistic children. III. Generalized descriptive phrases. *Journal of Autism and
Developmental Disorders, 17*, 217–230.

Carr, E. G., Newsom, C. D., & Binkoff, J. A. (1976). Stimulus control of self-
destructive behavior in a psychotic child. *Journal of Abnormal Child Psychology,
4*, 139–153.

Carr, E. G., Schreibman, L., & Lovaas, O. I. (1975). Control of echolalic speech in
psychotic children. *Journal of Abnormal Child Psychology, 3*, 331–351.

Charlop, M. H. (1983). The effects of echolalia on acquisition and generalization of
receptive labeling in autistic children. *Journal of Applied Behavior Analysis, 16*,
111–126.

Charlop, M. H., & Greenberg, F. (1985a). *The use of self-stimulation as a reinforcer:
A close look at a feasible approach.* Paper presented at a meeting of the Association for Behavior Analysis, Columbus, Ohio.

Charlop, M. H., & Greenberg, F. (1985b). *Using ritualistic and stereotypic responses
as reinforcers for autistic children.* Paper presented at the annual meeting of the
American Psychological Association, Los Angeles.

Charlop, M. H., & Kurtz, P. F. (1987). *Using aberrant behaviors as reinforcers with
autistic children.* Paper presented at a meeting of the Association for Behavior
Analysis, Nashville, TN.

Charlop, M. H., Schreibman, L., & Thibodeau, M. G. (1985). Increasing spontaneous
verbal responding in autistic children using a time delay procedure. *Journal of
Applied Behavior Analysis, 18*, 155–166.

Charlop, M. H., Schreibman, L., & Tryon, A. S. (1983). Learning through observation: The effects of peer modeling on acquisition and generalization in autistic
children. *Journal of Abnormal Child Psychology, 11*, 355–366.

Chess, S. (1977). Follow-up report on autism in congenital rubella. *Journal of Autism
and Childhood Schizophrenia, 7*, 69–81.

Child is father. (1960, July). *Time*, 78.

Christian, W. P., Hannah, G. T., & Glahn, T. J. (Eds.). (1984). *Programming effective
human services.* New York: Plenum Press.

Chruch, R. M. (1963). The varied effects of punishment on behavior. *Psychological
Review, 70*, 369–374.

Churchill, D. W. (1971). Effects of success and failure in psychotic children. *Archives
of General Psychiatry, 25*, 208–214.

Churchill, D. W. (1972). The relation of infantile autism and early childhood schizophrenia to developmental language disorders of childhood. *Journal of Autism and
Childhood Schizophrenia, 2*, 182–197.

Churchill, D. W., Alpern, G. D., & DeMyer, M. K. (Eds.). (1971). *Infantile Autism.*
Springfield: Charles C Thomas.

Churchill, D. W., & Bryson, C. Q. (1972). Looking and approach behaviour of
psychotic and normal children as a function of adult attention and preoccupation.
Comparative Psychiatry, 13, 171–177.

Clarizio, H. F., & McCoy, G. F. (1983). *Behavior disorders in children* (3rd. Ed.). New York: Harper and Row.

Clark, P., & Rutter, M. (1977). Compliance and resistance in autistic children. *Journal of Autism and Childhood Schizophrenia, 7*, 33–48.

Clark, P., & Rutter, M. (1979). Task difficulty and task performance in autistic children. *Journal of Child Psychology and Psychiatry, 20*, 271–285.

Cohen, I. L., Campbell, M., Posner, D., Small, A. M., Triebel, D., & Anderson, L. T. (1980). Behavioral effects of haloperidol in young autistic children: An objective analysis using a within-subjects reversal design. *Journal of the Academy of Child Psychiatry, 19*, 665–677.

Coleman, M. (1976). Introduction. In M. Coleman (Ed.), *The autistic syndromes*. New York: American Elsevier.

Coleman, M., & Rimland, B. (1976). Familial autism. In M. Coleman (Ed.), *The autistic syndromes*. New York: American Elsevier.

Courchesne, E. (1987). A neurophysiological view of autism. In E. Schopler and G. Mesibov (Eds.), *Neurobiological issues in autism*. New York: Plenum Press.

Courchesne, E., Hesselink, J. R., Jernigan, T. L., & Yeung-Courchesne, R. (1987). Abnormal neuroanatomy in a non-retarded person with autism: Unusual findings using magnetic resonance imaging. *Archives of Neurology, 44*, 335–341.

Cox, A., Rutter, M., Newman, S., & Bartak, L. (1975). A comparative study of infantile autism and specific developmental receptive language disorder: II. Parental characteristics. *British Journal of Psychiatry, 126*, 146–159.

Creak, M. (1961). Schizophrenic syndrome in childhood: Progress report of a working party. *Cerebral Palsy Bulletin, 3*, 501–504.

Creak, M. (1963). Childhood psychosis: A review of 100 cases. *British Journal of Psychiatry, 109*, 84–89.

Creak, M., & Ini, S. (1960). Families of psychotic children. *Journal of Child Psychology and Psychiatry, 1*, 156–175.

Creak, M., & Pampiglione, G. (1969). Clinical and EEG studies on a group of 35 psychotic children. *Developmental Medicine and Child Neurology, 11*, 218–227.

Creedon, M. P. (1973). *Language development in nonverbal autistic children using a simultaneous communication system.* Paper presented at the Society for Research in Child Development Meeting, Philadelphia.

Dangel, R. F., & Polster, R. A. (1984). *Parent training: Foundations of research and practice.* New York: The Guilford Press.

Darley, F. L. (1964). *Diagnosis and appraisal of communication disorders.* Englewood Cliffs, NJ: Prentice-Hall.

Darr, G. C., & Worden, F. G. (1951). Case report twenty-eight years after an infantile autistic disorder. *American Journal of Orthopsychiatry, 21*, 559–570.

Davids, A. (1975). Childhood psychosis: The problem of differential diagnosis. *Journal of Autism and Childhood Schizophrenia, 5*, 129–138.

Dawson, G. D. (1979). *Early infantile autism and hemispheric specialization.* Unpublished doctoral dissertation, University of Washington.

Dawson, G. D., Warrenburg, S., & Fuller, P. (1982). Cerebral lateralization in individuals diagnosed as autistic in early childhood. *Brain and Language, 15*, 353–368.

DeMyer, M. K. (1975). Research in infantile autism: A strategy and its results. *Biological Psychiatry, 10*, 433–450.

DeMyer, M. K. (1979). *Parents and children in autism*. Toronto: John Wiley and Sons.

DeMyer, M. K., Alpern, G. D., Barton, S., DeMyer, W. E., Churchill, D. W., Hingtgen, J. N., Bryson, C. Q., Pontius, W., & Kimberlin, C. (1972). Imitation in autistic, early schizophrenic and non-psychotic subnormal children. *Journal of Autism and Childhood Schizophrenia, 2*, 264–287.

DeMyer, M. K., Barton, S., Alpern, G. D., Kimberlin, C., Allen, J., Yang, E., & Steele, R. (1974). The measured intelligence of autistic children. *Journal of Autism and Childhood Schizophrenia, 4*, 42–60.

DeMyer, M. K., Barton, S., DeMyer, W. E., Norton, J. A., Allen, J., & Steele, R. (1973). Prognosis in autism: A follow-up study. *Journal of Autism and Childhood Schizophrenia, 3*, 199–246.

DeMyer, M. K., Barton, S., & Norton, J. A. (1972). A comparison of adaptive, verbal, and motor profiles of psychotic and nonpsychotic subnormal children. *Journal of Autism and Childhood Schizophrenia, 2*, 359–377.

DeMyer, M. K., Churchill, D. W., Pontius, W., & Gilkey, K. M. (1971). A comparison of five diagnostic systems for childhood schizophrenia and infantile autism. *Journal of Autism and Childhood Schizophrenia, 1*, 175–189.

DeMyer, M. K., Hingtgen, J. N., & Jackson, R. K. (1981). Infantile autism reviewed: A decade of research. *Schizophrenia Bulletin, 7*, 388–451.

DeMyer, M. K., Pontius, W., Norton, J. A., Barton, S., Allen, J., & Steele, R. (1972). Parental practices and innate activity in normal, autistic, and brain-damaged infants. *Journal of Autism and Childhood Schizophrenia, 2*, 49–66.

Denkla, M. B. (1986). New diagnostic criteria for autism and related behavioral disorders—guidelines for research protocols. *Journal of the American Academy of Child Psychiatry, 25*, 221–224.

DesLauriers, A. M. (1978). Play, symbols, and the development of language. In M. Rutter & E. Schopler (Eds.), *Autism: A reappraisal of concepts and treatment*. New York: Plenum Press.

Despert, J. L. (1951). Some considerations relating to the genesis of autistic behavior in children. *American Journal of Orthopsychiatry, 21*, 335–350.

Deykin, E. Y., & MacMahon, B. (1979). The incidence of seizures among children with autistic symptoms. *American Journal of Psychiatry, 136*, 1310–1312.

Dietz, S. M., & Repp, A. L. (1973). Decreasing classroom misbehavior through the use of DRL schedules of reinforcement. *Journal of Applied Behavior Analysis, 6*, 457–463.

Donnellan, A. M., & Neel, R. S. (1986). New directions in educating students with autism. In R. H. Horner, L. H. Meyer, & H. D. Fredericks (Eds.), *Education of learning with severe handicaps: Exemplary service strategies*. Baltimore: Paul H. Brookes Publishing Co.

Drabman, R. S., Spitalnik, R., & O'Leary, K. D. (1973). Teaching self-control to disruptive children. *Journal of Abnormal Psychology, 82*, 10–16.

Duchan, J. F. (1983). Autistic children are noninteractive: Or so we say. *Seminars in Speech and Language, 4*, 53–61.

Dunlap, G., Koegel, R. L., & Egel, A. L. (1979). Autistic children in school. *Exceptional Children, 45*, 552–558.

Dunlap, G., Koegel, R. L., Johnson, J., & O'Neill, R. E. (1987). Maintaining performance of autistic clients in community settings with delayed contingencies. *Journal of Applied Behavior Analysis, 20*, 185–191.

Dunlap, G., Koegel, R. L., & O'Neill, R. E. (1985). Pervasive developmental disorders. In P. H. Bornstein & A. E. Kazdin (Eds.), *Handbook of clinical behavior therapy with children*. Homewood, IL: Dorsey Press.

Eason, L. J., White, M. J., & Newsom, C. D. (1982). Generalized reduction of self-stimulatory behavior: An effect of teaching appropriate play to autistic children. *Analysis and Intervention in Developmental Disabilities, 2*, 157–169.

Egel, A. L. (1981). Reinforcer variation: Implications for motivating developmentally disabled children. *Journal of Applied Behavior Analysis, 14*, 345–350.

Egel, A. L., Richman, G. S., & Button, C. (1982). Integration of autistic children with normal children. In R. L. Koegel, A. Rincover, & A. L. Egel (Eds.), *Educating and understanding autistic children*. San Diego: College Hill Press.

Egel, A. L., Richman, G. S., & Koegel, R. L. (1981). Normal peer models and autistic children's learning. *Journal of Applied Behavior Analysis, 14*, 3–12.

Eimas, P. (1969). Multiple-cue discrimination learning in children. *Psychological Record, 19*, 417–424.

Eisenberg, L. (1956). The autistic child in adolescence. *American Journal of Psychiatry, 112*, 607–612.

Eisenberg, L., & Kanner, L. (1956). Early infantile autism: 1943–1955. *American Journal of Orthopsychiatry, 26*, 55–65.

Epstein, L. H., Doke, L. A., Sajwaj, T. E., Sorell, S., & Rimmer, B. (1974). Generality and side effects of overcorrection. *Journal of Applied Behavior Analysis, 7*, 385–390.

Favell, J. E., McGimsey, J. F., & Jones, M. L. (1978). The use of physical restraint in the treatment of self-injury and as positive reinforcement. *Journal of Applied Behavior Analysis, 11*, 225–241.

Fay, W. H. (1967). Childhood echolalia: A group study of late abatement. *Folia Phoniatrica, 19*, 297–306.

Fay, W. H. (1969). On the basis of autistic echolalia. *Journal of Communication Disorders, 2*, 38–47.

Fay, W. H. (1979). Personal pronouns and the autistic child. *Journal of Autism and Developmental Disorders, 9*, 247–260.

Fay, W. H., & Schuler, A. L. (1980). *Emerging language in autistic children*. Baltimore: University Park Press.

Fein, D., Pennington, B., Markowitz, P., Braverman, M., & Waterhouse, L. (1986). Towards a neuropsychological model of autism: Are the social deficits primary? *Journal of the American Academy of Child Psychiatry, 25*, 198–217.

Ferster, C. B. (1961). Positive reinforcement and behavioral deficits of autistic children. *Child Development, 32*, 437–456.

Ferster, C. B., & DeMyer, M. K. (1961). The development of performance in autistic children in an automatically controlled environment. *Journal of Chronic Diseases, 13*, 312–345.

Ferster, C. B., & DeMyer, M. K. (1962). A method for the experimental analysis of the behavior of autistic children. *American Journal of Orthopsychiatry, 32*, 89–98.

Fischer, M. A., & Zeaman, D. (1973). An attention-retention theory of retardate discrimination learning. In N. R. Ellis (Eds.), *International review of research in mental retardation* (Vol. 6). New York: Academic Press.

Fish, B., Shapiro, T., & Campbell, M. (1966). Long-term prognosis and the response of schizophrenic children to drug therapy: A controlled study of trifluoperazine. *American Journal of Psychiatry, 123*, 32–39.

Fish, B., Shapiro, T., Campbell, M., & Wile, R. A. (1968). A classification of schizophrenic children under five years. *American Journal of Psychiatry, 124*, 1415–1423.

Folstein, S., & Rutter, M. (1977). Genetic influences and infantile autism. *Nature, 265*, 726–728.

Forehand, R., & Atkeson, B. M. (1977). Generality of treatment effects with parents as therapists: A review of assessment and implementation procedures. *Behavior Therapy, 8*, 575–593.

Fox, J.J., Gunter, P., Brady, M. J., Bambara, L. M., Spiegel-McGill, P., & Shores, R. E. (1984). Using multiple peer-exemplars to develop generalized social responding of an autistic girl. *Monographs in Behavior Disord:rs, 7*, 17–26.

Foxx, R. M., & Azrin, N. J. (1972). Restitution: A method for eliminating aggressive-disruptive behavior of retarded and brain-damaged patients. *Behavior Therapy, 10*, 15–27.

Foxx, R. M., & Azrin, N. J. (1973). The elimination of autistic self-stimulatory behavior by overcorrection. *Journal of Applied Behavior Analysis, 6*, 1–14.

Frankel, F., & Simmons, J. Q. (1976). Self-injurious behavior in schizophrenic and retarded children. *American Journal of Mental Deficiency, 80*, 512–522.

Freeman, B. J., & Ritvo, E. R. (1976). Parents as paraprofessionals. In E. R. Ritvo (Ed.), *Autism: Diagnosis, current research, and management.* New York: Spectrum Publications.

Freeman, B. J., & Ritvo, E. R. (1984). The syndrome of autism: Establishing the diagnosis and principles of management. *Pediatric Annals, 13*, 284–305.

Freeman, B. J., Ritvo, E. R., Guthrie, D., Schroth, P., & Ball, J. (1978). The Behavior Observation Scale for Autism: Initial methodology, data analysis, and preliminary findings on 89 children. *Journal of the American Academy of Child Psychiatry, 17*, 576–588.

Freeman, B. J., Ritvo, E., & Miller, R. (1975). An operant procedure to teach an echolalic, autistic child to answer questions appropriately. *Journal of Autism and Childhood Schizophrenia, 5*, 169–176.

Funderburk, S. J., Carter, J., Tanguay, P., Freeman, B. J., & Westlake, J. R. (1983). Parental reproductive problems and gestational hormonal exposure in autistic and schizophrenic children. *Journal of Autism and Developmental Disorders, 13*, 325–332.

Fyffe, C., & Prior, M. (1978). Evidence for language recording in autistic, retarded and normal children: A re-examination. *British Journal of Psychology, 49*, 393–402.

Geller, E., Ritvo, E. R., Freeman, B. J., & Yuwiler, A. (1982). Preliminary observations on the effect of fenfluramine on blood serotonin and symptoms in three autistic boys. *New England Journal of Medicine, 307*, 165.

Gillberg, C. (1980). Maternal age and infantile autism. *Journal of Autism and Developmental Disorders, 10*, 293–297.

Gillberg, C. (1983). Identical triplets with infantile autism and the fragile X syndrome. *British Journal of Psychiatry, 143*, 256–260.

Gillberg, C., & Gillberg, I. C. (1983). Infantile autism: A total population study of reduced optimality in the pre, peri-, and neonatal period. *Journal of Autism and Developmental Disorders, 13*, 153–166.

Gillberg, C., & Schaumann, H. (1982). Social class and infantile autism. *Journal of Autism and Developmental Disorders, 12*, 223–228.

Gittelman, M., & Birch, H. G. (1967). Childhood schizophrenia: Intellect, neurological status, perinatal risk, prognosis and family pathology. *Archives of General Psychiatry, 17*, 16–25.

Glogower, F., & Sloop, W. E. (1976). Two strategies of group training of parents as effective behavior modifiers. *Behavior Therapy, 7*, 177–184.

Goldfarb, W. (1956). Receptor preferences in schizophrenic children. *Archives of Neurology and Psychiatry, 76*, 643–652.

Goldfarb, W. (1961). *Childhood schizophrenia.* Cambridge, MA: Harvard University Press.

Goldfine, P. E., McPherson, P. M., Adair, G., Hardesty, V. A., Beauregard, L. J., & Gordon, S. B. (1985). Association of fragile X syndrome with autism. *American Journal of Psychiatry, 142*, 108–110.

Gordon, S. B., & Davidson, N. (1981). Behavioral parent training. In A. S. Gurman & D. P. Kniskern (Eds.), *Handbook of family therapy.* New York: Brunner/Mazel.

Graziano, A. M. (1977). Parents as behavior therapists. In M. Hersen, R. M. Eisler, & P. M. Miller (Eds.), *Progress in behavior modification*, Vol. 4. New York: Academic Press.

Greenfeld, J. (1972). *A child called Noah: A family journey.* New York: Holt, Rinehart, & Winston.

Griffith, R., & Ritvo, E. R. (1967). Echolalia: Concerning the dynamics of syndrome. *Journal of the American Academy of Child Psychiatry, 6*, 184–193.

Hale, G. A., & Morgan, J. S. (1973). Development trends in children's component selection. *Journal of Experimental Child Psychology, 15*, 302–314.

Hall, R. V., & Broden, M. (1967). Behavior changes in brain-injured children through social reinforcement. *Journal of Experimental Child Psychology, 5*, 463–479.

Halle, J. W. (1982). Teaching functional language to the handicapped: An integrative model of the natural environment teaching techniques. *Journal of the Association for the Severely Handicapped, 7*, 29–36.

Halle, J. W., Marshall, A. M., & Spradlin, J. E. (1979). Time delay: A technique to increase language use and facilitate generalization in retarded children. *Journal of Applied Behavior Analysis, 12*, 431–439.

Handleman, J. S., & Harris, S. L. (1984). Can summer vacation be detrimental to learning? An empirical look. *The Exceptional Child, 31*, 151–159.

Hanson, D. R., & Gottesman, I.I. (1976). The genetics, if any, of infantile autism and childhood schizophrenia. *Journal of Autism and Childhood Schizophrenia, 6*, 209–234.

Harris, S. L. (1984). Intervention planning for the family of the autistic child: A multilevel assessment of the family system. *Journal of Marital and Family Therapy, 10*, 157–166.

Harris, S. L. (1986). Families of children with autism: Issues for the behavior therapist. *The Behavior Therapist, 9*, 175–177.

Harris, S. L., & Wolchik, S. A. (1979). Suppression of self-stimulation. Three alternative strategies. *Journal of Applied Behavior Analysis, 12*, 185–198.

Harris, S. L., Wolchik, S. A., & Milch, R. E. (1983). Changing the speech of autistic children and their parents. *Child and Family Behavior Therapy, 4*, 151–173.

Harris, S. L., Wolchik, S. A., & Weitz, S. (1981). The acquisition of language skills by autistic children: Can parents do the job? *Journal of Autism and Developmental Disorders, 11*, 373–384.

Hart, B. (1980). Pragmatics and language development. In B. B. Lahey and A. E. Kazdin (Eds.), *Advances in clinical child psychology*, Volume 3. New York: Plenum.

Hart, B., & Risley, T. R. (1980). In vivo language intervention: Unanticipated general effects. *Journal of Applied Behavior Analysis, 13*, 407–432.

Hartman, H., Kris, E., & Lowenstein, R. (1946). Comments on the formation of the psychic structure. *Psychoanalytic Study of the Child, 2*, 11–38.

Haslam, J. (1809). *Observations on madness and meloncholy*. London: Hayden.

Hécaen, H. (1976). Acquired aphasia in children and the ontogenesis of hemispheric functional specialization. *Brain and Language, 3*, 114–134.

Helm, D. T., & Kozloff, M. A. (1986). Research on parent training: Shortcomings and remedies. *Journal of Autism and Developmental Disorders, 16*, 1–22.

Hemsley, R., Howlin, P. A., Berger, M., Hersov, L., Holbrook, D., Rutter, M., & Yule, W. (1978). Training autistic children in a family context. In M. Rutter & E. Schopler (Eds.), *Autism: A reappraisal of concepts and treatment*. New York: Plenum Press.

Herendeen, D. L., Jeffrey, D. B., & Graham, M. C. (1974). *Reduction of self-stimulation in institutionalized children: Overcorrection and reinforcement for nonresponding*. Paper presented at the eighth annual meeting of the Association for Advancement of Behavior Therapy, Chicago.

Hermelin, B., & O'Connor, N. (1968). Measures of the occipital alpha rhythm in normal, subnormal and autistic children. *British Journal of Psychiatry, 114*, 603–610.

Hermelin, B., & O'Connor, N. (1970). *Psychological experiments with autistic children*. Oxford: Pergamon.

Hetzler, B., & Griffin, J. (1981). Infantile autism and the temporal lobe of the brain. *Journal of Autism and Developmental Disorders, 11*, 317–330.

Holman, J., & Baer, D. M. (1979). Facilitating generalization of on-task behavior through self-monitoring of academic tasks. *Journal of Autism and Developmental Disorders, 9*, 429–446.

Holroyd, J. (1974). The questionnaire on resources and stress: An instrument to measure family response to a handicapped family member. *Journal of Community Psychology, 2*, 92–94.

Horner, R. H., Dunlap, G., & Koegel, R. L. (Eds.), (1988). *Generalization and maintenance: Lifestyle changes in applied settings*. New York: Pergamon.

Horner, R. H., Meyer, L. H., & Fredericks, H. D. (Eds.). (1986). *Education of learning with severe handicaps: Exemplary service strategies*. Baltimore: Paul H. Brookes Publishing Co.

Howlin, P. A. (1981). The effectiveness of operant language training with autistic children. *Journal of Autism and Developmental Disorders, 11*, 89–105.

Howlin, P. A. (1986). An overview of social behavior in autism. In E. Schopler & G. Mesibov (Eds.), *Social behavior in autism*. New York: Plenum Press.

Hung, D. W. (1978). Using self-stimulation as reinforcement for autistic children. *Journal of Autism and Childhood Schizophrenia, 8*, 355–366.

Hutt, C. (1975). Degrees of novelty and their effects on children's attention and preference. *British Journal of Psychology, 66*, 487–492.

Hutt, S. J., & Hutt, C. (Eds.). (1970). *Behaviour studies in psychiatry*. Oxford: Pergamon.

Hutt, S. J., Hutt, C., Lee, D., & Ounsted, C. (1964). Arousal and childhood autism. *Nature, 204*, 908–909.

Hutt, C., & Vaizey, M. J. (1966). Differential effects of group density on social behaviour. *Nature, 209*, 1371–1372.

Itard, J.M.G. (1801). *The wild boy of Aveyron*. English translation of two reports by G. and M. Humphrey, 1932. New York: Appleton-Century-Crofts, 1962.

Iwata, B. A., Dorsey, M. F., Slifer, K. J., Bauman, K. E., & Richman, G. S. (1982). Toward a functional analysis of self-injury. *Analysis and Intervention in Developmental Disabilities, 2*, 3–20.

Janicki, M. P., Lubin, R. A., & Friedman, E. (1983). Variations in characteristics and service needs of persons with autism. *Journal of Autism and Developmental Disorders, 13*, 73–85.

Johnson, C. A., & Katz, R. C. (1973). Using parents as change agents for their children: A review. *Journal of Child Psychology and Psychiatry, 14*, 181–200.

Johnson, J., & Koegel, R. L. (1982). Behavioral assessment and curriculum development. In R. L. Koegel, A. Rincover, & A. L. Egel (Eds.), *Educating and understanding autistic children*. San Diego, CA: College-Hill Press.

Kanner, L. (1943). Autistic disturbances of affective contact. *Nervous Child, 2*, 217–250.

Kanner, L. (1949). Problems of nosology and psychodynamics of early infantile autism. *American Journal of Orthopsychiatry, 19*, 416–426.

Kanner, L. (1954). To what extent is early infantile autism determined by constitutional inadequacies? Reprinted in L. Kanner (1973) *Childhood psychosis: Initial studies and new insights*. Washington, D. C.: V. H. Winston & Sons.

Kanner, L. (1973). *Childhood psychosis: Initial studies and new insights*. Washington, D.C.: V. H. Winston & Sons.

Kanner, L., & Eisenberg, L. (1955). Note on the follow-up studies of autistic children. In P. H. Hoch & J. Bubin (Eds.), *Psychopathology of childhood*. New York: Greene and Stratton.

Kaufman, I., Rosenblum, E., Heims, L., & Willer, L. (1957). Childhood schizophrenia: Treatment of children and parents. *American Journal of Orthopsychiatry, 27*, 683–690.

Kazdin, A. E., & Moyer, W. (1976). Training teachers to use behavior modification. In S. Yen & R. McIntire (Eds.), *Teaching behavior modification*. Kalamazoo: Behaviordelia.

Keeler, W. R. (1958). Autistic patterns and defective communication in blind children with retrolental fibroplasia. In P. H. Hoch & J. Zubin (Eds.), *Psychopathology of communication*. New York: Grune & Stratton.

Kern, L., Koegel, R. L., Dyer, K., Blew, P. A., & Fenton, L. R. (1982). The effects of physical exercise and self-stimulation and appropriate responding in autistic children. *Journal of Autism and Developmental Disorders, 12*, 399–419.

Knoblock, H., & Pasamanick, B. (1962). Some etiological and prognostic factors in early infantile autism and psychosis. *Pediatrics, 33*, 182–191.

Knoblock, H., & Pasamanick, B. (1975). Etiologic factors in "early infantile autism" and "childhood schizophrenia." Paper presented at the 10th International Congress of Pediatrics. Lisbon.

Koegel, R. L., & Covert, A. (1972). The relationship of self-stimulation to learning in autistic children. *Journal of Applied Behavior Analysis, 5*, 381–387.

Koegel, R. L., Dyer, K., & Bell, L. K. (1987). The influence of child preferred activities on autistic children's social behavior. *Journal of Applied Behavior Analysis, 20*, 243–252.

Koegel, R. L., & Egel, A. L. (1979). Motivating autistic children. *Journal of Abnormal Psychology, 88*, 418–426.

Koegel, R. L., Egel, A. L., & Dunlap, G. (1980). Learning characteristics of autistic children. In W. S. Sailor, B. Wilcox, and L. J. Brown (Eds.), *Methods of instruction with severely handicapped students*. Baltimore: Brookes Publishers.

Koegel, R. L., Firestone, P. B., Kramme, K. W., & Dunlap, G. (1974). Increasing spontaneous play by suppressing self-stimulation in autistic children. *Journal of Applied Behavior Analysis, 7*, 521–528.

Koegel, R. L., Glahn, T. J., & Nieminen, G. S. (1978). Generalization of parent training results. *Journal of Applied Behavior Analysis, 11*, 95–109.

Koegel, R. L., & Koegel, L. K. (1986). Promoting generalized treatment gains through direct instruction of self-monitoring skills. *Direct Instruction News, 5*, 13–15.

Koegel, R. L., & Koegel, L. K. (1986). Generalization issues in the treatment of autism. *Seminars in Speech and Language, 8*, 241–256.

Koegel, R. L., Koegel, L. K., & Ingham, J. M. (1986). Programming rapid generalization of correct articulation through self-monitoring procedures. *Journal of Speech and Hearing Disorders, 51*, 24–32.

Koegel, R. L., & Mentis, M. (1985). Motivation in childhood autism: Can they or won't they? *Journal of Child Psychology and Psychiatry and Allied Disciplines, 26*, 185–191.

Koegel, R. L., O'Dell, M. C., & Koegel, L. K. (1987). A natural language teaching paradigm for nonverbal autistic children. *Journal of Autism and Developmental Disorders, 17*, 187–200.

Koegel, R. L., & Rincover, A. (1974). Treatment of psychotic children in a classroom environment: I. Learning in a large group. *Journal of Applied Behavior Analysis, 7*, 45–59.

Koegel, R. L., & Rincover, A. (1977). Research on the difference between generalization and maintenance in extra-therapy responding. *Journal of Applied Behavior Analysis, 10*, 1–12.

Koegel, R. L., Rincover, A., & Egel, A. L. (1982). *Educating and understanding autistic children*. San Diego: College-Hill Press.

Koegel, R. L., Rincover, A., & Russo, D. C. (1982). Classroom management: Progression from special to normal classrooms. In R. L. Koegel, A. Rincover, & A. L. Egel (Eds.), *Educating and understanding autistic children*. San Diego, CA: College Hill.

Koegel, R. L., Russo, D. C., & Rincover, A. (1977). Assessing and training teachers in the generalized use of behavior modification with autistic children. *Journal of Applied Behavior Analysis, 10*, 197–205.

Koegel, R. L., Russo, D. C., Rincover, A., & Schreibman, L. (1982). Assessing and training teachers. In R. L. Koegel, A. Rincover, & A. L. Egel (Eds.), *Educating and understanding autistic children*. San Diego: College Hill Press.

Koegel, R. L., & Schreibman, L. (1977). Teaching autistic children to respond to simultaneous multiple cues. *Journal of Experimental Child Psychology, 24*, 299–311.

Koegel, R. L., Schreibman, L., Britten, K. R., Burke, J. C., & O'Neill, R. E. (1982). A comparison of parent training to direct clinic treatment. In R. L. Koegel, A. Rincover, & A. L. Egel (Eds.), *Educating and understanding autistic children*. San Diego: College Hill Press.

Koegel, R. L., Schreibman, L., Johnson. J., O'Neill, R. E., & Dunlap, G. (1984). Collateral effects of parent training on families with autistic children. In R. F. Dangel & R. A. Polster (Eds.), *Parent training: Foundations of research and practice*. New York: Guilford.

Koegel, R. L., Schreibman, L., O'Neill, R. E., & Burke, J. C. (1983). The personality and family-interaction characteristics of parents of autistic children. *Journal of Consulting and Clinical Psychology, 51*, 683–692.

Koegel, R. L., & Wilhelm, H. (1973). Selective responding to the components of multiple visual cues by autistic children. *Journal of Experimental Child Psychology, 15*, 442–453.

Koegel, R. L., & Williams, J. (1980). Direct vs. indirect response-reinforcer relationships in teaching autistic children. *Journal of Abnormal Child Psychology, 4*, 536–547.

Kolvin, I. (1971). Studies in the childhood psychoses. I. Diagnostic criteria and classification. *British Journal of Psychiatry, 118*, 381–384.

Kolvin, I., Ounsted, C., & Roth, A. (1971). Studies in childhood psychoses. V. Cerebral dysfunction and childhood psychoses. *British Journal of Psychiatry, 118*, 407–414.

Konstantareas, M. M., Oxman, J., & Webster, C. D. (1977). Simultaneous communication with autistic and other severely dysfunctional nonverbal children. *Journal of Communication Disorders, 10*, 267–282.

Korein, J., Fish, B., Shapiro, T., Gerner, E. W., & Levidow, L. (1971). EEG and behavioral effects of drug therapy in children. Chlorpromazine and diphenhydramine. *Archives of General Psychiatry, 24*, 552–563.

Kozloff, M. A. (1973). *Reaching the autistic child: A parent training program*. Champaign, IL: Research Press.

Kozloff, M. A. (1974). *Educating children with learning and behavioral problems*. New York: Wiley.

Krug, D. A., Arick, J. R., & Almond, P. J. (1979). Autism Screening Instrument for Educational Planning: Background and development. In J. Gilliam (Ed.), *Autism: Diagnosis, instruction, management, and research*. Austin, TX: University of Texas at Austin Press.

Kugelmass, N. I. (1970). *The autistic child*. Springfield, IL: Charles C Thomas.

L'Abate, L. (1972). Early infantile autism: A reply to Ward. *Psychological Bulletin, 77*, 49–51.

Lansing, M. D., & Schopler, E. (1978). Individualized education: A public school model. In M. Rutter & E. Schopler (Eds.), *Autism: A reappraisal of concepts and treatment*. New York: Plenum Press.

Laski, K. E., Charlop, M. H., & Schreibman, L. (in press). Training parents to use the natural language paradigm to increase their autistic children's speech. *Journal of Applied Behavior Analysis*.

Levine, M. D., Brooks, R., & Schonkoff, J. P. (1980). *A pediatric approach to learning disorders*. New York: Wiley.

Levine, M. D., & Olson, R. P. (1968). Intelligence of parents of autistic children. *Journal of Abnormal Psychology, 73*, 215–217.

Levitt, E. E. (1957). The results of psychotherapy with children: An evaluation. *Journal of Consulting Psychology, 21*, 189–196.

Levitt, E. E. (1963). Psychotherapy with children: A further evaluation. *Behaviour Research and Therapy, 1*, 45–51.

Lichstein, K. L., & Schreibman, L. (1976). Employing electric shock with autistic children: A review of the side effects. *Journal of Autism and Childhood Schizophrenia, 6,* 163–174.

Links, P. S., Stockwell, M., Abichandani, F., & Simeon, J. (1980). Minor physical anomalies in childhood autism. Part I. Their relationship to pre- and perinatal complications. *Journal of Autism and Developmental Disorders, 10,* 273–285.

Litt, M. D., & Schreibman, L. (1981). Stimulus specific reinforcement in the acquisition of receptive labels by autistic children. *Analysis and Intervention in Developmental Disabilities, 1,* 171–186.

Lockyer, L., & Rutter, M. (1969). A five to fifteen year follow-up study of infantile psychosis: III. Psychological aspects. *British Journal of Psychology, 115,* 865–882.

Lockyer, L., & Rutter, M. (1970). A five to fifteen year follow-up study of infantile psychosis: IV. Patterns of cognitive ability. *British Journal of Social and Clinical Psychology, 9,* 152–163.

Lotter, V. (1966). Epidemiology of autistic conditions in young children. I. Prevalence. *Social Psychiatry, 1,* 124–137.

Lotter, V. (1967). Epidemiology of autistic conditions in young children. II. Some characteristics of the parents and children. *Social Psychiatry, 1,* 163–173.

Lotter, V. (1974). Factors related to outcome in autistic children. *Journal of Autism and Childhood Schizophrenia, 4,* 263–277.

Lotter, V. (1978). Childhood autism in Africa. *Journal of Child Psychology and Psychiatry, 19,* 231–244.

Lovaas, O. I. (1966). A program for the establishment of speech in psychotic children. In J. K. Wing (Ed.), *Early childhood autism*. London: Pergamon.

Lovaas, O. I. (1977). *The autistic child*. New York: Irvington.

Lovaas, O. I. (1979). Contrasting illness and behavioral models for the treatment of autistic children: A historical perspective. *Journal of Autism and Developmental Disorders, 9,* 315–323.

Lovaas, O. I. (1987). Behavioral treatment and normal educational and intellectual functioning in young autistic children. *Journal of Consulting and Clinical Psychology, 55,* 3–9.

Lovaas, O. I., Berberich, J. P., Perloff, B. F., & Schaeffer, B. (1966). Acquisition of imitative speech in schizophrenic children. *Science, 151,* 705–707.

Lovaas, O. I., Freitag, G., Gold, V. J., & Kassorla, I. C. (1965). Experimental studies in childhood schizophrenia. I. Analysis of self-destructive behavior. *Journal of Experimental Child Psychology, 2,* 67–84.

Lovaas, O. I., Freitag, G., Kinder, M. I., Rubenstein, B. D., Schaeffer, B., & Simmons, J. Q. (1966). Establishment of social reinforcers in two schizophrenic children on the basis of food. *Journal of Experimental Child Psychology, 4,* 109–125.

Lovaas, O. I. Freitag, G., Nelson, K., & Whalen, C. (1967). The establishment of imitation and its use for the development of complex behavior in schizophrenic children. *Behaviour Research and Therapy, 5,* 171–181.

Lovaas, O. I., Koegel, R. L., & Schreibman, L. (1979). Stimulus overselectivity in autism: A review of research. *Psychological Bulletin, 86,* 1236–1254.

Lovaas, O. I., Koegel, R. L., Simmons, J. Q., & Long, J. S. (1973). Some generalization and follow-up measures on autistic children in behavior therapy. *Journal of Applied Behavior Analysis, 6,* 131–166.

Lovaas, O. I., Litrownik, A., & Mann, R. (1971). Response latencies to auditory stimuli in autistic children engaged in self-stimulatory behavior. *Behaviour Research and Therapy, 9,* 39–49.

Lovaas, O. I., & Newsom, C. D. (1976). Behavior modification with psychotic children. In H. Leitenberg (Ed.), *Handbook of behavior modification and behavior therapy.* Englewood Cliffs, NJ: Prentice Hall.

Lovaas, O. I., Newsom, C. D., & Hickman, C. (1987). Self-stimulatory behavior and perceptual reinforcement. *Journal of Applied Behavior Analysis, 20,* 45–68.

Lovaas, O. I., Schaeffer, B., & Simmons, J. Q. (1965). Building social behavior in autistic children by use of electric shock. *Journal of Experimental Research and Personality, 1,* 99–109.

Lovaas, O. I., & Schreibman, L. (1971). Stimulus overselectivity of autistic children in a two-stimulus situation. *Behaviour Research and Therapy, 9,* 305–310.

Lovaas, O. I., Schreibman, L., Koegel, R. L., & Rehm, R. (1971). Selective responding by autistic children to multiple sensory input. *Journal of Abnormal Psychology, 77,* 211–222.

Lovaas, O. I., & Simmons, J. Q. (1969). Manipulation of self-destruction in three retarded children. *Journal of Applied Behavior Analysis, 2,* 143–157.

Lovaas, O. I., Varni, J., Koegel, R. L., & Lorsch, N. L. (1977). Some observations on the non-extinguishability of children's speech. *Child Development, 48,* 1121–1127.

MacMillan, D. L. (1971). The problem of motivation in the education of the mentally retarded. *Exceptional Children, 37,* 579–586.

Mahler, M. (1952). On child psychosis and schizophrenia, autistic and symbiotic infantile psychoses. *Psychoanalytic Study of the Child, 7,* 286–305.

Marcus, L. M., Lansing, M. D., Andrews, C. E., & Schopler, E. (1978). Improvement of teaching effectiveness in parents of autistic children. *Journal of the American Academy of Child Psychiatry, 17,* 625–639.

McAdoo, G. W., & DeMyer, M. K. (1978). Personality characteristics of parents. In M. Rutter & E. Schopler (Eds.), *Autism: A reappraisal of concepts and treatment.* New York: Plenum Press.

McGee, G. G., Krantz, P. J., Mason D., & McClannahan, L.E.S. (1983). A modified incidental-teaching procedure for autistic youth: Acquisition and generalization of receptive object labels. *Journal of Applied Behavior Analysis, 16,* 329–338.

McGee, G. G., Krantz, P. J., & McClannahan, L.E.S. (1985). The facilitative effects of incidental teaching on preposition use by autistic children. *Journal of Applied Behavior Analysis, 18,* 17–31.

McMahon, R. J., Forehand, R., & Griest, D. L. (1981). Effects of knowledge of social learning principles on enhancing treatment outcome and generalization in a parent training program. *Journal of Consulting and Clinical Psychology, 49,* 526–532.

Menolascino, F. J. (1971). The description and classification of infantile autism. In D. W. Churchill, G. D. Alpern, & M. K. DeMyer (Eds.), *Infantile autism.* Proceedings of the Indiana University Colloquium. Springfield, IL: Charles C Thomas.

Merritt, G. C. (1968). Review of "The Empty Fortress" by B. Bettelheim. *American Journal of Orthopsychiatry, 38,* 926–930.

Mesibov, G. B., & Dawson, G. D. (1986). Pervasive developmental disorders and schizophrenia. In J. M. Reisman (Ed.), *Behavior disorders in infants, children, and adolescents* (1st ed.). New York: Random House.

Metz, J. R. (1965). Conditioning generalized imitation in autistic children. *Journal of Experimental Child Psychology, 2*, 389–399,

Mirenda, P., Donnellan, A. M., & Yoder, D. (1983). Gaze behavior: A new look at an old problem. *Journal of Autism and Developmental Disorders, 13*, 397–409.

Moreland, J. R., Schwebel, S. B., Beck, S., & Wells, R. (1982). Parents as therapists: A review of the behavior therapy parent training literature—1975 to 1981. *Behavior Modification, 2*, 250–276.

Mulhern, I., & Baumeister, A. A. (1969). An experimental attempt to reduce stereotypy by reinforcement procedures. *American Journal of Mental Deficiency, 74*, 69–74.

Murphy, G., & Wilson, B. (1985). *Self-injurious behavior.* Kidderminster, UK: BIMH Publications.

National Institute of Mental Health, Research Task Force. (1975). *Research in the service of mental health.* Rockville, MD: Author.

Neef, N. A., Walters, J., & Egel, A. L. (1984). Establishing generative yes/no responses in developmentally disabled children. *Journal of Applied Behavior Analysis, 17*, 453–460.

Newsom, C. D., & Rincover, A. (1982). Autism. In E. J. Marsh and L. G. Terdal (Eds.), *Behavioral assessment of childhood disorders.* New York: The Guilford Press.

Nordquist, V. M., & Wahler, R. G. (1973). Naturalistic treatment of an autistic child. *Journal of Applied Behavior Analysis, 6*, 79–87.

O'Connor, N., & Hermelin, B. (1967a). Auditory and visual memory in autistic and normal children. *Journal of Mental Deficiency Research, 11*, 126–131.

O'Connor, N., & Hermelin, B. (1967b). The selective visual attention of psychotic children. *Journal of Child Psychology and Psychiatry, 8*, 167–179.

O'Dell, M. C., Dunlap, G., & Koegel, R. L. (1983). *The importance of reinforcing verbal attempts during speech training with nonverbal children.* Paper presented at the American Psychological Association Annual Convention, Los Angeles.

O'Dell, M. C., & Koegel, R. L. (1981). *The differential effects of two methods of promoting speech in nonverbal autistic children.* Paper presented at the American Speech-Language-Hearing Association, Los Angeles, November.

O'Dell, S. L. (1974). Training parents in behavior modification: A review. *Psychological Bulletin, 81*, 418–433.

O'Dell, S. L. (1985). Progress in parent training. In M. Hersen, R. M. Eisler, & P. M. Miller (Eds.), *Progress in behavior modification*, Vol. 19. New York: Academic Press.

O'Dell, S. L., Krug, W. W., Patterson, J. N., & Faustman, W. O. (1980). An assessment of methods for training parents on the use of time-out. *Journal of Behavior Therapy and Experimental Psychiatry, 11*, 21–25.

Odom, S. L., & Strain, P. S. (1986). A comparison of peer-initiation and teacher-antecedent interventions for promoting reciprocal social interaction of autistic preschoolers. *Journal of Applied Behavior Analysis, 19*, 59–71.

O'Gorman, G. (1970). *The nature of childhood autism.* London: Butterworths.

Olson, D. R. (1971). Information-processing limitations of mentally retarded children. *American Journal of Mental Deficiency, 75*, 478–486.

Orne, M. T. (1962). On the social psychology of the psychological experiment: With particular reference to demand characteristics and their implications. *American Psychologist, 17,* 776–783.

Ornitz, E. M. (1969). Disorders of perception common to early infantile autism and schizophrenia. *Comprehensive Psychiatry, 10,* 259–274.

Ornitz, E. M. (1985). Neurophysiology of infantile autism. *Journal of the American Academy of Child Psychiatry, 24,* 251–262.

Ornitz, E. M., Brown, M. B., Sorosky, A. D., Ritvo, E. R., & Diedrich, L. (1970). Environmental modification of autistic behavior. *Archives of General Psychiatry, 22,* 560–565.

Ornitz, E. M., & Ritvo, E. R. (1968). Perceptual inconstancy in early infantile autism. *Archives of General Psychiatry, 18,* 76–98.

Ornitz, E., & Ritvo, E. (1976). The syndrome of autism: A critical review. *The American Journal of Psychiatry, 133,* 609–621.

Parks, S. L. (1983). The assessment of autistic children: A selective review of available instruments. *Journal of Autism and Developmental Disorders, 3,* 255–267.

Peterson, R. F., Cox, M. A., & Bijou, S. W. (1971). Training children to work productively in classroom groups. *Exceptional Children, 37,* 491–500.

Piggott, L., Gdowski, C., Villanueva, D., Fischhoff, J., & Frohman, C. (1986). Side effects of fenfluramine in autistic children. *Journal of the American Academy of Child Psychiatry, 25,* 287–289.

Pitfield, M., & Oppenheim, A. N. (1964). Child-rearing attitudes of mothers of psychotic children. *Journal of Child Psychology and Psychiatry and Allied Disciplines, 5,* 51–57.

Prior, M. (1984). Developing concepts of childhood autism: The influence of experimental cognitive research. *Journal of Consulting and Clinical Psychology, 52,* 4–16.

Prior, M., & Bence, R. (1975). A note on the validity of the Rimland Diagnostic Checklist. *Journal of Clinical Psychology, 31,* 510–513.

Prior, M., & Bradshaw, J. L. (1979). Hemispheric functioning in autistic children. *Cortex, 15,* 73–81.

Prior, M., & Gajzago, C. (1974). Recognition of early signs of autism. *Medical Journal of Australia, 8,* 183.

Prior, M., & Isaacs, J. (1979). Language acquisition in autistic and developmental aphasic children. In *Proceedings of Aphasia Convention.* Melbourne, Victoria, Australia: Victorian Branch Australian Association of Speech and Hearing.

Prizant, B. M., & Duchan, J. F. (1981). The functions of immediate echolalia in autistic children. *Journal of Speech and Hearing Disorders, 46,* 241–249.

Ragland, E. U., Kerr, M. M., & Strain, P. S. (1978). Effects of peer social initiations on the behavior of withdrawn autistic children. *Behavior Modification, 2,* 565–578.

Rank, B. (1955). Intensive study and treatment of preschool children who show marked personality deviations, or "atypical development," and their parents. In G. Caplan (Ed.), *Emotional problems of early childhood.* New York: Basic Books.

Rank, B., & MacNaughton, D. (1950). A clinical contribution to early ego development. *Psychoanalytic Study of the Child, 5,* 53–65.

Reichler, R. J., & Schopler, E. (1976). Developmental therapy: A program model for providing individualized services in the community. In E. Schopler & R. J. Reichler (Eds.), *Psychopathology and child development.* New York: Plenum.

Reynolds, B. S., Newsom, C. D., & Lovaas, O. I. (1974). Auditory overselectivity in autistic children. *Journal of Abnormal Child Psychology, 2*, 253–263.

Ricks, D. M., & Wing, L. (1975). Language, communication, and the use of symbols in normal and autistic children. *Journal of Autism and Childhood Schizophrenia, 5*, 191–222.

Rimland, B. (1964). *Infantile autism.* New York: Appleton-Century-Crofts.

Rimland, B. (1971). The differentiation of childhood psychoses: An analysis of checklists for 2,218 psychotic children. *Journal of Autism and Childhood Schizophrenia, 1*, 161–174.

Rimland, B. (1973). High dosage levels of certain vitamins in the treatment of children with severe mental disorders. In D. Hawkins and L. Pauling (Eds.), *Orthomolecular psychiatry.* San Francisco: Freeman.

Rimland, B. (1978). Inside the mind of an autistic savant. *Psychology Today, 12*, 68–80.

Rincover, A. (1978). Variables affecting stimulus-fading and discriminative responding in psychotic children. *Journal of Abnormal Psychology, 87*, 541–553.

Rincover, A., Cook, R., Peoples, A., & Packard, D. (1979). Sensory extinction and sensory reinforcement principles for programming multiple adaptive behavior change. *Journal of Applied Behavior Analysis, 12*, 221–233.

Rincover, A., & Koegel, R. L. (1975). Setting generality and stimulus control in autistic children. *Journal of Applied Behavior Analysis, 8*, 235–246.

Rincover, A., & Koegel, R. L. (1977a). Classroom treatment of autistic children: II. Individualized instruction in a group. *Journal of Abnormal Child Psychology, 5*, 113–126.

Rincover, A., & Koegel, R. L. (1977b). Research on the education of autistic children: Recent advances and future directions. In B. B. Lahey & A. E. Kazdin (Eds.), *Advances in clinical child psychology* (Vol. 1). New York: Plenum Press.

Rincover, A., Koegel, R. L., & Russo, D. C. (1978). Some recent behavioral research on the education of autistic children. *Education and Treatment of Children, 1*, 31–45.

Rincover, A., Newsom, C. D., Lovaas, O. I., & Koegel, R. L. (1977). Some motivational properties of sensory stimulation in psychotic children. *Journal of Experimental Child Psychology, 24*, 312–323.

Risley, T. R. (1968). The effects and side effects of punishing the autistic behaviors of a deviant child. *Journal of Applied Behavior Analysis, 1*, 21–34.

Risley, T. R., & Wolf, M. M. (1967). Establishing functional speech in echolalic children. *Behaviour Research and Therapy, 5*, 73–88.

Ritvo, E. R. (Ed.). (1976). *Autism: Diagnosis, current research, and management,* New York: Spectrum Publications.

Ritvo, E. R. (1981). *Genetic and immuno-hematologic studies on the syndrome of autism.* Paper presented at the International Conference on Autism, Boston.

Ritvo, E. R., & Freeman, B. J. (1978). National Society for Autistic Children definition of the syndrome of autism. *Journal of Autism and Childhood Schizophrenia, 8*, 162–167.

Ritvo, E. R., Freeman, B. J., Geller, E., & Yuwiler, A. (1983). Effects of fenfluramine on 14 outpatients with the syndrome of autism. *Journal of the American Academy of Child Psychiatry, 22*, 549–558.

Ritvo, E. R., Freeman, B. J., Mason-Brothers, A., Mo, A., & Ritvo, A. M. (1985). Concordance for the syndrome of autism in 40 pairs of afflicted twins. *American Journal of Psychiatry, 142*, 74–77.

Ritvo, E. R., Freeman, B. J., Sheibel, A. B., Duong, T., Robinson, R., Guthrie, D., & Ritvo, A. M. (1986). Lower Purkinje cell counts in the cerebella of four autistic subjects: Initial findings of the UCLA-NSAC autopsy research report. *American Journal of Psychiatry, 143*, 862–866.

Ritvo, E. R., Freeman, B. J., Yuwiler, A., Geller, E., Yokota, A., Schroth, P., & Novak, P. (1984). Study of fenfluramine in outpatients with the syndrome of autism. *The Journal of Pediatrics, 105*, 823–828.

Ritvo, E. R., Spence, M. A., Freeman, B. J., Mason-Brothers, A., Mo, A., & Marazita, M. L. (1985). Evidence for autosomal recessive inheritance in 46 families with multiple incidences of autism. *American Journal of Psychiatry, 142*, 187–192.

Ritvo, E. R., Yuwiler, A., Geller, E., Kales, A., Rashkis, S., Schicor, A., Plotkin, A., Axelrod, R., & Howard, C. (1971). Effects of L-dopa on autism. *Journal of Autism and Childhood Schizophrenia, 1*, 190–205.

Rodda, M. (1977). Language and language-disordered children. *Bulletin of the British Psychological Society, 30*, 139–142.

Runco, M. A., & Schreibman, L. (1983). Parental judgments of behavior therapy efficacy with autistic children: A social validation. *Journal of Autism and Developmental Disorders, 13*, 237–248.

Runco, M. A., & Schreibman, L. (1987). Brief report: Socially validating behavioral objectives in the treatment of autistic children. *Journal of Autism and Developmental Disorders, 17*, 141–147.

Runco, M. A., & Schreibman, L. (in press). Children's judgment of autism and social validation of behavior therapy efficacy. *Behavior Therapy*.

Russo, D. C., & Koegel, R. L. (1977). A method for integrating an autistic child into a normal public-school classroom. *Journal of Applied Behavior Analysis, 10*, 579–590.

Rutt, C. N., & Oxford, D. R. (1971). Prenatal and perinatal complications in childhood schizophrenics and their siblings. *Journal of Nervous and Mental Disorders, 152*, 324–331.

Ruttenberg, B. A. (1971). A psychoanalytic understanding of infantile autism and its treatment. In D. Churchill, G. Alpern, & M. DeMyer (Eds.), *Infantile autism: Proceedings, Indiana University Colloquium*. Springfield, IL: Charles C Thomas.

Ruttenberg, B. A., Dratman, J. L., Fraknoi, J., & Wenar, C. (1966). An instrument for evaluating autistic children. *Journal of the American Academy of Child Psychiatry, 5*, 453–478.

Ruttenberg, B. A., Kalish, B. I., Wenar, C., & Wolf, E. G. (1977). *Behavior rating instrument for autistic and other atypical children* (Rev. Ed.). Philadelphia: Developmental Center for Autistic Children.

Ruttenberg, B. A., & Wolf, E. G. (1967). Evaluating the communication of the autistic child. *Journal of Speech and Hearing Disorders, 32*, 314–324.

Rutter, M. (1965). Speech disorders in a series of autistic children. In A. W. Franklin (Ed.), *Children with communication problems*. London: Pitman.

Rutter, M. (1966a). Behavioural and cognitive characteristics of a series of psychotic children. In J. Wing (Ed.), *Early childhood autism*. Oxford: Pergamon.

Rutter, M. (1966b). Prognosis: Psychotic children in adolescence and early adult life. In J. K. Wing (Ed.), *Early childhood autism: Clinical, educational and social aspects*. London: Pergamon Press.

Rutter, M. (1968). Concepts of autism: A review of research. *Journal of Child Psychology and Psychiatry, 9*, 1–25.

Rutter, M. (1970). Autistic children: Infancy to adulthood. *Seminars in Psychiatry, 2*, 435–450.

Rutter, M. (1971). The description and classification of infantile autism. In D. W. Churchill, G. D. Alpern, & M. K. DeMyer (Eds.), *Infantile autism*. Springfield IL: Charles C Thomas.

Rutter, M. (1972). Childhood schizophrenia reconsidered. *Journal of Autism and Childhood Schizophrenia, 2*, 315–337.

Rutter, M. (1978a). Diagnosis and definition. In M. Rutter & E. Schopler (Eds.), *Autism: A reappraisal of concepts and treatment*. New York: Plenum Press.

Rutter, M. (1978b). Diagnosis and definition of childhood autism. *Journal of Autism and Childhood Schizophrenia, 8*, 139–161.

Rutter, M. (1983). Cognitive deficits in the pathogenesis of autism. *Journal of Child Psychology and Psychiatry, 24*, 513–531.

Rutter, M., & Bartak, L. (1973). Special educational treatment of autistic children: A comparative study. II. Follow-up findings and implications for services. *Journal of Child Psychology and Psychiatry, 14*, 241–270.

Rutter, M., Bartak, L., & Newman, S. (1971). Autism—a central disorder of cognition or language? In M. Rutter (Ed.), *Infantile autism: Concepts, characteristics and treatment*. London: Churchill-Livingstone.

Rutter, M., & Cox, A. (1975). A comparative study of infantile autism and specific developmental receptive language disorder. I. The children. *British Journal of Psychiatry, 126*, 127–145.

Rutter, M., & Garmezy, N. (1983). Childhood psychopathology. In M. Hetherington & P. H. Mussen (Eds.), *Carmichael's manual of child psychology*. New York: John Wiley & Sons.

Rutter, M., Greenfield, D., & Lockyer, L. (1967). A five- to fifteen-year follow-up of infantile psychosis. II. Social and behavioral outcome. *British Journal of Psychiatry, 113*, 1187–1199.

Rutter, M., & Lockyer, L. (1967). A five to fifteen year follow-up study of infantile psychosis. I. Description of sample. *British Journal of Psychiatry, 113*, 1169–1182.

Rutter, M., Yule, W., Berger, M., & Hersov, L. (1977). An evaluation of a behavioural approach to the treatment of autistic children. *Final Report to the Department of Health and Social Security*, London.

Sahley, T. L., & Panksepp, J. (1987). Brain opioids and autism: An updated analysis of possible linkages. *Journal of Autism and Developmental Disorders, 17*, 201–216.

Sajwaj, T. E., Twardosz, S., & Burke, M. (1972). Side effects of extinction procedures in a remedial preschool. *Journal of Applied Behavior Analysis, 5*, 163–175.

Sanders, M. R., & James, J. E. (1983). The modification of parent behavior: A review of generalization and maintenance. *Behavior Modification, 7*, 3–27.

Sasso, G. M., Simpson, R. L., & Novak, C. G. (1985). Procedure for facilitating integration of autistic children in public-school settings. *Analysis and Intervention in Developmental Disabilities, 5*, 233–246.

Schaffer, H. R. (1965). Changes in developmental quotient under two conditions of maternal separation. *British Journal of Social and Clinical Psychology, 4*, 39–46.

Schopler, E. (1965). Early infantile autism and receptor processes. *Archives of General Psychiatry, 13*, 327–335.

Schopler, E. (1978). On confusion in the diagnosis of autism. *Journal of Autism and Childhood Schizophrenia, 8*, 137–138.

Schopler, E. (1986). Editorial: Treatment abuse and its reduction. *Journal of Autism and Developmental Disorders, 16*, 99–104.

Schopler, E., Andrews, C. E., & Strupp, K. (1979). Do autistic children come from upper-middle-class parents? *Journal of Autism and Developmental Disorders, 9*, 139–152.

Schopler, E., Brehm, S. S., Kinsbourne, M., & Reichler, R. J. (1971). Effect of treatment structure on development in autistic children. *Archives of General Psychiatry, 24*, 415–421.

Schopler, E., & Loftin, J. (1969). Thinking disorder in parents of young psychotic children. *Journal of Abnormal Psychology, 14*, 281–287.

Schopler, E., & Mesibov, G. B. (1983). *Autism in adolescents and adults.* New York: Plenum Press.

Schopler, E., Mesibov, G. B., & Baker, A. (1982). Evaluation of treatment for autistic children and their parents. *Journal of the American Academy of Child Psychiatry, 21*, 262–267.

Schopler, E., Mesibov, G. B., Shigley, R. H., & Bashford, A. (1984). Helping autistic children through their parents: The TEACCH model. In E. Schopler & G. B. Mesibov (Eds.), *The effects of autism on the family.* New York: Plenum.

Schopler, E., & Olley, J. G. (1982). Comprehensive educational services for autistic children: The TEACCH model. In C. R. Reynolds & T. R. Gutkin (Eds.), *The handbook of school psychology.* New York: Wiley.

Schopler, E., & Reichler, R. J. (1971). Developmental therapy by parents with their own autistic child. In M. Rutter (Ed.), *Infantile autism: Concepts, characteristics, and treatment.* London: Churchill-Livingstone.

Schopler, E., & Reichler, R. J. (1979). *Individualized assessment and treatment for autistic and developmentally disabled children.* Baltimore: University Park Press.

Schopler, E., Reichler, R. J., DeVellis, R. F., & Daly, K. (1980). Toward objective classification of childhood autism: Childhood Autism Rating Scale (CARS). *Journal of Autism and Developmental Disorders, 10*, 91–103.

Schreibman, L. (1975). Effects of within-stimulus and extra-stimulus prompting on discrimination learning in autistic children. *Journal of Applied Behavior Analysis, 8*, 91–112.

Schreibman, L. (1983). Are we forgetting the parent in parent training? *The Behavior Therapist, 6*, 107–109.

Schreibman, L. (1988). Parent training as a means of facilitating generalization in autistic children. In R. H. Horner, G. Dunlap, & R. L. Koegel (Eds.), *Generalization and maintenance: Lifestyle changes in applied settings.* New York: Pergamon.

Schreibman, L., & Britten, K. R. (1984). Training parents as therapists for autistic children: Rationale, techniques, and results. In W. P. Christian, G. T. Hannah, & T. J. Glahn (Eds.), *Programming effective human services.* New York: Plenum.

Schreibman, L., & Carr, E. G. (1978). Elimination of echolalic responding to questions through the training of a generalized verbal response. *Journal of Applied Behavior Analysis, 11*, 453–463.

Schreibman, L., & Charlop, M. H., (1987). Autism. In V. B. Van Hasselt & M. Hersen (Eds.), *Psychological evaluation of the developmentally and physically disabled.* New York: Plenum Press.

Schreibman, L., Charlop, M. H., & Britten, K. R. (1983). Childhood autism. In R. Morris & T. Kratochwill (Eds.), *Practice of therapy with children.* New York: Pergamon Press.

Schreibman, L., Charlop, M. H., & Koegel, R. L. (1982). Teaching autistic children to use extra stimulus prompts. *Journal of Experimental Child Psychology, 33*, 475–491.

Schreibman, L., Charlop, M. H., & Tryon, A. S. (1981). *The acquisition and generalization of appropriate spontaneous speech in autistic children.* Paper presented at the Annual Convention of the American Psychological Association, Los Angeles, August.

Schreibman, L., & Koegel, R. L. (1981). A guideline for planning behavior modification programs for autistic children. In S. M. Turner, K. S. Calhoun, & H. E. Adams (Eds.), *Handbook of clinical behavior therapy.* New York: John Wiley & Sons.

Schreibman, L., Koegel, R. L., & Craig, M. S. (1977). Reducing stimulus overselectivity in autistic children. *Journal of Abnormal Child Psychology, 5*, 425–436.

Schreibman, L., Koegel, R. L., Mills, D. L., & Burke, J. C. (1984). Training parent-child interactions. In E. Schopler & G. B. Mesibov (Eds.), *The effects of autism on the family.* New York: Plenum.

Schreibman, L., Koegel, R. L., Mills, J. I., & Burke, J. C. (1981). The social validation of behavior therapy with autistic children. *Behavior Therapy, 12*, 610–624.

Schreibman, L., Kohlenberg, B., & Britten, K. R. (1986). Differential responding to content and intonation components of a complex auditory stimulus by nonverbal and echolalic autistic children. *Analysis and Intervention in Developmental Disabilities, 6*, 109–125.

Schreibman, L., & Lovaas, O. I. (1973). Overselective response to social stimuli by autistic children. *Journal of Abnormal Child Psychology, 1*, 152–168.

Schreibman, L., & Mills, J. I. (1983). Infantile autism. In T. J. Ollendick & M. Hersen (Eds.), *Handbook of child psychopathology.* New York: Plenum.

Schreibman, L., Oke, N. J., Mills, D. L., & Ploog, B. O. (1986). *Behavioral group training for siblings of autistic children.* Paper presented at the annual convention of the American Psychological Association, Washington, D.C.

Schreibman, L., O'Neill, R. E., & Koegel, R. L. (1983). Behavioral training for siblings of autistic children. *Journal of Applied Behavior Analysis, 16*, 129–138.

Schreibman, L., Runco, M. A., Mills, J. I., & Koegel, R. L. (1982). Teachers' judgments of improvements in autistic children in behavior therapy: A social validation. In R. L. Koegel, A. Rincover, & A. L. Egel (Eds.), *Educating and understanding autistic children.* San Diego: College Hill Press.

Schwartz, S., & Johnson, J. H. (1985). *Psychopathology of childhood: A clinical-experimental approach* (2nd Edition). New York: Pergamon Press.

Seibert, T., & Oller, D. K. (1981). Linguistic pragmatics and language intervention strategies. *Journal of Autism and Developmental Disorders, 11*, 75–88.

Shapiro, T. (1978). Therapy with autistic children. In M. Rutter & E. Schopler (Eds.), *Autism: A reappraisal of concepts and treatment*. New York: Plenum Press.

Shapiro, T., Roberts, A., & Fish, B. (1970). Imitation and echoing in young schizophrenic children. *Journal of American Child Psychiatry, 9*, 548–567.

Shea, V., & Mesibov, G. B. (1985). The relationship of learning disabilities and higher-level autism. *Journal of Autism and Developmental Disorders, 15*, 425–435.

Short, A. B. (1984). Short-term treatment outcome using parents as co-therapists for their own autistic children. *Journal of Child Psychology and Psychiatry and Allied Disciplines, 25*, 443–458.

Silberg, J. (1978). The development of pronoun usage in the psychotic child. *Journal of Autism and Childhood Schizophrenia, 8*, 413–425.

Simmons, J. Q., & Baltaxe, C. A. (1975). Language patterns of adolescent autistics. *Journal of Autism and Childhood Schizophrenia, 5*, 333–351.

Simon, N. (1976). Echolalic speech in childhood autism. In S. Chess & A. Thomas (Eds.), *Annual progress in child psychiatry and child development*. New York: Brunner/Mazel.

Smolev, S. R. (1971). The use of operant techniques for the modification of self-injurious behavior. *American Journal of Mental Deficiency, 76*, 295–305.

Solnick, J. V., Rincover, A., & Peterson, C. R. (1977). Determinants of the reinforcing and punishing effects of time-out. *Journal of Applied Behavior Analysis, 10*, 415–428.

Sorosky, A. D., Ornitz, E. M., Brown, N. B., & Ritvo, E. R. (1968). Systematic observations of autistic behavior. *Archives of General Psychiatry, 18*, 439–449.

Spence, M. A., Simmons, J. Q., Brown, M. B., & Wikler, L. (1973). Sex rating in families of autistic children. *American Journal of Mental Deficiency, 77*, 405–407.

Spitz, R. A. (1945). Hospitalism: An inquiry into the genesis of psychiatric conditions in early childhood. *Psychoanalytic Study of the Child, 1*, 153–172.

Spitz, R. A. (1965). *The first year of life*. New York: International Universities Press.

Stanley, A. E. (1985). *Toward a functional analysis of stereotypy*. Unpublished doctoral dissertation. University of California, San Diego.

Stokes, T. F., & Baer, D. M. (1977). An implicit technology of generalization. *Journal of Applied Behavior Analysis, 10*, 349–368.

Strain, P. S. (1980). Social behavior programming with severely handicapped and autistic children. In B. Wilcox & A. Thompson (Eds.), *Critical issues in educating autistic children and youth*. NSAC, The National Society for Children and Adults with Autism.

Strain, P. S. (1983). Generalization of autistic children's social behavior change: Effects of developmentally integrated and segregated settings. *Analysis and Intervention in Developmental Disabilities, 3*, 23–24.

Strain, P. S., Kerr, M. M., & Ragland, E. U. (1979). Effects of peer-mediated social initiations and prompting/reinforcement procedures on the social behavior of autistic children. *Journal of Autism and Developmental Disorders, 9*, 41–54.

Tanguay, P. E. (1976). Clinical and electro-physiological research. In E. R. Ritvo (Ed.), *Autism: Diagnosis, current research, and management*. New York: Spectrum Publications.

Tanner, B. A., & Zeiler, M. (1975). Punishment of self-injurious behavior using aromatic ammonia as the aversive stimulus. *Journal of Applied Behavior Analysis, 8,* 53–57.

Tate, B. G., & Baroff, G. S. (1966). Aversive control of self-injurious behavior in a psychotic boy. *Behaviour Research and Therapy, 4,* 281–287.

Tiegerman, E., & Primavera, L. (1984). Imitating the autistic: Facilitating communicative gaze behavior. *Journal of Autism and Developmental Disorders, 14,* 27–38.

Tinbergen, E. A., & Tinbergen, N. (1972). Early childhood autism: An ethological approach. In *Advances in Ethology, 10,* Supplement to *Journal of Comparative Ethology.* Berlin and Hamburg: Verlag Paul Pany.

Touchette, P. E., MacDonald, R. F., & Langer, S. N. (1985). A scatter plot for identifying stimulus control of problem behavior. *Journal of Applied Behavior Analysis, 18,* 343–351.

Treatment and education of autistic and related communication handicapped children (TEACCH). Annual report, 1985–1986. University of North Carolina at Chapel Hill.

Treffert, D. A. (1970). Epidemiology of infantile autism. *Archives of General Psychiatry, 22,* 431–438.

Tsai, L. Y., Stewart, M. A., & August, G. J. (1981). Implication of sex differences in the familial transmission of infantile autism. *Journal of Autism and Developmental Disorders, 11,* 165–173.

Tsai, L. Y., Stewart, M. A., Faust, M., & Shook, S. (1982). Social class distribution of fathers of children enrolled in the Iowa autism program. *Journal of Autism and Developmental Disorders, 12,* 211–221.

Turkewitz, H., O'Leary, K. D., & Ironsmith, M. (1975). Generalization and maintenance of appropriate behavior through self-control. *Journal of Consulting and Clinical Psychology, 43,* 577–583.

Turkington, C. (1987, January). Opioid system role suspected in autism. *APA Monitor,* p. 8.

Turner, B. L. (1978). *The effects of choice of stimulus materials on interest in the remediation process and the generalized use of language training.* Unpublished master's thesis, University of California, Santa Barbara.

Twardosz, S., & Nordquist, V. M. (1987). Parent training. In M. Herson & V. B. Van Hasselt (Eds.), *Behavior therapy with children and adolescents: A clinical approach.* New York: Wiley.

Vaillant, G. E. (1962). John Haslam on early infantile autism. *American Journal of Psychiatry, 119,* 356.

Van Riper, C. (1963). *Speech correction.* Englewood Cliffs, NJ: Prentice-Hall.

Varni, J., Lovaas, O. I., Koegel, R. L., & Everett, N. L. (1979). An analysis of observational learning in autistic and normal children. *Journal of Abnormal Child Psychology, 7,* 31–43.

Voeltz, L. M. (1984). Program and curriculum innovations to prepare children for integration. In N. Certo, N. Haring, & R. York (Eds.), *Public school integration of severely handicapped students: Rational issues and progressive alternatives.* Baltimore: Paul H. Brookes Publishing Co.

Wahler, R. G. (1969). Setting generality: Some specific and general effects of child behavior therapy. *Journal of Applied Behavior Analysis, 2,* 239–246.

Wahler, R. G., Sperling, K. A., Thomas, M. R., Teeter, N. C., & Luper, H. L. (1970). The modification of childhood stuttering: Some response-response relationships. *Journal of Experimental Child Psychology, 9,* 411–428.

Wakabayashi, S. (1979). A case of infantile autism associated with Down's syndrome. *Journal of Autism and Developmental Disorders, 9,* 31–36.

Ward, A. J. (1970). Early infantile autism: Diagnosis, etiology and treatment. *Psychological Bulletin, 73,* 350–362.

Watson, L. S. (1973). *Child behavior modification: A manual for teachers, nurses, and parents.* New York: Pergamon Press.

Weiland, H., & Rudnick, R. (1961). Considerations of the development and treatment of autistic childhood psychosis. *Psychoanalytic Study of the Child, 16,* 549–563.

Wenar, C., & Ruttenberg, B. A. (1976). The use of BRIAC for evaluating therapeutic effectiveness. *Journal of Autism and Childhood Schizophrenia, 6,* 175–191.

Wetherby, A. (1982). Communicative, cognitive, and social development in autistic children. Unpublished dissertation, University of California, San Francisco.

Wetherby, A., & Koegel, R. L. (1982). Audiological testing. In R. L. Koegel, A. Rincover, & A. L. Egel (Eds.), *Educating and understanding autistic children.* San Diego: College Hill Press.

Wetzel, R. J., Baker, J., Roney, M., & Martin, M. (1966). Outpatient treatment of autistic behavior. *Behaviour Research and Therapy, 4,* 169–177.

White, G. D., Nielsen, G., & Johnson, S. M. (1972). Time-out duration and the suppression of deviant behavior in children. *Journal of Applied Behavior Analysis, 5,* 111–120.

Wilcox, B., & Thompson, A. (Eds.). (1980). *Critical issues in educating autistic children and youth.* U.S. Department of Education, Office of Special Education, November.

Wilhelm, H., & Lovaas, O. I. (1976). Stimulus overselectivity: A common feature in autism and mental retardation. *American Journal of Mental Deficiency, 81,* 227–241.

Wing, L. (1969). The handicaps of autistic children—a comparative study. *Journal of Child Psychology and Psychiatry, 10,* 1–40.

Wing, L. (1972). *Autistic children: A guide for parents.* New York: Brunner/Mazel.

Wing. L. (1976). Diagnosis, clinical description, and prognosis. In L. Wing (Ed.), *Early childhood autism: Clinical, educational and social aspects* (2nd Ed.). Oxford: Pergamon Press.

Wing, L., & Gould, J. (1979). Severe impairments of social interaction and associated abnormalities in children: Epidemiology and classification. *Journal of Autism and Developmental Disorders, 9,* 11–29.

Wolf, M. M., Risley, T. R., & Mees, H. (1964). Applications of operant conditioning procedures to the behavior problems of an autistic child. *Behaviour Research and Therapy, 1,* 305–312.

Wolff, S., & Chess, S. (1964). A behavioural study of schizophrenic children. *Acta Psychiatrica Scandinavica, 40,* 438–466.

Yarbrough, E., Santat, U., Perel, I., Webster, C. D., & Lombardi, R. (1987). Effects of fenfluramine on autistic individuals residing in a state developmental center. *Journal of Autism and Developmental Disorders, 17,* 303–314.

Yarrow, M. R. (1963). Problems of methods in parent-child research. *Child Development, 34,* 215–226.

Yarrow, M. R., Waxler, C. Z., & Scott, P. M. (1971). Child effects on adult behavior. *Developmental Psychology, 5,* 300–311.

Young, S. (1969). *Visual attention in autistic and normal children: Effects of stimulus novelty, human attributes, and complexity.* Unpublished doctoral dissertation, University of California at Los Angeles.

Yuwiler, A., Ritvo, E. R., Geller, E., Glousman, R., Schneiderman, G., & Matsuno, D. (1975). Uptake and efflux of serotonin and platelets of autistic and non-autistic children. *Journal of Autism and Childhood Schizophrenia, 5,* 83–98.

Zaslow, R. W. (1967). *A psychogenic theory of the etiology of infantile autism and implications for treatment.* Paper presented at a meeting of the California State Psychiatric Association, San Diego.

Zaslow, R. W., & Breger, L. (1969). A theory and treatment of autism. In L. Breger (Ed.), *Clinical-cognitive psychology.* Englewood Cliffs, NJ: Prentice-Hall.

Zipf, G. K. (1949). *Human behavior and the principle of least effort.* New York: Hafner.

AUTHOR INDEX

177

SUBJECT INDEX

ABOUT THE AUTHOR

Laura Schreibman (Ph.D., University of California, Los Angeles) is Professor of Psychology at the University of California, San Diego, where she directs a clinical research program focusing on the analysis and treatment of autism. Her research interests include the analysis of attentional and language deficits in autistic children, parent training for families of autistic children, and generalization and maintenance of behavior change. She has served as an Associate Editor of the *Journal of Applied Behavior Analysis* and *Analysis and Intervention in Developmental Disabilities*. Her editorial board memberships have included the *Journal of Experimental Child Psychology, Journal of Autism and Developmental Disorders, Behavior Modification, Journal of Behavioral Assessment, The Behavior Analyst*, and *Clinical Behavior Therapy Review*. She is the co-author of *Teaching Autistic and Other Severely Handicapped Children*, with Robert L. Koegel.

NOTES

NOTES

NOTES